Dan Christian is one of the w

best-travelled all-round crickete

20 one-day and 23 T20 internat

in T20 leagues in England, India, South Africa and the West Indies, as well as his own country, where he has represented teams in every state bar Western Australia. He is a proud Wiradjuri man from Narranderra in New South Wales and in 2018 captained the Australian Aboriginal XI to England in the sesquicentenary of the famous indigenous team of 1868. He is based in Sydney.

Gideon Haigh has written for more than a hundred newspapers and magazines, and published more than 40 books, most recently *The Brilliant Boy: Doc Evatt and the Great Australian Dissent*. He is a life member of South Yarra CC, where he has played for almost 30 years.

DAN CHRISTIAN

WITH GIDEON HAIGH

THE ALL-ROUNDER

HarperCollinsPublishers

Aboriginal and Torres Strait Islander readers are respectfully advised this book contains names and descriptions of people who have died.

HarperCollins*Publishers*
Australia • Brazil • Canada • France • Germany • Holland • Hungary
India • Italy • Japan • Mexico • New Zealand • Poland • Spain • Sweden
Switzerland • United Kingdom • United States of America

First published in Australia in 2022
by HarperCollins*Publishers* Australia Pty Limited
Level 13, 201 Elizabeth Street, Sydney NSW 2000
ABN 36 009 913 517
harpercollins.com.au

A catalogue record for this book is available from the National Library of Australia

ISBN 978 1 4607 6117 5 (paperback)
ISBN 978 1 4607 1420 1 (ebook)

Cover design by Hazel Lam, HarperCollins Design Studio
Front cover images (from left to right): BBL – Sixers v Heat by Chris Hyde / Getty Images; Surrey v Nottinghamshire – T20 Vitality Blast 2020 Final by Alex Davidson / Getty Images; VIC v TAS – Sheffield Shield by Robert Cianflone / Getty Images
Back cover photographs courtesy of the Christian family archives (clockwise): Celebrating on the outfield at the SCG after our Big Bash League final win, 7 February 2021; Travelling lightly in the West Indies, 29 June 2021; And travelling hygienically with Jorgia in Chennai, 15 April 2021.
All internal photographs are courtesy of the Christian family archives unless otherwise indicated.
Typeset in Sabon LT Std by Kirby Jones
Printed and bound in the UK using 100% Renewable Electricity at CPI Group (UK) Ltd

For Jorgia and Harper

Contents

FOREWORD

Most books by cricketers are the initiative of either a publisher, a player agent, or both. *The All-Rounder* is an exception. Dan Christian is too unassuming to crave much attention. I had to talk him into this journal of his year, which started as an account of his experiences in the Indian Premier League, but took on a life of its own as the early 2020s threw up challenge after challenge.

Having an interest in cricket as a life as well as a game, I have a bit of a weakness for cricket diaries. A bit over a decade ago, I helped my friend Ed Cowan put his thoughts in order for a diary of his season as a first-class cricketer with Tasmania in 2010–11. I had since been looking around for someone who might help update my understandings of the cricketer's day-to-day world. I'd interviewed Dan a couple of times, liked his take on things, and mentioned my idea to a mutual friend. A couple of days later, I started chatting to Dan in Chennai on Zoom, and off we went, yarning every few days, usually with the lovely Jorgia in the background. I subsequently came back with a publisher, and everything went from there.

I say 'everything went' advisedly. Because one of the notable contrasts with Ed's book, which captured the last Australian season before the Big Bash League and featured a regular succession of matches in the Sheffield Shield and Ryobi One-Day Cup, is how little the modern player can now be sure of.

At the outset of *The All-Rounder*, Dan was scheduled to play the Pakistan Super League for the Karachi Kings, the Indian Premier League for Royal Challengers Bangalore, the Vitality Blast for Notts Outlaws, The Hundred for the Manchester Originals and the Big Bash League for the Sydney Sixers, with the chance of a berth in Australia's squad for the T20 World Cup.

Only the Sixers panned out as planned. The PSL and IPL were both wracked by COVID-19. Dan and Jorgia had to grope their way to England via the Maldives and Bahrain, only for Dan to be summoned back to Australia to undertake a white-ball tour of the West Indies and Bangladesh before completing the second half of his RCB commitments in the UAE. One bio-secure bubble succeeded another. One hotel room melted into the next. A running gag became the curtains by which Dan would usually be framed when he joined each Zoom meeting, a personal favourite being the set lying on the floor in Dhaka, having come away in Dan's hand the night before. The imagined glamour of the freelance cricketer's life is decidedly superficial.

Then there was the business of trying to lead something resembling a normal life. Dan and Jorgia learned at the commencement of the IPL that they would be becoming parents before the end of the year; he set about finding a new home in Sydney while in Chennai, bought it while in Bahrain, settled on it while in St Lucia, but did not sleep in it until after returning from Dhaka. He played for the Sixers the night before Jorgia gave birth to Harper, and took them on the road soon after.

A professional cricketer for almost two decades, Dan has become a veteran at contouring his personal life to cricket, but this experience was, of course, intensified by the pandemic. Most of us accepted in this time that international travel was too difficult. Dan had no choice but to keep it up, with all that this involved: constant tests, regular isolations, endless rigmarole and reorganising. About viruses and vaccines, he knows a great deal more than I do: he has had to.

Dan coped. Of course he did: he is personable and practical, even-tempered and good-humoured, never too high or too low but fundamentally optimistic. He puts games behind him quickly; he does not fuss about what he cannot control; but he also cares and empathises, takes counsel and thinks things through. He's the kind of guy, in fact, you'd like to share a dressing room with – which, in addition to his talent and record, explains why he has played so long, so widely and so popularly. I like him. You would too. And we hope you enjoy *The All-Rounder* as much as we did putting it together.

Gideon Haigh

1

BEGINNINGS

T20 is my life today, but it wasn't always. I'm an old-fashioned country cricketer. I'm also a Wiradjuri man. Now I get to play with Virat Kohli and AB De Villiers. It's as much fun as it sounds.

Monday, 5 April 2021

These days I'm not much of a cricket watcher. Even of games I've played in. Cricket's developed a bit of an obsession with studying video, to analyse technique and correct faults. But Andrew McDonald, who was my coach at Victoria and at the Melbourne Renegades, used to say that we spent too much time watching the 5 per cent of cricket where we did things wrong, to the exclusion of the 95 per cent of the time we did things well. And I reckon he's right.

There's one exception to that. I enjoy looking at images of the teams I've played with celebrating victory – those moments where everyone's united, enjoying their own success and each other's. No cricketer can win anything on their own. You can't bat without a partner or bowl without fielders. So I like looking round the faces, enjoying my memories of the hard work we did together and thinking about the bonds of friendship we established. By now, there are a lot of bonds.

In many ways, I'm quite a conventional cricketer. I played 83 first-class and 119 List A matches, including 19 one-day internationals for Australia. For me, first-class cricket is still the benchmark. It wasn't my choice to stop playing it: Victoria simply didn't renew my contract. I could still play it now; actually, I think I'd be at least as good as I was before, if not better.

Around the time I was taking my first steps in elite cricket, a new kind of game appeared. Twenty20 or T20 cricket was so novel that, in my second season for New South Wales, I played with Andrew Johns, probably history's greatest rugby league player. Which was great, because he'd been a childhood hero of mine, but it showed what the attitude was to the new format – it was treated as a novelty. Times have changed. It's on T20's growth that my career has been carried forward. I was recently asked if I could name all the T20 franchises I have played for, and while I did it successfully, some did come to mind more easily than others – and on the various team songs I mostly drew a blank. Still, like I said, something that never loses its attraction for me is being part of a winning side.

Three years ago, I thought I was pretty much done. I was 34 and Victoria had let me go. I played a season at the Delhi Daredevils, where I only started four times and had little impact. Knowing I might not have much time left in top-level cricket, I set out simply to enjoy it. It turned out I was on the brink of the most successful phase of my career – one that would take me to England, South Africa, the West Indies, the UAE and Pakistan.

I was part of a win in the Caribbean Premier League for the Trinbago Knight Riders, and in the Mzansi Super League with the Jozi Stars. The Notts Outlaws are my fourth county, following spells at Hampshire, Middlesex and Gloucestershire. I've led them to two T20 Blast titles. The Sydney Sixers are my fourth Big Bash League franchise, after stints at the Brisbane Heat, the Hobart Hurricanes and the Melbourne Renegades. When we won the BBL 10 at the Sydney Cricket Ground on 6 February 2021, it was the ninth T20 competition I'd been involved in winning in less than a decade, with six of these titles in the last four years.

In modern cricket, there's not much chance to lay memories down. There's always another game. Even when you win, you're usually on your way somewhere else the next day. But after stepping down from the BBL winners' podium, my Sixers teammates and I had the luxury of four days together. It was a rare opportunity for me to enjoy the moment.

The summer had been a lucky break really. I'd not enjoyed my last season at the Renegades, and they'd withdrawn an offered contract extension. So I said to my friend Moises Henriques, who captains the Sixers: 'Any room on your list?' And they found one. It was also an opportunity to be coached by Greg Shipperd, who'd been my coach with Victoria. Greg trained as a school teacher, and he's brilliant at running meetings, talking through scenarios, getting everyone to contribute – it's just good cricket talk, like a post-match beer. I made a thirty-ball hundred in a practice match against the Thunder at North Sydney Oval, and straight away it was like I'd played my whole career there. We lost a tight one to the Hurricanes first up, but next we thrashed the Renegades, which naturally I enjoyed. I made 50 off 16 balls against the Strikers, aiming to sweep every ball Rashid Khan bowled, and we were away.

Some of the matches of 2020–21 are going to end up among my favourite games. Against the Heat at Metricon, I came in at four for 54 chasing 149. I decided to block out Mujeeb Ur Rahman's last over and back myself against their pace bowlers: my unbeaten 61 off 38 got us home off the last ball. Later I came in at five for 103 chasing 178 against the Stars, and got us home with an unbeaten 49 off 23. We won close games, which is always a great feeling: Jason Holder got us over the line against the Renegades; Daniel Hughes played really well when we met the Stars again; Josh Philippe was consistently excellent; James Vince batted brilliantly in the final, where I contributed a couple of wickets and a quick 20. As we celebrated in the days following, it felt like I could play cricket forever.

That's how I come to be setting these thoughts down in the Leela Palace hotel in Chennai, in between stints at a conditioning camp at the Centre for Sports Science as part of the squad for the Royal Challengers Bangalore ahead of the 14th Indian Premier League. RCB are one of the IPL's foundation franchises. They're led by Virat Kohli, the world's best-known cricketer, and also feature AB de Villiers, the supreme all-format batter/keeper. In past seasons they have boasted Rahul Dravid, Chris Gayle, Jacques Kallis, Kevin Pietersen, Mitchell Starc and Shane Watson. But they've never won the title, and have been runners-up three times. Their hashtag, funnily enough, is #WeAreChallengers. They're hoping – we're hoping – that my experience will help make them champions

*

The IPL has already changed my life once. In January 2011, I was sitting in another hotel room, in Canberra, where I was to represent the Prime Minister's XI the next day. I was on the phone to my great mate Shaun Tait, and we were following the player auction in Bangalore on our laptops – it wasn't broadcast then and you followed via a chatroom. We saw my name come up: 'D. Christian, South Australia, allrounder: reserve price US$50,000.' What I didn't know was that three Australian IPL coaches – the aforementioned Greg Shipperd at the Delhi Daredevils, Darren Lehmann at the Deccan Chargers, and Geoff Lawson at the Kochi Tuskers Kerala – were all keen to get me. The price just kept going up. It got to US$400,000. Then it stopped for a minute. Then it came back at US$800,000. I was finally knocked down to the Chargers for US$900,000 a year, for two years, with an option for a third. In a few minutes, I'd gone from being a fringe international all-rounder to a cricket millionaire.

I'd be the first to admit I didn't justify it. In two seasons, I averaged 21 with the bat and 31 with the ball. In some ways, it was a very confronting experience. I'd just started using social media, so I heard a lot about how I wasn't worth what they'd paid for me. From a team point of view, it was also a letdown. We had a lot of good players, including Shikhar Dhawan, Ishant Sharma, Dale Steyn and Kumar Sangakkara. But we finished seventh and eighth, and in September 2012 the franchise dissolved. I never did get that third year. Instead I went to RCB, but I played only two games and wasn't retained.

In 2017 I had a stint at the Rising Pune Supergiants, who with the Gujurat Lions filled the void left as the Rajasthan Royals and the Chennai Super Kings served two-year suspensions for betting offences. But I didn't set the world on fire. That year's final, against the Mumbai Indians, is one of the few games of T20 I feel really disappointed about. I'd taken a couple of key wickets, made a runout, and with five balls to go was sitting with my pads on, with us on three for 123 and needing nine runs to win. Then we lost wickets from consecutive deliveries, and somehow I ended up needing six from the last two balls. Off Mitchell Johnson I could only scrape two twos; I was run out attempting the run that would have got us into a Super Over. I've replayed that game in my head many times, as I believe I should have been capable of winning it.

It's during the BBL that players start thinking about the IPL – about which franchises might be looking for what type of player, and where they might make a difference. And if you play well, your mates will start taking the piss: 'That'll help you at the auction.' This year I knew it would be a bit different, being a mini-auction: franchises were looking to fill gaps, often with all-rounders. So I had feeling I might attract some interest again.

By the time the auction came around, I was about to start the Pakistan Super League with the Karachi Kings. Ironically, although the auction is broadcast on television now, I couldn't get it at Karachi's Mövenpick Hotel, because no Indian TV is allowed in Pakistan. Via social media I learned that Chris Morris had gone for a bucket to the Rajasthan Royals, and Kyle Jamieson likewise to RCB. But I saw none of the activity until Shaun Tait texted to tell me my name had just been read out.

Ten years after we'd followed that auction via a chatroom, he Facetimed me and held his phone up to the television screen

Three all-rounders of different generations. Arm in arm with the excellent Mohammad Nabi and the all-time great Wasim Akram at the Karachi Kings.

so I could watch myself being sold. It wasn't as wild as the three-way tussle of 2011, but the paddles started going up on two tables: RCB and the Kolkata Knight Riders. Finally, after RCB bid 4.8 crore rupees – about $850,000 – I saw a head shake among the KKR crew. That was when I knew I would be rejoining Virat – and, as coach, Simon Katich, who had been my first captain for New South Wales. I soon received a generous message from Brendon McCullum at KKR: they'd been very keen to get me, he said, but the price had just got too high.

At times like these there's always a bit of disappointment going round. I had half a bottle of good Scotch left from the celebrations at the Sixers, and I shared it with Alex Hales, a teammate at the Notts Outlaws, a crosstown rival at the Sydney Thunder, and now an opponent at Islamabad United. He's been an unlucky cricketer. He had a brilliant BBL season, but because most IPL franchises were already bulging with good batters, he'd not attracted a bid. That night he said he must now hold a record as the cricketer most often left unsold at IPL auctions.

*

The PSL is a terrific competition – the standard is probably second only to the IPL. All the top Pakistani players play. Every franchise has a couple of local guys bowling 145 km/h who swing the new ball and reverse the old. The West Indians attend, headlined by Chris Gayle; so do the world's premier T20 spinners, Rashid Khan and Mujeeb Ur Rahman, along with their Afghani countryman Mohammad Nabi. Because the time of year suits them, you get a fair few good county players. There are also usually a handful of Aussies – including, this year, Ben Cutting, Chris Lynn, Ben Dunk and Fawad Ahmed.

I have to say, though, that there was an uneasy feeling throughout this edition. We were COVID-tested at the start, then not again. We were in the changing rooms and the dugouts together. We were high-fiving, shaking hands, hugging after games. With all six teams at the Mövenpick, you'd be having breakfast with different people every day. And the place was packed. You'd say to someone: 'Are you part of the bubble?' And they'd say: 'Oh yes, in the bubble.' But people were everywhere, and you sensed it couldn't be right. Then we heard that Fawad, Alex's teammate at Islamabad, had returned a positive test for COVID-19 and shown symptoms, leading to the postponement of a game against the Quetta Gladiators. And I knew from what had happened in Australia how quickly one case could become a few, then many.

There was nothing we could do for Fawad now that he was in 14-day quarantine, but I started talking to the other Aussie guys, and to Brendan Drew at the Australian Cricketers' Association, about getting out. The PSL were obviously desperate to keep the competition going, so they organised to obtain 400 vaccines – I guess you can do that

With my Dubai practice partner, friend and rival Chris Lynn.

when your president used to be a great cricketer. But by then there were seven active cases in the hotel, so I arranged an Emirates flight to Dubai at noon on 4 February. That way I could avoid serving a quarantine period – if you test negative on arrival in the UAE, you're good to go. I was a bit quicker than the others, and was leaving the hotel as Lynny and Cuttsy were getting up. But they followed me later that day, as the announcement was made that the tournament had been postponed. It's due to restart on 1 June.

Because there was about a month until the first match of the IPL, the three of us decided to make Dubai our training base. RCB organised for us to use the ICC Academy facilities, which at this time of year is often full of county teams doing their pre-seasons, but it was quiet because of COVID. Cuttsy had a mate there, Qasim Ali, who organised some net bowlers, including a few from the UAE team. The setting was really relaxed – we played a lot of golf. The weather was perfect – 33 or 34 degrees every day, just like what we'd experience in India. My girlfriend, Jorgia, joined me on our last night so that we could fly to India and quarantine in Chennai together; we were among the earliest overseas arrivals. Kane Richardson, who has just become a father, is spending a few extra days at home. Adam Zampa has been having a hard time: he and his fiancée's first attempt to get married, a year ago, was foiled by the COVID-19 lockdown; now the outbreak in Brisbane has just foiled their second attempt. Incredible.

The COVID situation in India, of course, is another thing altogether. They're reporting more than 100,000 cases per day, and yet you look out the window and realise that this is just not a country you can shut down – at least not in the way we did in Australia in 2020. RCB have already had two cases. Devdutt Padikkal tested positive before I arrived, and now Daniel Sams has too, probably as a result of passing through the airport. We're tested every few days. Samsy tested negative the first time, but positive three days later, so now he'll spend at least nine days in isolation. I was chatting to him yesterday and he says he feels okay – he only has a few mild symptoms. But he needs back-to-back negative tests before he can join us in the bio-bubble.

In some ways, this still doesn't feel too different to a standard IPL so far. Other than in Delhi and Mumbai, where there are some bars and restaurants the players favour, we tend not to go beyond the precincts of the hotel anyway, except to play and train. Our RCB group of 100 people – players, staff, management, drivers, hotel workers, kitchen workers – have taken over the entire Leela Palace hotel. There's a communal dining area, a physiotherapy area, meeting rooms, and a big team room full of beanbags, screens, video games and table games. The facilities at the Centre for Sports Science, or CSS, where I've joined in the conditioning camp after my week in quarantine, are excellent. We've just played a practice match, and I've caught up with all the players save Virat and AB, who are still isolating.

This year's RCB is different from the one I remember from 2013. Back then the owner was Vijay Mallya, who'd occasionally land his helicopter on the hotel roof and sweep through with his son. Now the owner is Diageo India, and their CEO Anand Kripalu, the chairman of RCB, is in the bubble with us – where it's safest.

Tuesday, 6 April 2021

Look closely at my Kookaburra bats when I come in and you'll notice something different about them: colourful stickers on the front and back from original paintings by Emma MacNeill. I came across Emma in 2018 on Instagram, as you do these days. She's a Yamatji Martu woman, the partner of Mitch Robinson from the Brisbane Lions. I loved the designs she was doing for the boots and jumpers of Indigenous AFL players like Buddy Franklin, and wanted to ask her to do something similar for cricket. Maybe it would inspire an Indigenous kid to take up cricket rather than football – the way I did.

I'm Wiradjuri on my father's side; my mother's background is British and Irish Catholic. I'm an only child and spent my first 12 years in the Riverina town of Narrandera, where Dad still lives. I've always been conscious of my ancestry, and proud of it. Wiradjuri Australians include Evonne Goolagong, Laurie Daley and Josh Addo-Carr. My great aunt, my grandfather's sister, was the famous Mum Shirl, Shirley Smith, a founder of the Aboriginal Legal Service and the Tent Embassy, who, before her death in 1998, was acknowledged as a National Living

Treasure. My uncle Trevor was a boxer, Riverina champion in three divisions simultaneously, narrowly missed selection in the 1960 Olympic team, then spent 35 years as an official. He later served as CEO of the Aboriginal Legal Service, and received an Order of Australia for services to the indigenous community.

Interestingly, probably because of my pale skin, nobody made any fuss about my heritage until I played for Australia, and I wasn't inclined to. I was just enjoying myself, playing all sports, trying to make up my mind which to pursue.

That choice ended up being made for me towards the end of my time at St Gregory's College in Campbelltown. I loved my rugby league growing up, and was a captain at junior levels; I was also playing first-grade cricket for the University of New South Wales, and under-17s cricket for New South Wales, bowling fast and having a go in the lower order. But around that time I was starting to play league against guys who were in junior programs for the Wests Tigers. They were getting massive and I was getting belted. One of my coaches said to me: 'If I were you, I'd go for cricket.' Then one day I was knocked out cold. I never played another minute.

In January 2002, I played four games in the Australian team that won the under-19 World Cup, alongside guys like Cameron White, who I'd play a lot of cricket with, and George Bailey, who I'd play a lot against. That led to my being part of the last intake at the old AIS Cricket Academy in Adelaide, along with Tim Paine, Ben Hilfenhaus and Shaun Tait. I played my first game for New South Wales against Taity in the Ford Ranger Cup in October 2006. Then the following season, when I moved to South Australia, I played with him. So I've been used to changing sides from my earliest days.

It's one of the things I most like about my cricket now. You check in with guys you played with 20 years ago, and it's like you don't miss a beat. Thanks to T20, wherever I go in the world there will always be someone I know who I can catch up with. Maybe I've been lucky, but I've hardly ever met a dickhead playing cricket. I can honestly say that there are very few guys with whom I wouldn't happily play again.

I drew inspiration from an earlier team too. The first time I ever heard about the Indigenous side that toured England in 1868 was when Ian Chappell talked about it at an Allan Border Medal presentation dinner. I was fascinated. They played 47 matches in conditions that could not have been more different from where they came from, in Victoria's Western District. It meant that when, 140 years later, I was offered the chance to lead another Indigenous team to England, this time organised by Cricket Australia, I jumped at the chance. I was the senior guy in what was mainly a development team, with players aged between 18 and 21. We played a dozen one-dayers, wearing a maroon shirt with a white sash like our forebears had, and we also did cultural demonstrations like they had. Mostly we just hung out, had lunch and dinner together, and played touch footy in the park next door. It was a great tour to be part of, representing our heritage on the other side of the world.

In 2018, the sesquicentenary of the 1868 tour, I captained another, stronger, squad of Indigenous men, alongside a squad of Indigenous women led by Ash Gardner. A film crew made a documentary about the tour called *Walkabout Wickets.* That may have been an even better experience. Even as we were engrossed in our games, we had the feeling that we were representing something bigger, that we were moving in the right direction. We linked up with the Australian team at Lord's, and there was a real sense we were making a statement about cricket being for everyone.

As I get older and more confident, I'm happier to speak out on issues affecting Aboriginal people. Last summer, in fact, I pissed off a few people when I tweeted critically about the Prime Minister's response to our taking a knee at the Sydney Sixers during the Big Bash League, and then playing down Brittany Higgins' allegations about being sexually assaulted at Parliament House. I got a lot of unsought advice of how I should stick to cricket from the likes of Mark Latham, the One Nation state leader in New South Wales, and Gerard Rennick, the climate change denialist LNP senator from Queensland.

I'm actually quite circumspect on Twitter. I never tweet straightaway. I always give myself ten minutes to think things over, and maybe to talk to someone else. I've got a lot of things sitting in my drafts. The responses to my tweets were interesting. At the outset, about 40 per cent were hostile; within a few days that had dropped to about 10 per cent. By then, I guess, most of the trolls had found something else to be outraged about.

Centre wicket training under the watchful eye of Simon Katich, Devdutt Padikkal at the non-striker's end.

EXIDE
muthoot
FINCORP
MAX
LIFE

And while it may sound strange, I feel more optimistic about positive change than I did a year ago. There are lots of little signs that things are getting better. It's a trivial example perhaps, but today I was talking to Kookaburra about Emma's fantastic bat stickers. The Sydney Thunder's teenage batter Anika Learoyd, a Gumbaynggirr woman, has been using the bats recently, and Kookaburra wants to make them more widely available next season. That they'll be on show in India can only be good.

Wednesday, 7 April 2021

In preparing for a tournament, you start thinking about situations you could find yourself in – they call it scenario training. You might have a certain number of runs to get, or to defend, off a certain number of balls, or particular opponents to confront. You're also getting your volume of practice up, because once you start playing, your training loads naturally taper. I'm at the stage where I don't need to bat lots – just enough to feel good. Bowling's different. I need to bowl lots of overs so that I get to the stage where I can almost shut my eyes and put the ball where I want it.

At the CSS ground today we had a practice match, where five for 224 was overtaken in the last over by five for 228, thanks to Rajat Patidar, who made 104 from 49 balls – he's likely to make our starting XI for the first time this week. It felt good to get a few out of the middle at the back end and pick up three-for. Then things got better.

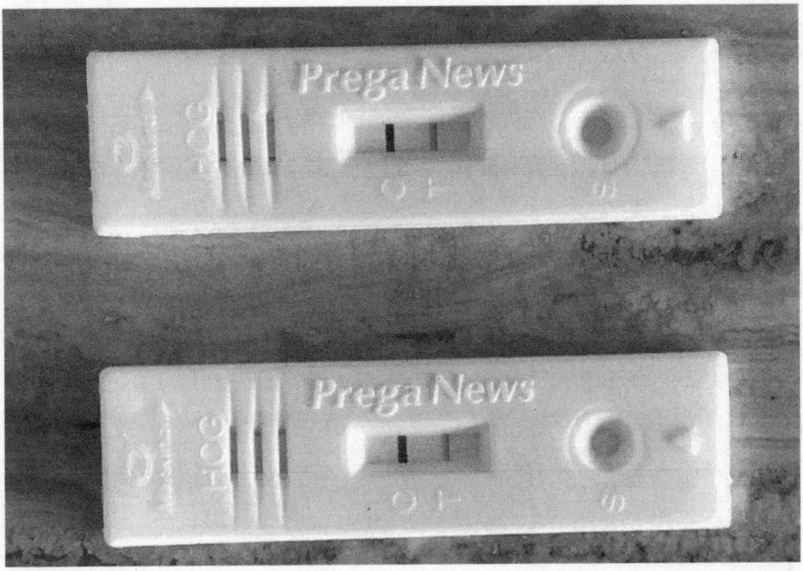

Jorgia hadn't been feeling well. Then, in Chennai, we learned why.

When Jorgia and I arrived in Chennai, she was unwell for a couple of days, which I told her was standard for India – she was just getting used to the food. But while I was out today, she was in the bathroom for hours, and Glenn Maxwell's fiancée, Vini, who has a pharmacy degree, gave her some anti-nausea tablets. Finally, when I got back, we asked the Leela Palace liaison people for a couple of pregnancy tests, and they came back positive. We're now 99 per cent sure that Jorgia is expecting.

It's all happened extremely quickly. Although we've spoken about it, we haven't been trying to start a family, but we're happy all the same. We've both got friends and family, as I'm sure everyone does, who have either been trying for a while or who have had trouble conceiving in the past, so we certainly weren't expecting anything. The planets have just aligned for us. This IPL hasn't even started yet, but already for me it's been memorable.

Thursday, 8 April 2021

'You know what,' Maxy said to me today. 'I think I've worked it out.' We were standing behind the nets at Chidambaram Stadium watching Virat Kohli and AB de Villiers have their first net sessions since coming out of quarantine – and, well, it was awesome. The light wasn't that good. Neither were the surfaces. The bowling was pretty tasty. You had Navdeep Saini and Mohammed Siraj, who were so good against Australia last summer. But Virat and AB seemed to have all the time in the world, and smashed everything. 'Yeah,' says Maxy, 'I've worked it out. They're just better than everybody else.'

They're different too. When I played at RCB the first time, what struck me about Virat was his absolute self-belief. The way I was taught to cope with failure is by being honest about what I've done wrong. Virat simply doesn't admit failure. If he gets out, it is never his fault. It was a bad decision; the wicket did something; the guy bowled an unbelievable ball; his partner made a bad call. Consequently, he's never out of form. You'd look at him in the dressing room and think: 'This guy is just at another level.'

AB's similar. I played against him in the Mzansi Super League back in November 2018. I was bowling and gave him a good slower ball – it landed right where I wanted it to. He just stood there, waited for it and hit it out of Centurion Park. Waiting is the hardest thing about slower balls, and it was something I was struggling with at the time. So I went to him after the match and asked: 'How do you do that? Is there something you do to prepare for playing the ball that way, to help you wait and hold your shape? What are you thinking about?'

He said: 'I don't think about it.'

What's also amazing about AB is that he's not playing anything but one or two T20 leagues. That's really hard. You watch guys in the BBL who've stopped playing four-day cricket, and they really taper off. AB has lost nothing.

After the session, Virat talked to everyone. He said he wanted us to play at full intensity all the time, but also to have fun and enjoy ourselves. Pretty obvious messages, but good to hear, especially as we're up against the title holders in our first match, the Mumbai Indians – the team to which I was so disappointed to lose four years ago.

Mumbai are the benchmark in the IPL. Rohit Sharma at the top and Kieron Pollard in the middle form their nucleus, along with the Pandya boys, Hardik and Krunal. They used to have Lasith Malinga and Mitch McClenaghan; since then it's been Trent Boult and Jasprit Bumrah.

To prepare, I've been playing scenarios, watching videos and thinking about who I'll be facing. I've seen a fair bit of Trent Boult, who I played with at Delhi, so I know his slower balls, and how he can sometimes miss his yorker. As I tend to come in around the 15th or 16th over, I might get an over of spin from either Krunal Pandya, who I've faced a bit, or Rahul Chahar, who I played with when he was a kid at the Rising Pune Supergiants. Then there'll probably be Nathan Coulter-Nile.

These days, there's a lot of analysis of strike rates against particular kinds of bowling, but it's often misleading. For instance, people point out that my strike rate against spin is a good deal slower than against pace bowling. But that's largely because I come in when I do: I tend to face at best an over of spin before the pace bowlers come back, who I then have to really attack. Since the 2018 IPL final, apparently only Pollard has scored more T20 runs than I have in the last four overs of innings, at a strike rate of 193. I guess that's one of the reasons I'm here, as last season RCB struggled in the back end of their innings. So if I can get 30 or 40 off 15 balls every so often after Virat and AB have batted deep, I'll be justifying my recruitment.

Looking around our hotel room tonight, I can see the five Kookaburra bats, wearing Emma's stickers, that I hope will see me through this IPL. When I started in professional cricket, I used a brand called Screaming Cat, made by Julian Millichamp from the bat maker Millichamp and Hall. They were beautiful bats but the business wasn't quite sustainable. So I've been with Kookaburra since 2008. It might be slightly different now, but back then when you played international cricket you were paid a retainer; then you might get bonuses for the number of internationals you played, or when you scored a century. You received an equipment allowance up to a certain limit, which tended to be so high you'd never reach it.

I have one match bat, which has lasted me about two and a half years. On average, I only face 15 or 20 balls per match, so the wear and tear on it isn't heavy, and repairs can keep a bat going. The other four are for the nets, and they only last a month to six weeks – all those yorkers at training take their toll.

It's common to say now that the bats are better than ever before, and they are – but they're also not. The middles are the same as always. I don't hit a ball out of the middle any farther than I did ten years ago. What's different is how far the mis-hits travel. I don't know what it's like for other players, but

I reckon I get about half my shots out of the middle. I make perfect contact for about half of my sixes; the rest of it is muscle and bat speed.

As a batter, you know it, too. When you look down in your stance, you draw confidence from the profile of the bat you're holding – and confidence is everything. Sometimes you'll hear commentators talk about 'accessing the short boundary'. It's not a matter of distance so much as of psychology. You hit stronger in that direction – because you know the margin for error is in your favour, you tend to hold your shape better, and you end up clearing the boundary by 20 metres. The bats also have a psychological impact on the bowlers, because they know that if they miss even slightly, they're gone. Miss a yorker by a foot or be a foot out with the height of a bouncer, and the ball's out of the park. That's T20.

I'm ready to play some.

2

GAME TIME

The Royal Challengers Bangalore dressing room contains a staggering array of talent. We're going to take a lot of beating in IPL14. But can we beat the most intimidating opponent? The global COVID pandemic, which has already led to the truncation of the Pakistan Super League, is bearing down on everyone.

Friday, 9 April 2021

'Welcome back, youngster,' said Virat as we walked out onto Chidambaram Stadium tonight, his arm around my shoulder, a big smile on his face. It was classic Virat – he's a fierce competitor, but personally so generous and welcoming. He was in a good mood, too, having won the toss and sent Mumbai in. It was a gesture of confidence in the depth of our batting, and a precaution against the evening dew making the ball slippery.

The welcome from the stadium? Well, of course, there wasn't one. The last time I played an IPL match, almost three years ago, the stands at Rajiv Gandhi Stadium in Hyderabad were heaving. Now the only crowd noise was recorded. I'd had a taste of this in the T20 Blast. Finals day in the Blast can be pretty rowdy, in front of people who've had their first drink at 10 am even though the final starts at 8 pm. But last season when we played Surrey, the stands at Edgbaston were bare, and our celebrations afterwards echoed around the empty stands. The effect here was magnified: there were all these superstars on show and nobody to watch them. The early part of the game reflected this: there were plays and misses, misfields, a few cobwebs. Then the game turned on one bit of brilliance from our captain.

Before the match, we were shown a crazy stat: that Mumbai win something like 90 per cent of their games when Rohit faces more than 20 balls. It's not exactly 'get Rohit and you win the game', but he's clearly a key part of their winning formula. Anyway, Mumbai were 24 off 23 balls when Chris Lynn pushed Yuzvendra Chahal into the covers and gave Rohit the old 'yes ... no' when Virat appeared in the gap. Virat then had the presence of mind to bounce his throw to the non-striker's stumps, where Yuzi took off the bails. It was a huge moment. Rohit had just hit the first six of the innings; but we'd cut him off after 17 balls. Lynny put on 70 in seven overs with Suryakumar Yadav, and Ishan Kishan belted 28 off 19, but we made steady inroads, and Harshal Patel got Pollard and both Pandyas cheaply to keep them under eight runs per over.

My two wicketless overs cost 21. I bowled the ninth and the 15th overs, conceded three boundaries, bowled three dots. Hardly a day out, but I wasn't unhappy about the way I'd bowled. The first boundary was a lovely cut by Suryakumar off the top of off; the second wouldn't have gone for four except that we didn't have Washington Sundar in quite the right place and his foot touched the boundary rope as he slid to collect the ball on the dewy outfield. The third was from probably my only bad ball, something juicy and full that Hardik Pandya smashed past me at head height.

It was one of those nights – and they probably happen about half the time – that the figures didn't reflect the quality of my bowling. I mean, you can bowl beautifully in T20 and take none for 35 off four, or you can bowl badly and grab three wickets – that's the kind of game it is, and you have to accept it. The final game I played in the PSL, I went for 32 in my last over. I didn't quite nail a couple of yorkers, and I bowled a good slower-ball bouncer, which the umpire called a wide and which then beat the keeper. An hour and a bit later, I hit a four and a six and won the match. That's also the kind of game T20 is.

After we lost a couple of early ones, Virat and Maxy looked like they were doing it easily, with Maxy really enjoying the chance to bat at four. He's an amazing player. I've never seen him play with any kind of self-doubt. He always backs himself; he always thinks he's going to do the job for the team; he always thinks he can hit every ball for six. I've no doubt that he's been in the best six batsmen in Australia at several stages of his career, yet he's never played a home Test match. It's almost like his short-form prowess has stopped people seeing what a good first-class player he is. It's not that long since he made 278 for Victoria. You don't get 278 just slogging.

We lost our way a bit after Bumrah got Virat lbw. There was a fair bit of bad luck, really. You hardly ever see guys caught at leg gully, but Maxy was. Shahbaz Ahmed hit a beautiful pull but picked out backward square. I nailed a cut but found point. On the highlights, Mark Nicholas says 'Shot!' as it leaves my bat; a yard either side or above the fielder, Rahul Chahar, and it was four. It was disappointing, because the situation was tailor-made for what I've been doing the last few years, but I also played the shot because I have confidence in our depth, which proved well-founded. We lost AB and Kyle Jamieson to run-outs but still got over the line. One from one – the perfect start.

A final slight strangeness. One of the nice features of the IPL is the handshake and the chat with your opponents afterwards. Franchise T20 being what it is, many of them are former teammates, and it's always good to catch up. After the game tonight, however, we were not allowed to interact with the Mumbai players, because one of their staff had returned a positive COVID test. I suspect it won't be the last time that happens.

Saturday, 10 April 2021

Today we had our reviews with the backroom staff. I sat down with our bowling coach, Adam Griffith, to talk over my dozen balls, to look at where we might improve – whether, for example, we had our leg-side field quite right for Lynny, who doesn't really play the lap sweep but is such a danger when he can free his arms. If all the wickets are as slow as this one, I think I'll try to jam guys up in this IPL; it seems the way to go.

It felt like both teams were a bit rusty. Each of us had two run-outs, including of top batsmen (Rohit and AB). Running between the wickets is the skill of cricket that only gets practised in the middle. Way back when I was at South Australia, I remember Dean Jones putting us through running drills, emphasising things like staying low in the turns. Since then, I've hardly ever heard it discussed, except as something it would be good to be better at. AB got out yesterday mainly because he didn't come back for the second run in a straight line. But he's been doing that half-circle for 20 years, so I can't see him changing now.

It's funny we don't think about running between wickets more, because some of it is counterintuitive. A few years ago Jarrod Kimber published an analysis of T20 cricket's most and least frequent run-out casualties. Chris Gayle was comfortably the least run out, although he's notoriously nonchalant between wickets, and can sometimes put pressure on partners who want to turn the strike over. David Warner was near the top, although there's hardly anyone quicker or more aggressive. The takeaway was that the quicker you are, the more you risk. That interested me, because personally I think run-outs in T20 are a shocking waste, except maybe in the death overs; you're donating the opposition a bonus wicket, and the new batter will inevitably slow the innings. But for whatever reason – maybe because the economy of T20 is geared to churning out boundaries – nobody's looked all that closely at running between wickets as a key skill.

T20 lends itself to being reviewed. It goes by so quickly that it's easy to overlook things; it's short enough that you can, if you want, analyse all 240 balls. But I also believe there's such a thing as paralysis by analysis – I reckon you should trust what you're doing at training and stick with that to get the job done. One of the best things about T20 is that it's easy to put a bad result behind you. During the Big Bash League, my Sixers teammate Jack Edwards was picking my brains about what it took to be a successful cricketer, to perform under pressure. I said: 'You think I'm successful, do you? Well, at least ten times I've been hit for six off the last ball of a game and lost. Did you know that?'

He said: 'No.'

I said: 'People don't remember that. So why should I, and let it get me down? Just focus on the good stuff.'

The good stuff in our first game is that we won a close match against a great team without really playing to our full potential. Regardless of my contribution, I'm happy with that.

Sunday, 11 April 2021

Back at training at 2 pm, which at Royal Challengers is something of an event, because it's live-streamed to our fans via the RCB app. You can't buy this from the app store in Australia, but in India it gets a big audience – and when you've got Virat and AB going through their paces, that's not really surprising. We were joined today for the first time by Finn Allen, and rejoined by Devdutt Padikkal after his COVID quarantine period. Daniel Sams is still serving his.

You can't avoid noticing that COVID is a bigger deal elsewhere. The daily cases are getting over 150,000, up towards 200,000. It doesn't surprise me. I was just looking at a piece in *Time* that talked about a survey about six months ago drilling into the data, which estimated that there were about 30 infections in India for every reported case of the virus. So 150,000 reported cases implies 4.5 million infections. In a day. Even in a country of 1.3 billion, that's a lot.

In the meantime, it's official: Jorgia and I are going to be parents. The RCB team doctor, whose responsibilities include all the families as well as the squad members and staff, did a blood test today to confirm the presence of the hCG hormone. It's very early – our due date is 16 December – so we're keeping it quiet for the moment. What a place and time for it to happen. But that's the nature of modern cricket. All the things that make up a life – births, deaths, marriages, family celebrations, friendships – have to be fitted in around the relentless schedule.

Jorgia has quickly become adept at this. In her professional life, she's a project manager for a firm of Adelaide architects. When I'm not around, she's busy working, emailing and Zooming. When we're together, we're spending a lot of time house hunting online, concentrating on Sydney's Eastern Suburbs. Now Jorgia's pregnancy has added some urgency to that need to find a home. We'll almost certainly have to buy something without actually stepping inside it first. But that's just the way it is.

Monday, 12 April 2021

Further training in the heat of the day – 35 degrees, 80 per cent humidity, no let-up. It takes about 40 minutes to get to the CSS ground from the Leela Palace hotel but about an hour and a half in the afternoon to get back, which can be trying when you're exhausted, and a bit frustrating even if you're not. It's a long way to go if all you want is two dozen throwdowns.

I like training. I took to heart the motto of St Gregory's: *Quae Seminaveris Metes* translates as 'what you sow, so shall you reap'. And I'm probably fitter at this stage of my career than I've ever been. Last year I had no cricket between the end of the Big Bash League and the delayed start of the Vitality Blast, and I worked really hard on getting fit – started running for the first time in my life and really enjoyed it. But India can be as tough to practise in as to play. When I was in Delhi in 2018, I remember we were training through that period when the pollution was just off the charts. You'd get back to the hotel, blow your nose and the black gunk would pour out; your ears were full of it too. Imagine what was getting into people's lungs.

Still, it's a foretaste of our weekend game against Kolkata Knight Riders – one of our two day-time matches for the tournament. And sometimes it's amazing just to watch India go by. There've been elections here recently for the Tamil Nadu Legislative Assembly, and tonight our coach passed through a political rally. There were people as far as the eye could see. Maybe five of them were wearing masks.

Tuesday, 13 April 2021

Ahead of our match tomorrow night against the Sunrisers Hyderabad, we're restricted to the Leela Palace hotel. That means the gym, the pool, the team room. It's not quite the setup of the Mumbai Indians, who have villas on the beach. Lynny went surfing the other day. That's what happens when you've got the Ambanis behind you.

There are still things to do. There's a lot of social media, including an RCB YouTube channel, and we have huge Twitter and Instagram followings. The franchises keep everyone busy. Steve Smith might not have been picked for the Delhi Capitals' first match but there's a video circulating of him on Twitter dancing the dilli baraati with his teammates Ajinkya Rahane, Rishabh Pant, Shikhar Dhawan, Chris Woakes and Ravichandran Ashwin. Today, in fact, it's our turn to perform – although thankfully not dancing. We had to participate in advertisements for our commercial partners, like Exide Industries, Muthoot Fincorp and Dubai Ports World.

There's probably more of this than ever, but it's always been a feature of the IPL. By far the most embarrassing I can remember was a 7 Up commercial I did at RCB in 2013, which involved, yes, Bollywood dancing. Virat was in it. He's a natural. Andrew McDonald too. He's not. When inevitably it turned up on Twitter again a week or two ago, I made sure to send a link to Ronny. Thanks to the internet, everything's forever.

Wednesday, 14 April 2021

Match day. We set off on the 15-minute drive along Marina Beach to Chepauk in the late afternoon in two buses: one for players, the other for support staff, management and the players' partners, including Jorgia, who watch the game from a separate box. The squad was finally at full strength, with Zamps and Kane having served their quarantine, and Samsy having rejoined the bio-bubble after two negative COVID tests.

I had my most significant interaction before the game with David Warner, the Sunrisers' captain. When we were out there looking at the pitch, he started talking about their recent match against KKR. He said that the pitch had been ordinary, but that both teams had bowled poorly – his guys had been too full, and allowed too many step hits. I went back to our guys and said: 'They're probably going to bowl more into the pitch tonight, with a bit more variety.' Sure enough, they did.

We made a reasonable start – we were two for 91 after 12 overs – then we lost Virat, and Rashid Khan bowled a brilliant spell, removing AB and Washington Sundar. Turned out to be another of those surfaces where it was really hard to start, and Maxy showed amazing patience and game awareness, only attacking when the odds were in his favour: he hit 38 in boundaries from eight balls, and 21 from his other 33. Wonderful calculation.

I was the victim of some wonderful calculation myself, from T Natarajan. These days, when someone pushes mid-off and mid-on back, you're expecting them to bowl straight. He threw in a wide one, which took a bit of guts without third man on the fence or a deep point, but it was the perfect double bluff, and I chased it so far that the bat turned in my hand. In fact, I wasn't actually sure I connected. The umpire took a long time to give it, and because we had the review left, Maxy and I thought: bugger it, let's send it upstairs. But there was a spike, and a pretty big one, although I can honestly say I didn't feel anything.

Normally you'd be disappointed with 149, but it looked defendable. Teams have struggled this week to maintain momentum. KKR had been none for 72 on Tuesday night, then lost seven for 68 in 65 balls. So even when Davey got going with Manish Pandey, it felt like seven or eight an over was going to be hard to get, and we were a wicket away from being right back in it – which duly came when Davey hit Kyle Jamieson down my throat at long-on. Then, in the 17th over, Virat threw the ball to Shahbaz, whose left-arm tweakers he thought would hold up in the surface. Result: a three-wicket over, leaving two new batsmen. In the 18th over, Virat caught Vijay Shankar off Harshal Patel; in the 19th I caught Jason Holder off Mohammed Siraj, who then ran out Rashid Khan with two balls left. 'That's a real win,' said Virat, pumping his fist as we entered the dressing room. Too right.

The fashion in recent years in T20 has been to chase. But so far at Chepauk, nobody's been able to score with any freedom, and batting's become harder the deeper the match has gone. If you can take a wicket or two around the 14 or 15 over mark, you're a good chance of shutting the game down altogether. It's partly the surfaces. They're not terrible, but they're deteriorating so that you need to score early. I'm pretty sure they've re-laid the middle four tracks on the square since I was last here, because there's a height change in the middle of the square and a distinct difference in colour. Chepauk pitches have traditionally been a red clay – flat, glassy, rolled mud where it skids on beautifully. You still see that red clay on the outside of the square, but the soil colour towards the centre is different and there's more grass cover. And rather than the dew making it more difficult for the bowlers, it's been softening and weighing the ball down, making it harder for the batters to get away. All this is not making for spectacular cricket, but it is intriguing.

Thursday, 15 April 2021

They talk about parenthood changing your life. For Jorgia and me, it has already. Today, because we needed to get a six-week ultrasound, RCB had to create what's called a 'green corridor', which is what they do when a guy gets injured and has to get a scan or an MRI. They close the part of the hospital where you're going to go and sanitise everything. You put on a full hazmat suit, leave your bubble hotel in your bubble car, step out into the hospital lift and go straight into the room with the ultrasound machine; you don't see a soul except for about half a dozen medical staff done up like astronauts. After an hour, it was back into our bubble car and back to our bubble hotel. As Jorgia said, it felt like we were royalty.

Our news has added to the general good vibe at RCB: everyone's pretty happy at the moment, including those at the top. Players tend to be philosophical about winning and losing – we know how narrow the gap can be. Management is more cut-and-dried about these things: how you're treated depends very heavily on how you're going on the field. Lose a few and management starts pressuring staff, calling the coach in, asking why this guy's playing but not that guy. That was certainly the case at the Deccan Chargers, where after a while it seemed like Boof Lehmann was always in with the owners.

The mood was reflected in a function this evening, where the squad was divided into three groups, led by Virat, AB and Yuzvendra Chahal, who each had to perform a skit based on a fairy tale. Yuzi's group had Little Red Riding Hood, with Maxy as the Big Bad Wolf. AB's group had Cinderella, including Mohammed Siraj in the title role and me as the fairy godmother. Virat was the Ugly Duckling – having an actress wife, he was very good, while Zamps as narrator did a lot of ad-libbing. The judging panel of backroom staff and partners made them the winner. It was a really fun night – and nights have a way of being fun when you've won consecutive matches.

Friday, 16 April 2021

A decent night's sleep at last, which I'm grateful for. Your hours go haywire during an IPL. On a playing day you're never in bed before 3 am, by the time you've packed up and returned to the hotel, because you normally spend at least some time in the team room afterwards. Which is bad for me – I'm a naturally early riser, so there are lots of nights I don't get more than three or four hours' rest. Eight last night was a big improvement.

It was nice to have something positive for my new Oura Ring to report. We were issued these wearables a few days ago; they're in use in the PGA, NBA, WNBA and even NASCAR. The ring tracks my sleep stages, steps, heartbeat, body temperature and so on via two infrared LED sensors, two negative thermal coefficient body temperature sensors, a 3D accelerometer and a gyroscope. It'll take a couple of weeks to get to know my baseline metrics before giving me a daily readiness measure I'll be able to read on my phone. And, of course, so will RCB. They haven't actually told us how they're going to use the data, but when you've paid so much for cricketers, you're probably entitled to know all about them.

Being watched is what a sportsperson's life is all about. I caught up this morning with the result of last night's game between the Rajasthan Royals and the Delhi Capitals, where the South African Chris Morris blazed 36 off 18, including four sixes, to win the game with two balls to spare. Morris, of course, was the priciest player at the recent auction, fetching US$2.2 million.

Players aren't bothered about stuff like that. It's not like you went looking for all this money – it's not your fault the paddles kept going up. It's the luck of the draw. You might take the piss out of one another now and again. You're at the bar and you say: 'I think you can get this one, Maxy.' But the public nature of the player deals, which is unique to the IPL, is hard to ignore: definitely the fans, and potentially some owners, pay attention to how much you're on, which does introduce pressure. When you miss out, it can feel like your fault. You feel the eyes watching, watching. You're being judged. I didn't handle it well the first time around. I understand now, as I didn't then, that a big contract for a young player can be a mixed blessing.

Saturday, 17 April 2021

It's going to be an interesting one tomorrow. I almost went to KKR, who are captained by Eoin Morgan and include Pat Cummins. At about 4 pm in Chennai a bit of a breeze comes in, but until then it'll be really challenging. Rain this week has worsened the humidity. The dew won't be a factor, so maybe we'll want 60 to 70 in the powerplay rather than being satisfied with 50.

Surprisingly, the time of day a T20 match starts can make a big difference. A couple of years ago I was playing the PSL in Sharjah. You'd play a game in the afternoon, and the scores would be around 160, because there was no dew, the ball was reversing, and batting at the end was really hard. There'd be a second game on the same pitch in the evening, and the scores would be 40 runs per innings higher because those factors were not in play.

Most of our games in England are day games, but they're different again. The pitches are slower and don't turn much; medium-pacers can be hard to get away. Plus, of course, it's cold! In golf the ball doesn't travel as far when it's cold, and I assume it's the same in cricket. Sometimes it's argued that conditions don't play a big part in T20 because the game's so short, but I've always felt they can be hugely influential.

Sunday, 18 April 2021

Match day – and I don't play. It's hardly unprecedented. The reality is that I've not played more often than I've played in the IPL: 42 games in six seasons. If I'm honest, it's a let-down.

It was a late call too, during the warm-ups. I was just about to measure my run-up when Kat came up to me and explained that, after looking at the pitch, they thought they were going to get a lot of spin in the powerplay, so they were going to play Rajat Patidar as an extra top-order bat. Kat and I go way back. He's been my teammate, my captain and now my coach. An advantage of that is that we can have honest conversations, and I told him frankly that I'd have been fine had I been told in the morning, but to learn at the last minute was tough. You're pretty annoyed for the first half-hour after you've been left out, and you need the chance to compose yourself. It was also strange to return to a bench with four other international cricketers: Zamps, Samsy, Kane and Finn Allen. I can't recall playing an IPL game when the starting XI included only three internationals; the maximum permitted is four. So at first I was thinking to myself: 'What's going on here?'

Of course, you get over these things, and the match turned out to be brilliant. KKR did start with spin: we lost Virat and Rajat in the second over to Varun Chakravarthy to leave us two for nine. But Eoin Morgan then decided to hold Varun back to bowl to AB, and Maxy played the perfect innings under the circumstances, zooming to 50 in 28 balls. The daytime heat was hellish and the perspiration was pouring off him, but you could tell it was Morgs who was really sweating. When AB came in to join Maxy, they took 17 off Varun's last over, and AB then smashed 38 off two overs from Andre Russell. With 56 in the last three overs, we surged to four for 204, which was well over par. The pitch was no better than the other two we've played on – Maxy and AB are just freaks. Chasing ten runs per over was going to be a huge challenge for KKR.

I got on the field as a sub for Maxy, who was pretty cooked after his innings, and from mid-on I watched Shubman Gill get off to a flier, flaying consecutive sixes over the off-side from Jamieson. There was nothing wrong with the deliveries – they were probably hitting the top of the stumps – but Gill's an amazing player. The next ball, though, slightly slower, he cross-batted and miscued towards me. I went to my right and dived at the last second as it started to tail away, catching it in both hands. So, despite not playing, I was a contributor on the day, which felt good. Our spinners then bowled tighter than KKR's, Russell came in too late to do much damage, and Harshal Patel didn't give away a boundary.

So we're three from three after one of the best team performances I've seen. Just a shame I didn't feature in it.

Monday, 19 April 2021

A normal IPL involves a constant flit from one city to the next. Obviously, this one is different. We'll be travelling less often and more comprehensively. The move from Chennai to Mumbai today was unlike any trip I can remember. Our party was ushered from the Leela Palace hotel in three coaches, with everyone in a mask, shield and gloves. We bypassed the international airport and arrived at a satellite terminal to take our two-hour charter flight to the Chhatrapati Shivaji airport, seeing only the security staff at each end and the in-flight crew, who were dressed in full PPE, along the way. It was amazingly smooth. I literally put my bag outside my door in Chennai in the morning, and it turned up outside my door two minutes after I arrived in my room at the Taj Land's End.

All the features of our stay in Chennai are replicated here. We have exclusive use of four levels; we have the pool, the gym, the team room, a dedicated kitchen. The hotel workers we interact with have been living here for a month already. We'll have no contact with anyone outside the bubble. In Chennai, we were still allowed to use Zoomato, the Indian version of Uber Eats. Orders were dropped outside and had to pass through some kind of UV scanner before you got them. That's now off the menu. It feels a great deal safer than the PSL; it will want to be, because the COVID news worsens daily. Today, more than a quarter of a million cases have been reported. As I said earlier, I can't help feeling that this is an underestimate.

Tuesday, 20 April 2021

A training day. In previous years I've stayed at the Trident, at Nariman Point. The Taj is closer to the airport, but further from the ground. Our coach passes through the busy streets where life is somehow going on regardless of the fact – a staggering statistic I heard today – that *half* the people of Mumbai have suffered a COVID-19 infection.

As cut off as we are, it is hard not to think about the strangeness of what we're doing – carrying on a cricket tournament in the midst of a pandemic that in India alone has killed more than 180,000 people and infected more than

15 million. To be frank, it would have made far more sense had this IPL been held, like last year's, in the UAE. When I was in Dubai a month ago, life was almost completely normal. Eighty-five per cent of the population had received the vaccine; I imagine everyone's been vaccinated by now. I understand the optics of it. The Board of Control for Cricket in India have the T20 World Cup later in the year, and they want to prove they can make it work. But it is a huge expense and effort.

I've given a lot of thought to whether it's right to carry on under the circumstances. I can certainly see why some would doubt it, in the face of such an emergency in a country that's both very rich and very poor. On balance I think we're doing the right thing, providing joy and satisfaction to cricket watchers, in the same way as footy made life more liveable in Australia in 2020. Being able to see live sport on television during lockdown distracted people from the daily agony of restrictions, case numbers and deaths. Plus we're keeping people employed here – staff, broadcasters, media, hotel workers, drivers and the rest – who would otherwise not be working. If there were no IPL, there would still be a pandemic – it would just be a pandemic without the IPL.

I've had a few Pakistanis in my Twitter timeline complaining that I took a different attitude to the PSL. That's a fair enough criticism, except for two factors. For one, things were a great deal more dangerous in Karachi. The bio-security was nowhere near as exacting as it has been here, and it felt like an accident waiting to happen. For another thing, and

I'll be quite honest here, do the math. My contract with RCB is worth ten times what I earned from the Kings. And we're flying. We've got Kohli, AB and Maxy making runs. We've got no superstar bowlers – no Bumrah, no Rashid – but everyone's doing their job. Kyle's taking wickets. Siraj has been tight. The spinners, Yuzi and Washy Sundar, are bowling well, and Harshal Patel's been terrific at the death. So I'm part of a winning franchise. Which is what I play for.

Wednesday, 21 April 2021

A long training session today under lights in Mumbai, ahead of our game tomorrow against the Rajasthan Royals. Of course now I'm not sure I'll play. When Kat dropped me on Sunday, he said it was due to the conditions, although not that it was a one-off. The pitches at Wankhede Stadium look to be better than the pitches we got in Chepauk, with a bit more pace and carry. But I also know from experience that when you're left out as an overseas player, it's like you drop down to the bottom of the pecking order: you have to work your way back up.

Still, you can't afford to let being left out get you down in the IPL, and it actually causes less trouble than you might think. Especially when you're winning, and guys in the starting XI are set in their roles, which is the situation here. Because franchises always have more talent than they need on any given day, they've given a bit of thought to this. A guy who it's known has a problem with being left out isn't going to last. Word will spread. He'll start missing out.

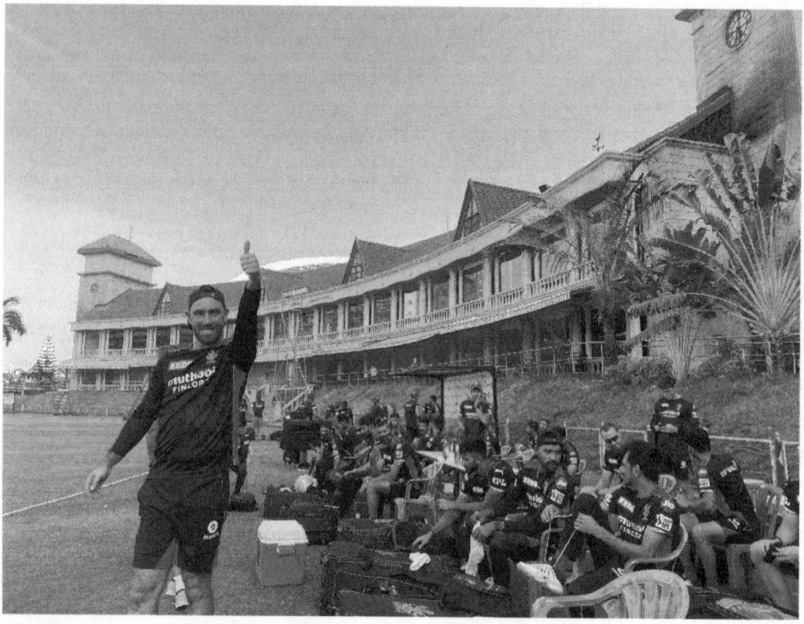

Ready for training in Mumbai, Maxy leading the way.

I've some experience to draw on in this respect. I was 12th man in two Tests. I was playing well at the time, but each time the guy I was pushing for a place was Mike Hussey, and I was hardly going to play ahead of him! The standard in the IPL is so high that it's not like you'll ever be missing out to an obviously inferior cricketer. You just have to be patient and contribute in other ways.

Thursday, 22 April 2021

Four from four – our most convincing win yet, by ten wickets. Without Ben Stokes or Jofra Archer, the Royals were not quite ripe for the picking, but they were clearly vulnerable. Again I didn't play, although I could follow the logic. The pitch at Wankhede is quicker, so there was an argument for an extra quick, and that turned out to be Kane Richardson.

We thought a score of 210 would be par. The other night KKR had been five for 31 against the Chennai Super Kings and still made 202. Jos Buttler was clearly the key wicket. We talked in the bowling meeting about trying to bowl tight at his stumps, posting a backward square and a fine leg, in the hope he'd try to back away and access the off-side – which is exactly what he did to Siraj, and was bowled. Siraj then bowled an absolute rocket to get David Miller lbw, and though the Royals rallied in the middle overs, 177 was never enough.

Shreyas Gopal has a great record against us: he's got Virat three times and AB four times. So we weren't surprised that the Royals started with him, but Devdutt Padikkal as a leftie helped neutralise him. It was the first time I'd seen Devdutt really get going, and he is amazingly impressive, tall and elegant, with an effortless pull shot that goes for miles. At one point he was 70 and Virat was about 20. By the time we overtook KKR, the gap had closed a little: Devdutt ended up 101 off 52, Virat 72 off 47.

After the game, Zamps, Kane and I had a yarn to Rob Cassell, the Royals' bowling coach, about the midseason trade period coming up. The Royals have three overseas spots to fill, now that Liam Livingstone has gone home, and they can only fill them from other franchises, because otherwise the player would have to serve a quarantine period, then perhaps also quarantine on the way home. At the moment, though, you wouldn't want to leave RCB. Virat's found a great balance between relaxation and competitiveness. We were laughing about him in the dugout the other night. At the reviews after beating the Sunrisers, he gave this talk about how we'd made a great start, but he didn't want anyone getting too excited – we were going to stay level and calm and steady. Next game, of course, Virat's just on fire. He's charging out of the huddle, he's leading these massive wicket celebrations, he's pointing to the badge on his shirt, all that stuff. The guys saw the funny side of that – he just can't help himself. He loves the contest, whether it's a game of T20 or table tennis in the team room.

Tonight after the match we had the run of the pool area, and there were multiple celebrations to be had. Finn Allen and Malolan Rangarajan, our fielding coach, were celebrating birthdays, while Adam Griffith's wife has had a baby. He watched the birth on Zoom. They found out she was pregnant three days before the last IPL, and he's hardly been home over summer, going from bubble to bubble. That's definitely something for me to think about, now that Jorgia and I are expecting.

It was the kind of gathering you might find at any club – and also not. My first club was the University of New South Wales CC, where I went when I was 14, in 1996, out of St Gregory's. I'd tried out for the Campbelltown Green Shield team and not made it; Uni were running a Green Shield team for the first time, so they ended up with all the leftovers, including me. There was a strong country connection, with quite a few guys who'd come to make it in the big smoke. I was from Narrandera, there were four guys from Dubbo, one from Mudgee, one from Griffith, guys from the South Coast – and from Wagga, of course, Geoff Lawson, who's probably been the single biggest influence on my career. The guys I played with then are probably my oldest friends, and it's still a fantastic club. When I played half a dozen games there before the Big Bash League last summer, I could see it hadn't really changed.

The relationships you form in franchise T20 are wider but shallower. The community is constantly turning over. You'll almost always have played with some members of the opposition, and one of the nice things is catching up after the game for a beer – although this season it's been more like a

Gatorade out on the ground. You get to know some people pretty well; with others it's more superficial. There are more families. For instance, AB's wife, three kids and mother-in-law are here, although he's still very much part of the team. Tonight, when Danielle went to bed about 2 am, AB said: 'Oh, I'll just stay for one more.' And before we knew it, it was dawn. The last four of us standing at 7.30 am were AB, Maxy, me and Kat. And AB and Maxy were winding Kat up, saying: 'C'mon, mate, just play Dan.' Which was good!

Friday, 23 April 2021

An example of that community: after the KKR match the other night, I was chatting to Pat Cummins about our house hunting and he recommended a buyers' agent. So this morning we had a Zoom call with one, which went well – Jorgia felt confident enough afterwards to start closing all the real estate tabs on her laptop. Life goes on, around the cricket, under the COVID shadow.

A big result tonight. The Punjab Kings beat the Mumbai Indians by nine wickets on another of those very average Chennai pitches. That leaves as our nearest rival CSK, who we play on Sunday. Will I play? My near-term prospects aren't so good. The pitch at Wankhede is starting to dry out because they're just using the three in the middle of the square, so the only change I can foresee is that maybe Zamps will come in for Kane. The batting depth is good with Jamo at seven and Harshal Patel at eight. I also know they like having Devdutt,

Sundar and Shahbaz as left-handers to use against leg-spin. But I have to stay ready. You're only ever an injury or a coach's match-up idea away from playing.

Saturday, 24 April 2021

The COVID-19 news gets worse and worse. Cases in India have soared to 350,000 a day, with around 3000 deaths. More significantly for us, the news has hit Australia – and I'm getting a message every 20 minutes from home to see if I'm all right. I'm fine, of course. We're probably the safest people in India, and among the best informed. The Australian Cricketers' Association have set up a WhatsApp group for the 40 Australians here – players, commentators, coaches, support staff. It keeps us up to date on news, health advice and government statements. There's talk of border closures in Australia.

I went to see RCB's director of cricket operations, Mike Hesson, to find out what's going on. For a while there's been rumours about the whole tournament taking place in Mumbai, using the four grounds in that city: Wankhede, DY Patil, the Brabourne Stadium and the Mumbai Cricket Association ground at the Bandra Kurla Complex. It would help minimise the travel, which is the biggest danger to the integrity of the bio-bubbles.

Mike asked what I wanted to do, and I said I was comfortable staying. We're being well looked after, and I'm not concerned about returning to Australia at the moment because from India I'm flying on to England – my first game for Notts is on 9 June. But I wasn't surprised when Richo and Zamps decided to go. Neither of them was in that good a place when they arrived, Richo having just become a father and Zamps having had the problems with his wedding. You could tell they were nervous when they saw the cases skyrocketing and were worried about getting home. Apparently Andrew Tye is leaving the Royals to get back to Perth. The news here is bad enough that I can understand why players wouldn't want to stay.

Sunday, 25 April 2021

On with the cricket. Our top-of-the-table clash with CSK today was a bit of a fizzer – we lost by 69 runs. It was closer than that, and after 88 balls of their innings, when they were three for 111, with two new batsmen, we were well on top. Padikkal had just caught Suresh Raina and I'd caught Faf du Plessis off consecutive deliveries from Harshal Patel. Then I let Ravi Jadeja off, Padikkal let the next one go for four and we paid heavily.

I'd come into the side to bat at number six and not bowl when we left out Kane and Shahbaz, and I can honestly say that I have never been hotter on a cricket field. When we left the Taj, there was a little bit of breeze coming from the beach, and we started going: 'Oh, this isn't so hard.' But the soaring stands at Wankhede shut out any wind, and the atmosphere got worse and worse. I was drinking so much water that it actually started making me feel sick; I felt like I was sweating out fluid as quickly as I absorbed it. AB looked like he was going to pass out, and he's super fit.

I actually did end up bowling, and delivered two good back-to-back overs, with AB up at the stumps. Raina hit me over the top once, and I bowled a wide, but apart from that I gave away just seven runs in 11 deliveries, with a lot of slower balls, which were just holding up enough to miss the middle of the bat. I was coming back for a third over when I started wondering whether I should. As a T20 captain, I know that third overs can be costly. You might have kept things quiet for two, but the batter's probably had a good look at you, and he'll be coming hard. In 350 games of T20, I reckon I've only bowled three consecutive overs ten times. I said to Maxy: 'I'm not sure I should be bowling this one.' So Virat threw it to Harshal Patel – the current holder of the Purple Cap, as the competition's leading wicket taker – and we got Raina and Faf. Good choice!

The pull shot from Jadeja came flat and, as sometimes happens in a day game, went out of light into shade – I'd certainly have caught it at night, although I really should have caught it in the day too. It hit the heel of my hand and bounced out. Initially, Jadeja didn't hurt us. He was 21 off 19. But from Patel's last over he plundered 37, benefiting from a no-ball full-toss above head height and a free hit, both of which he hit for six – effectively 13 runs off one ball.

I'd be interested to see the stats on day games in India, because I can't imagine that many chasing teams win, so tired are they from bowling and fielding – although nobody likes discussing that, because it can seem like you're unfit. I certainly suspect exhaustion from the heat undermined our chase. We got off to a flier, were going at ten runs per over in the powerplay, but I was in during the ninth over and then out in the tenth. AB jabbed one into the covers that bounced waist-high to Jadeja, so he didn't even have to stoop before throwing down the stumps, finding me a foot short. He also bowled AB and Maxy, and had Washington Sundar caught. No wonder CSK pay him a million dollars.

We weren't overly bothered about the loss, as it was pretty obvious where we went wrong. Virat said afterwards that we were bound to lose one, and it was better to lose it now than later. Still, after the game I muted my social media. I put my filters on Twitter and took my tags off Instagram; now the only comments and tags I'll receive are from people I follow. Nobody drops a catch deliberately, but on social media it's as though you have, and it's just not good for your mental health. I'll give it a couple of days.

3

GETTING OUT

RCB is on a roll, but India is on a more dangerous one. As we prepare to play at the world's biggest cricket stadium, time is against us. I'm about to get an unexpected and unwanted birthday present.

Monday, 26 April 2021

Another charter flight, this time to Ahmedabad. We're given our boarding passes on the buses, then driven through essentially the back gate of Mumbai's airport to a private jet terminal, where we're herded through security. A transfer bus takes us to the plane, the flight lasts 70 minutes, and we're in Gujarat.

I played cricket here against the Gujarat Lions four years ago, when I was part of the equally short-lived Rising Pune Supergiants. In fact, I have a favourite memory. Our hotel in

Indore was pretty average, but when we came down to breakfast there was a coffee cup for each of us with our names and faces on it. I still have mine. The Taj Skyline in Ahmedabad is only a year old, and feels new and comfortable – which is good because we're here for a couple of weeks. But the coffee cups are plain, my room overlooks a building site, and the home state of India's prime minister, Narendra Modi, has recorded 7000 deaths from COVID-19 – eight times more than all of Australia.

Tuesday, 27 April 2021

I wake up to the news that Australia has shut its borders to flights from India – which is on one hand predictable and on the other inconsistent. We didn't shut the borders to the United States when it had many more cases. There's inconsistency in the government's approach to us as well. At his press conference today, Prime Minister Scott Morrison insisted that he wouldn't be giving cricketers special treatment; then, soon after, it was announced that the Olympic team would be preferentially vaccinated. I appreciate that we're not on an international tour, but there are 40 Australians here, most of whom are either part of the Australian team or who have been, while India is one of Australia's five biggest trade partners. The prime minister's happy to hang around cricketers in summertime ...

We had our first sight of Narendra Modi Stadium, officially the world's biggest – bigger even than the MCG. My initial impression: yes, it's big. Extremely big. It's a 130,000-seat stadium for a city without an IPL team, although I dare say they'll be getting one when the IPL expands. The outfield is magnificent.

Second impression: without a crowd, it feels a bit apocalyptic. There's lot of incomplete construction work. There are weeds growing up through the concrete in the car park. Big grounds always feel extra empty. The pitches are a bit new, and a bit dead – from what we can tell, anyway, because we don't have the chance to practise.

But I'm yet to play there, because again I was left out at the last minute in favour of Rajat Patidar. Despite us playing such good cricket, the bosses seem to be changing their minds constantly this season; we haven't played the same XI in consecutive matches yet. It's partly because they have so many good cricketers to choose from, I guess. But we were all standing round the pitch at Modi Stadium five minutes before the toss saying: 'You playing?' 'No idea.' 'You playing?' 'No idea.' Eventually they also bought in Daniel Sams for his first game of the competition, although they only gave him two overs in the powerplay. It's all a bit confusing.

Despite that, we beat the Delhi Capitals, thanks mainly to AB taking 23 off the last over of our innings from Marcus Stoinis, then Jamo getting Shikhar Dhawan and Siraj nicking Steve Smith off inside the first four overs of their reply. Shimron Hetmyer hit four sixes, but Rishabh Pant needed to hit the last ball for six to win and could only just get bat on a wide one – fearless execution from Siraj. So we're five from six, and still well placed.

The world's biggest cricket stadium from ground zero.

Wednesday, 28 April 2021

The debate is continuing here about whether the IPL should go on. Last week I thought it should. Now I'm not sure. From the outside, I know it must look strange that the cricket is carrying on amid the chaos – the scenes in Delhi are astonishing. But if we stopped tomorrow, it's not like the broadcasters would go and spend the money they saved on oxygen trucks. Tens of thousands of people, too, depend on the IPL for their livelihood; it's not just a handful of millionaire cricketers. Pat Cummins has made a donation of US$50,000 to relief efforts, which is obviously admirable of him. There's some talk that the players here will be making a joint contribution to a cause. I hope we will. We haven't had a meeting about it, but Kat told me privately that something is in the works. On the Cricket Australia and Australian Cricketers' Association WhatsApp group chat, they've been recommending the UNICEF India Crisis Appeal.

For us, it's now probably easier to stay than to leave – we've just heard that there's a possibility the Mumbai Indians will receive their vaccinations on 1 May, and if they do we may not be far behind. Zamps and Kane, meanwhile, are in the middle of a 12-hour layover in Doha, waiting to board a Qatar Airways flight to Melbourne. They left our bubble when they stayed behind in Mumbai as we flew to Ahmedabad. Then, two hours later, ScoMo shut the borders. I don't know what that means for them, but I doubt it's good. In the meantime, I'm off for another COVID test, and then to training. That's life inside the bubble.

Thursday, 29 April 2021

Training again this afternoon. And training form is strangely significant in T20, because sometimes the matches provide so little evidence for judging a player. Get a few out of the middle in a practice session, bowl a few good deliveries, and it can do your chances a lot of good. Which means that a lot depends on good training facilities, and they can vary in quality. We worked so hard at CSS in Chennai that they ended up really average; the nets at Chepauk were poor; the nets at Wankhede were very good; the nets here are so-so.

Meanwhile, because Zamps and Kane booked their flights before the border closure was announced, they've been allowed to enter a 14-day quarantine in Melbourne. That loophole, however, is now closed. Another option that people are talking about on the WhatsApp is the Maldives. You can still go there, except to those islands populated exclusively by locals. But from there it's not clear what you can do, or how long you'll have to wait to re-enter Australia. The only certainty we seem to have is that the IPL is continuing – for the moment.

Friday, 30 April 2021

Another night looking on from the dugout as we lose our second game of the last three, although the eventual 34-run margin of the defeat by Punjab Kings doesn't reflect how the match fluctuated. They were 100 off ten overs after Chris Gayle and KL Rahul put on 80 from 45 balls: Gayle hit five fours off Jamo's second over, then two sixes off Yuvi's first. We did well to peg them back, but then leaked 50 in the last three, with Rahul taking Harshal for 23 in the last over.

Momentum shouldn't affect anyone, but if your last over goes for runs it always seems to affect your chase. It's a stat I'd like to know: what proportion of games do you win when the last over of your bowling innings goes for more than 20? Because if the openers don't get going straightaway, a dugout can get unsettled, and that seemed to happen tonight: we were run a ball for the first ten overs, and it felt like we could have gone up a gear. Their left-arm tweaker, Harpreet Brar, then got Virat, Maxy and AB in seven balls, and that was curtains for us, although Harshal and Jamo ensured that our net run rate didn't take too much of a hit. So it was a game we had the winning of at various stages but failed to clinch.

Saturday, 1 May 2021

Reviews for the Punjab Kings game. We're doing a lot of really good things at the moment, but we're just a touch off. Personally, I don't think our death bowling has been great. The figures have been distorted a bit by who we've been bowling at; we've faced set batsmen in the last three games and been belted. Jadeja was set for CSK; Pant and Hetmeyer were set for the Delhi Capitals, and we were lucky to get away with it; KL Rahul was set on Friday and made us pay.

Like I said, those last overs can affect your mindset when chasing. A dugout is different to a dressing room. Everyone's together; everyone's watching; everyone's responding to one another; you can feel the mood shift in a game, which is a reflection of your personnel, driven by the coach and the senior guys. I've played with coaches who've been very level, and with coaches who ride the wave. I've played with some who have changed: Greg Shipperd used to get very nervous, but these days he doesn't say much. That's the beauty of having older blokes in a side. We can say: 'Settle down, it'll be okay.' Kat is actually very good. He'll sit there taking his notes, very much in charge, in tune with what's going on. But it's important in a chase to stay ahead of the rate, because you'll lose wickets at certain points which will slow you down. And on Friday night, I think people could feel that pressure building. By the time AB came in, we needed 13 an over, and that was too much even for him.

Ultimately, it's been pretty clear what's happened in our two losses: Virat, Maxy and AB have got out at the same time, and we've had no one to back them up. Which may be my ticket. Maxy and AB being in the XI leaves two overseas spots up for grabs. Jamo hasn't played a bad game yet, and Samsy bowled beautifully the other night. But if Saini came in for one of those, I would be a chance to come in and lengthen the batting. Not playing is frustrating, because in the nets I feel really good. I've had three games and no sort of continuity. I've nailed a cut, nicked a wide and been run out.

But the other thing is that the internationals at an IPL franchise are a team within a team. While you want to be playing, you don't want to burn your overseas mates either – you want them to do well. That goes now for Scott Kuggeleijn, a Kiwi who's joined us to make up for Kane and Zamps leaving. He was on the reserve list at the Mumbai Indians and in their bubble in case anyone got injured; he's now done a bubble-to-bubble transfer. I'm sure I'll get another chance. It's just a matter of when.

Sunday, 2 May 2021

Outside the bubble, things are going from bad to worse. I was reading an article on SBS News this morning that recalled how earlier this year, when India got the cases down to fewer than 10,000 a day, the government relaxed all the restrictions; with a daily rate now of more than 400,000 cases, they're paying the penalty for that. The United States has just closed its borders to India, and the Morrison government has criminalised trying to return to Australia – they're threatening long jail terms and massive fines for those trying to get around the restriction. It seems a pretty extreme step. I even started googling the 'right of return' to one's own country. Because if you get COVID here you're fucked, particularly if you're vulnerable. That's what persuaded Michael Slater to head to the Maldives today, even though he's not sure how long he'll have to wait there before returning to Australia. Kevin Pietersen left today too.

Is it affecting our cricket? I don't think so – maybe the odd guy. When you're playing, you're not thinking about anything else. But while I haven't been concerned before now, now I am worried about being stuck here – and, of course, I'm concerned for Jorgia. She's suffering some nausea and tiredness, and didn't come to our last two games. Because everyone leaves for the ground at the same time, she would have been sitting in the heat for six hours.

There's also no doubt we're feeling the scrutiny: we've been asked not to post photos or videos of the team here at the Taj, and our Twitter and Instagram are now cricket only. One thing we have addressed is the franchise's contribution to the COVID relief effort, to which the Rajasthan Royals have made a commitment – individual players including Shikhar Dhawan, Jaydev Unadkat and Nicholas Pooran have followed Pat Cummins' original gesture. This afternoon we posted a video of Virat pledging a contribution to oxygen supplies, both via a lump sum and the auction of a special blue match kit, modelled on surgical scrubs, which we'll wear in a future match. But when that future match will be, it's hard to tell. The Delhi Capitals beat the Punjab Kings tonight, but our game against KKR tomorrow evening is starting to look doubtful.

Monday, 3 May 2021

Never mind our game. We woke to overnight reports of cases in two other franchises: the Chennai Super Kings have three support staff down with the virus, including Lakshmipathy Balaji, their batting coach; two players at KKR, Varun

Chakravarthy and Sandeep Warrier, have also tested positive. There are no problems with RCB's bubble, but that's the end of our KKR game, of course.

After lunch came news of positive tests for Wriddhiman Saha at Sunrisers Hyderabad and Amit Mishra at the Delhi Capitals. That added another layer of complication, because we're scheduled to play the Punjab Kings on Thursday, and they've just played Delhi. I was on WhatsApp with Moises Henriques, who is playing for Punjab, and asked him whether they'd been asked to isolate because they were close contacts of Mishra's. He said no. Which is crazy. In Sydney recently, there was a guy who went to four barbecue stores and a butcher's shop, and everyone who'd been at those places was told to isolate.

Even if we do play the Kings, what are we going to do then? Just go on playing the Kings? This now feels like the PSL: it seems a matter of time until they suspend the whole thing. Virat, who's been really strong throughout about player safety, has told the BCCI he won't agree to our playing the Kings – and when he talks, they tend to listen.

Tuesday, 4 May 2021

It's my birthday; it's also suspension day for the IPL, news of which came through in the afternoon. It couldn't have gone on. Only the United States and Brazil have had more COVID deaths than India; only the US has had more cases. It's too hard now to preserve the semblance of normality the

IPL represented. Personally, I don't feel in any danger. Today, in fact, we received the AstraZeneca jab, and we're luckier than some. Moises was telling me that the Punjab squad were all being offered it, then at the last minute were told that international players weren't eligible to receive it. Who knows what the deal was there? RCB have been great – really calm and conscientious throughout.

For me, there's also the consideration that Jorgia can't be vaccinated – not until she's at least 12 weeks pregnant. We're confident of the preventative measures the franchise has taken, but we'll both feel more comfortable in the Maldives, which is apparently where the Aussie players in the IPL are headed because of Australia's hard border with India. It's winding up quickly here. Virat has already gone; AB is heading home for South Africa with his family; eight of the 11 English players leave first thing tomorrow. We'll be following.

Wednesday, 5 May 2021

Leaving Ahmedabad meant leaving the bio-bubble for the first time. It wasn't easy. We travelled in the RCB team bus, which was hardly inconspicuous when we arrived at the airport – for the first time at an ordinary terminal. We were in full PPE, but when we set down, as always happens in India, people started flocking towards us with cameras. Knowing that one in two or three of them had probably been exposed to COVID was a bit alarming.

The Punjab Kings players were on board our charter to Bangalore, plus Pat Cummins, Ben Cutting and Dave Hussey from KKR. Missing was Dave's brother Mike, the batting coach at CSK, who's had the misfortune to test positive – apparently, he was sitting next to Balaji on the team bus. Now he's stuck in Chennai until he returns a negative test.

At Bangalore, the Aussies were joined on the charter flight to Malé, the capital of the Maldives, by Chris Gayle, Eoin Morgan, Kane Williamson and Mitchell Santner. Looking out the windows as we took off, it was hard to foresee when we would be back. What happens to the last 31 games of this year's IPL is anyone's guess.

Arriving, unobtrusively, in the RCB bus in Bangalore.

4

THE NOTTS CONNECTION

While most of my countrymen are locked down, I'm about to undertake a world tour of hotel rooms, from Bangalore to the Maldives to Bahrain to London to Nottingham. All in the name of cricket, though at times the game feels far away.

Thursday, 6 May 2021

So here we are at the Taj Exotica, on a private atoll of the southern end of the Maldives in the Laccadive Sea. We arrived by boat from Malé and, after three months cooped up in hotels, it immediately looked like a refuge. There are 40 of us occupying most of the 50 villas and it's stunning. You can swim and snorkel; there's a gym; you can run laps of the

Welcome to the Maldives, our temporary sanctuary.

CRICKET

island; people start heading for the bar around midafternoon. It's impossible to do anything but relax, at least for the moment – because now there's the consideration of how we'll get into England.

India was on the red list, from which it was impossible to get in; the Maldives is on the amber list, from which you can get in providing you self-isolate. But we've now been advised that the Maldives will be added to the red list shortly, so Jorgia and I will have to find another lily pad to land on. What a saga.

Friday, 7 May 2021

I'm glad we're out of India. It was starting to get a bit hairy there, and Jorgia and I both feel better for leaving it behind. Miraculously, the morning sickness and the fatigue Jorgia had been suffering disappeared as soon as we arrived in the Maldives. If we have other kids, she's going to expect to come back here for every pregnancy!

Everyone's comparing their COVID experiences, and it's obvious that most people feel the same way – although not everyone's happy being here. Michael Slater is still dealing with the negative commentary arising from his tweet a few days ago, when he had a crack at Scott Morrison. Slats has always been a bit volatile, but he stands by everything he said. I've been there – it can be stressful when you go out on a limb on social media for whatever reason. You've got to be willing to accept the blowback.

Saturday, 8 May 2021

Pat Cummins has brought his coffee machine with him, so I've been spending some time in his room ... this might become a frequent thing.

Our buyer's agent has put us onto a property that's up for auction in Clovelly, an apartment near the shops at the top of the hill. It's about ten minutes from Pat's house, and three minutes from Moises'. Sean Abbott lives around there too, and Daniel Hughes is house-hunting in the area. Looking at it, I have to admit that you don't get much for your buck in that part of Sydney. But I'd rather buy real estate than pay someone else's mortgage for a few years, and I made the mistake with my last house of buying something bigger too far out in Melbourne's South Caulfield.

Life admin! It seems like a bit of an adult job to be doing on an island paradise, but now I'm hassling my accountant to put my tax returns together so I can obtain pre-approval for financing. It's weird, of course: I'm trying to buy a home I've never even set foot in. But as a travelling cricketer, you get used to living this way. That's how I bought the place in South Caulfield.

Jorgia spent today drawing up the floor plans and fitting the furniture in – with room, of course, for the baby that, all being well, we'll be welcoming in December.

Sunday, 9 May 2021

Today we were meant to be playing the Sunrisers in Kolkata. Already the IPL feels far away, and I'm thinking about the next step in our journey. Eoin Morgan has contacts in Bahrain, so Jorgia and I will probably follow him there in a few days; the rest of the Aussies are heading home.

The IPL are still dealing with consequences of COVID. More players have tested positive. The fathers of Piyush Chawla and Chetan Sakariya are reported to have died. Virat has pledged US$270,000 to the COVID relief effort – it's a massively generous donation, but you also know it'll be swallowed up in the massive costs of this plague.

Monday, 10 May 2021

Just back from my pre-flight COVID test, ahead of our journey to Bahrain. It should be negative: the AstraZeneca vaccine is meant to offer 70 per cent protection for the first 12 weeks. Unfortunately, Jorgia still can't get vaccinated, although she'll eventually be in line for the Pfizer or Moderna shots. We've been reading the scientific literature on both in the case of pregnancy, and any side effects should be minimal.

The plan now is to get to London on 16 May, where a driver from Nottinghamshire will collect us at Heathrow. For those coming from an amber list location, it's ten days self-isolation, with the possibility of being released after five days if you get a negative test. However tough that might seem, it's easier than getting back into Australia.

Tuesday, 11 May 2021

Things got hairy, again, as we left the Maldives. A storm blew up as we left the island for the half-hour trip to Malé – it was actually the early stages of a cyclone that was about to batter the west coast of India. The irony was not lost on us: escape a pandemic only to drown at sea. But the flight was uneventful and the Fraser Suites in Bahrain, which RCB are still paying for, are a welcoming home – although we can't eat in the dining room or use the gym.

Wednesday, 12 May 2021

Apart from a fair bit of oil under a hell of a lot of sand, Bahrain is notable for its golf courses. Morgs and I tried one today, and it was like nowhere I've ever played: right next to a refinery, dotted with derricks, crisscrossed by pipes. Every now and again the wind changes and you get a colossal waft of oil straight up your nose.

There've been just over 800 COVID deaths and about 280,000 cases in Bahrain, so there's a coronavirus consciousness here. In fact, to get into places like restaurants and cafes, you need a government app with a vaccination passport on it. Unfortunately, India is so far behind with our paperwork that Morgs and I don't have our certification yet; Jorgia, by contrast, can go anywhere, because she has the passport of being pregnant. It makes no sense, but so little does these days.

A great venue if you like your golf and your oil.

Thursday, 13 May 2021

As I was having a beer today with Morgs at the Ritz-Carlton, where he's staying, I suddenly got a message from our buyer's agent: there's been a pre-auction offer on the apartment Jorgia and I have been looking at, and she recommended we make our own offer. We'd decided what we would spend, so I said go for it, even though I didn't have my finances arranged. It's hard to believe, but a few hours later we are home owners – of a property neither of us will set foot in for months! Such is the life of a nomadic cricketer.

Friday, 14 May 2021

Coming to Bahrain turns out to have made no difference. Because we've been in the Maldives, which is now a red zone (even though it wasn't while we were there), we have to spend a full ten days somewhere that stays an amber zone – if you can follow that. So now we have to wait almost a further week in Bahrain and hope that it doesn't become a red zone in the meantime. Amazingly, Israel is on the green list – Israel, which is basically at war at the moment. So it's easy to get to the United Kingdom if you don't mind dodging a few rockets. Anyway, it has been nice to do some ordinary things for the first time in ages. I played golf again today, then Jorgia and I went to a supermarket, bought some groceries and used the kitchenette to cook dinner like an everyday couple, which felt fantastic. I wonder when we'll get to do it in our new home.

Saturday, 15 May 2021

The rest of the Australians left the Maldives today, bound for home – after their hotel quarantine, anyway. In Bahrain, Jorgia said: 'Can we please go to the baby shop at the mall today?' So at least we've got something to show for the last few months.

Sunday, 16 May 2021

Contemplating my next few months. The Blast starts in June, takes a break in mid-July, after which The Hundred goes until 22 August. Then there's the Blast quarter-finals, followed by a three-week break that coincides with the Caribbean Premier League. Could I fit that in? During the IPL, I had a chat to Jason Holder about playing for Barbados. It's a bit easier than usual, because COVID is confining the whole tournament to St Kitts, to minimise the travel. But I also have Jorgia to think about, as it'll become increasingly difficult for her to travel as her pregnancy progresses.

There's talk now that the IPL will resume on 18 September, which is fine, except that it may overlap with finals day in the Blast. If I'm fully vaccinated by then, maybe I can fly back from the IPL to play that day, then turn around and go back with the minimum of quarantine. Kat has said that if I'm not in the RCB starting XI, he'd be happy for me to miss; we'll know roughly by 20 August. So much uncertainty, so much we used to take for granted.

Monday, 17 May 2021

Time is passing slowly here, and our movements are restricted: I can't even go to the beach. The mall is safe, though I have to stay outside places. There are a lot of prams to be looked at; we haven't bought one yet. We rented a car and drove to the bottom of the island today, which took about 40 minutes.

Some disappointing news today: my Notts teammate Harry Gurney has had to retire, aged just 34. His left-arm angle, slower balls and yorkers have been a crucial part of our success these last few years, but he had a shoulder operation a year ago and hasn't fully recovered. It's a setback for us, at Notts, and at Manchester – he'll be hard to replace.

Saturday, 22 May 2021

Finally it was time to leave Bahrain for England. We arrived in the evening. Coming from an amber-list country, we were escorted down one corridor for our arrival test. Those coming from red-list countries went down another corridor to goodness knows where. Notts had sent a van with a masked driver to collect us for the two-and-a-half-hour drive up the M1 to Nottingham.

Sunday, 23 May 2021

Today was meant to be the start of the IPL finals; instead, I'm in England. We're ahead of schedule and our accommodation isn't ready, so we're in a little apartment on Bridgford Road, which has been rebuilt by the club from an old hotel. Because

New quarters in Nottingham, but not for long.

we've done ten days in Bahrain, we can get out of self-isolation after five days if we pay for a release test, although as a professional athlete I'm allowed to train so I'll be heading to Trent Bridge tomorrow.

Monday, 24 May 2021

A month ago I reckoned I was as hot as I've ever been on a cricket field, during the game against CSK. This morning it was six degrees when I went for my morning run, and then it poured, which put paid to outdoor training, so I hit some balls indoors. Still, it's a great feeling to be here. This is my seventh year at Notts – very unusual in this day and age. County contracts now tend to be short and focused, so there's lots of traffic; it's all about filling gaps. I understand the industry – it's pretty cutthroat – but because we've had success, the county have always been keen to get me back, and I've always been keen to return.

I first came as a replacement for Daren Sammy when he had to go on international duty in 2015. I played seven one-dayers, made 251 runs at 63, took nine wickets at 19 and got a run in the T20s, where James Taylor was captain. We weren't bad, but we didn't quite have it; guys weren't quite certain of their roles. Then, at the end of the season, the coach Mick Newell asked me to take on the T20 captaincy, because James was working on his Test cricket – although he became unwell with a heart condition soon after and had to drop out.

The leadership offer came out of the blue. I had never been considered captaincy material in Australia. Even now I'm not sure what Mick's rationale was – he must have seen something in me in the half-season I was here. But I didn't need to be asked twice. I've always loved the tactical side of the game, and I get a lot of satisfaction from seeing guys do well. We had a great core unit: there were Harry, Alex Hales, Samit Patel and Steve Mullaney, while Jake Ball and Luke Fletcher were around.

I struck up a really good relationship with Peter Moores, who was Mick's assistant. He got me making some technical changes with my batting. He also clarified my role: I was to be the guy who comes in around the tenth over, gets himself in and is still there at the end. Peter would set little scenarios for me in the nets. 'It's the 13th over, you need eight an over, the field is here and you're not allowed to hit it in the air.' That was great for me: my pressure reliever has always been to try to hit a six, and now I wasn't allowed to do that, so I started getting across my stumps and knocking the ball into the leg side. So Peter really helped me loosen up some of the rigidity in my technique.

In 2016, we made the semi-final, only to stuff it up on the day. We let Northamptonshire reach eight for 161 after being three for 15; then we were three for 15 and didn't recover. The difference was Ben Duckett, who made 84 off 47 balls, which made us eager to get him to Nottinghamshire – and we did. In 2017, with Peter taking over as coach, we lost our first couple of games but then became unbeatable at home. The average score at Trent Bridge that summer was 209. We were absolutely slogging, then we'd have Harry bowling at the death and going for just eight an over. There was a game against Yorkshire where we chased 223 and won with five balls to spare, Alex making 101 off 47; in a match against Durham we chased 184 and won in 13.5 overs, with Alex making 95 off 30. That was the just the way we wanted to play. We went down to Edgbaston to play the final against Warwickshire, who'd beaten us in the first game, and blew them away, Harry taking four for 17.

In 2020 we won again, losing just one game for the season, and winning the semi-final and final at the Oval on 4 October. I collected both player-of-the-match awards as well as the trophy. But the success we've had here hasn't been about one-off performances. It's been underpinned by great clarity around our roles. The mainstays know exactly what they're doing and when they're doing it, so we prepare accordingly; the others feed off that energy.

Tuesday, 25 May 2021

Back to Trent Bridge on a clear day – such a great ground, beautiful pitches, fast outfield. Training with the four-day boys today, who are flying: three consecutive victories in the County Championship and top of their conference, having not won a first-class match for three years. Luke Fletcher is on fire, nipping it around, not bowling too quick. Ben Slater, who came to the club on his white-ball reputation, has been going beautifully with the red ball too.

There used to be an attitude that T20 and four-day cricket didn't mix, and it can certainly cause issues – you can get anxious about scoring, groove the wrong lengths. But I'm sure that over the years I played better Sheffield Shield after the Big Bash League. You'd think: 'I've just been smacking that ball for the last two months.' It simplified things: you were just dropping back to first or second gear.

I had a good chat with Stuart Broad today. He's loved his cricket this season, coming back from England duties to work with the younger guys. He said there's a confidence in the four-day side just like in the T20 team. They know that they can grind, take their opportunities and nail them – which is what they've been doing.

Wednesday, 26 May 2021

First serious chat of the season with Peter Moores, who's been so influential on my career. The knock on Peter is that he had two England stints but neither worked out. He's forever associated with a line at his last press conference, after England were eliminated from the 2015 World Cup, when he said the team would 'look at the data'. He was mocked for being 'the data guy', like his head was in the clouds. It's actually the complete reverse of the way he coaches. Peter is always exceptionally well prepared and researched, but really he is all about cricket smarts. I was pretty raw as a captain when I started, and he was so good to talk to about tactics. He also knew how to motivate me. Good coaches can make you feel like the world's best player, and Peter certainly does that with me: 95 per cent of the time he's blowing smoke up my arse, but in the other 5 per cent we're having a tough conversation. He's influenced lots of other guys too, including Kat, who played under him at Lancashire when Peter was there between his England stints. As coaches, and as people, they're quite alike.

Peter is a youthful 58, and has a son in our squad, Tom, an excellent left-handed keeper-bat. English coaches are often a bit older than Australian ones, and there's a respect for experience here that I appreciate more and more. Look at Darren Stevens: still playing at 45 and as good as ever. In Australia you hardly play cricket past 35. States are incentivised to produce Australian players, so it's in their interest to keep pumping kids through until they find someone good enough, rather than work with what they have – it becomes like glorified age group cricket. The system here has a better appreciation of what it takes to make a good cricketer: surrounding young guys with players who've been around a bit.

Our approach at Notts is simple: we build confidence. I hate the idea of people being 'challenged'. Very few players respond to it. I've seen too many guys get hung up on proving things to people – I've done it myself. I'm much happier with the idea of making people comfortable and secure so they can express themselves. I know it's fashionable to talk about 'being comfortable being uncomfortable'. But it's absolute fucking bullshit. Especially in T20 cricket, you have to be 100 per cent in everything you do, not 75 per cent and thinking about something else. And you have to be confident that you've got the support of everyone around you. It's so easy to get trapped into, say, knocking the ball around the field a bit longer than you should, rather than playing without fear of the consequences. In our team meetings at Notts, Peter and I talk about going out and putting on a show. At our practice sessions and matches, we encourage lots of experimentation. Don't be afraid to try that lap sweep over the keeper's head, or a reverse slog sweep. Just go out and do it.

Sitting down to consider our squad is a good feeling. I'm impressed with our options. The batting unit is basically the same as last year, and has a great look about it: Alex Hales, Joe Clarke, Steve Mullaney and Tom Moores, with Peter Trego, who we brought in last season and who's played a million games. The bowling's better still.

We've lost Harry, but we didn't have him last season either. We have Jake Ball as our number one quick, with me and Steve Mullaney backing up with our mediums. Because Jake's coming off four weeks on the sidelines with hotspots in his back, we'll bring in an extra seamer, whether it's Luke Fletcher, who's bowling the house down in the County Championship and has an excellent yorker, or Tom Barber, a left-armer who's got a yard on him and bowls in the mid-140s. We also have Dane Paterson, with whom I played in the Mzansi Super League. That's more depth than ever.

Thursday, 27 May 2021

The four-day team were down at Edgbaston playing Warwickshire today, so practice was low-key. Jorgia is excited about us both finally getting out of isolation. Others aren't so lucky. Chatting to Vini, Maxy's missus, I learned that Melbourne has gone back into lockdown. So the pair of them have gone straight out of quarantine into ... more quarantine.

Friday, 28 May 2021

We're out! Jorgia and I had thought about celebrating the end of isolation by going to London for the Bank Holiday weekend, but decided we'd done enough travelling so marked the occasion by going to the supermarket and buying a blender – a gesture towards domesticity. Nottingham is a pretty quiet city, and West Bridgford's really the only place to go, so it's pleasantly undemanding socially. We had dinner tonight with Jake Ball, our assistant coach Paul Franks, and their respective partners.

Saturday, 29 May 2021

Enjoying our new freedoms on a lovely sunny weekend, we went to a barbecue at Harry Gurney's place. He seems very content in his decision to retire, and he's done well for himself, investing money he's made as a T20 specialist in the Cat & Wickets Pub Company, which he started with Broady five years ago. I wonder whether he might have persevered with playing had he not had that to fall back on ... But he's

With my old Notts teammate Harry Gurney, a total legend.

had some good earning years, which probably made the decision a bit easier. Sometimes it can work that way. T20 can extend a career, but it can also make it possible to quit sooner.

Sunday, 30 May 2021

A bit of news for me from Kat, who's just finished his quarantine in Sydney: he expects to be back in the United Kingdom to start with the Manchester Originals in The Hundred in early July. Where I was going to be replacing Nicholas Pooran, I'm now going to come in full-time as a replacement for Shadab Khan, who can't make it. Harry Gurney's retirement has freed up a spot, which I'll take over. Someone else will take over from Shadab. I'll also captain when Jos Buttler isn't available, which could be a lot because of his other responsibilities; I think he's only going to be playing the first two or three matches.

Quite a lot to think about there. I love the idea of more captaincy, and it makes me wonder why I didn't do it more at home. I played with and against quite a few guys in Australia who were just not very good captains, and I always wondered: how did they get the job? I saw guys who were tactically hopeless and couldn't manage people who just went on and on in the role; I saw players who were natural leaders within groups who never got a go. Anyway, I'm excited about the chance to test myself again as leader in a new format.

Monday, 31 May 2021

My main focus now is helping Notts defend our Blast title. Who are our threats? Worcestershire, who we play in the first match, will be good, because Moeen Ali will be available most of the time. Somerset are always there or thereabouts. Surrey will be strong, as they were in the final last year, when they rolled out Hashim Amla, Reece Topley, Jason Roy and Ben Foakes. Sussex will have Rashid Khan, and Ben McDermott will be good for Derbyshire, although their squad is not deep.

To be honest, though, I don't think anyone is as good as us. We're bloody strong. It's why we've been there on four of the last five finals days. And while I know this is not a fashionable viewpoint, I don't believe in spending too long on the opposition. Much as we do at the Sixers, at Notts we focus on our own game and trust that we'll have the skill and nous to deal with anything that comes up. We'll do a little bit of preparation before each game, but the only factor we look hard at is how many batters in the opposition can play the lap sweep: they're the players who can get you to change normal fields, maybe to push your 45 back and bring your midwicket in. There are probably two players in each team who lap, and maybe three who reverse-sweep. The reverse really pays off in England, because the squares are so hard and the grounds are so small – a shot that will get you two in Australia races to the boundary. You don't see guys with the power game here; there are more deflectors. Which is what makes someone like Jos Buttler so exceptional: he can pump you back over your head or send one over the keeper's head. He's just so hard to bowl to.

I don't need data to tell me this, either – I'm sceptical it makes an ounce of difference. Even in the IPL, where you're swimming in information, you might get one wicket every five games from all your stuff. Apart from that, it's down to execution, pitch, luck. Data can never contain enough detail to be definitive. So-and-so has a bad strike rate against a particular bowler? Okay, but when and where has he batted against him? What was the wicket like? What was the scenario? Was it three for 20 or none for 100? Was it a small ground or a big ground? Which way was the wind blowing? Data excludes all these variables to produce a trend. It can't help but mislead you. So 'the data' says Alex Hales can't play leg-spin? Seriously? He can smash Matt Critchley from Derby all over the place; if it's Rashid Khan, different story.

So in my view, your cricketing common sense is your best guide. Data can only muddle your thinking.

Tuesday, 1 June 2021

After moving us into our new digs, I drove to Grantham for two afternoon practice T20s against Yorkshire on one of the out grounds – these were basically second XI games, in unfortunately poor conditions. I made 11 out of eight for 110 in the first, and I didn't play the second. Thirty-seven wickets fell in the day for 400 runs. Not quite the practice anyone wanted, really.

5

AN AUSSIE COMEBACK

I played 30 internationals between 2010 and 2017 without commanding a regular place, and the last time I was left out it felt like for good, although it's since then that I have played the best and most consistent cricket of my career. Would I like another opportunity? I'd jump at it – and I do. But touring in COVID times is tough, and the West Indies in their own backyard are tougher still.

Wednesday, 2 June 2021

Has there ever been a year like this one? Today I was on the golf course with Paul Franks when I got a message from George Bailey, my old rival and teammate who is now an Australian selector: 'Marcus Stoinis is 80 per cent certain to withdraw from the T20 tour of the Caribbean,' he tells me, 'so do you want to play?' The only problem is that, if I'm available, I'll have to come home, do a fortnight's quarantine and then go to a three-day camp. It would have been just too easy to fly from London to Barbados!

As annoying as more quarantine sounds, I'm not knocking this offer back. Of course I want to represent my country. It's what I dreamed of when I was a kid. I grew up idolising all those great players of the early 1990s: Steve and Mark Waugh, Craig McDermott and Glenn McGrath. Slats was from Wagga, 100 kilometres from where I grew up, which made it seem closer, and I loved watching him bat. I loved imitating the actions of visiting bowlers like Waqar Younis and Curtly Ambrose, too. I fantasised about playing against their successors.

Yes, it would be a massive inconvenience. More travelling. More hotels. More discomfort for Jorgia. I'll lose out financially too. But it's a chance for me to nail down a spot in the team ahead of the T20 World Cup, which is taking place in October and November. For me at 38, it's a last chance. I text back straightaway; I don't even have to think about it. Now I just have to wait until Stoin makes his decision, which they're expecting shortly. Four years after my last international match, I'm back in the hunt for a spot in the Australian side.

Thursday, 3 June 2021

To Manchester for two second XI practice T20s against Lancashire at Old Trafford. I gave Peter Moores and Mick Newell a heads-up about my possible selection for the

Caribbean tour. It's a headache for them, especially because Stoin has not made a final decision, which means they can't yet go looking for a replacement.

Still, they are supportive of me, and we talk about who should take over as captain. My suggestion is Alex Hales, for two reasons: one, that tactically he's really, really good; and two, I think it will help with the general perception of him as a cricketer. Runs alone won't get him back into the England team. Everyone knows he's good enough, and captaincy will tell the world he's matured, which he has, and that his peers think he's a leader.

Then it was into the field. I played the first game, made ten out of 180, and took two wickets and a couple of catches as we bowled them out for 100. I sat the second match out; the last thing I want to do now is ping a hamstring.

Friday, 4 June 2021

Life goes on; future life too. While we waited for Stoin to make up his mind, Jorgia and I went for her 12-week scan. It was pretty cool. Little thing wouldn't stop jumping around. I had no idea they moved so much at that time. Jorgia had her NIPT (Non-Invasive Pregnancy Test), for which we should get the results in the next ten days.

There would be an upside to coming home: Jorgia could settle into our new place – nesting, they call it! The downside is that I'll probably end up staying overseas, returning to England (depending on quarantine rules) for the back end of The Hundred and the finals of the Blast, before going to play the remainder of the IPL. Which is a long separation, but players have been getting used to that over the last year or so.

Saturday, 5 June 2021

Finally – I'm going. Stoin has pulled out, and Bails has messaged to say that I'm not heading to the Caribbean to sit on the bench – I'll be picked in the starting XI. Which is a better scenario than the last time I played for Australia. That was a rain-affected game in Ranchi in October 2017. I was one of five ins to the T20 squad after the boys had been belted 5–0 in the ODIs. I watched four wickets fall from the non-striker's end before Virat ran me out, and we made just over 100; they chased down the adjusted total in five overs, of which I bowled three balls.

T20 selection was such a mess in those days. I remember after the game, David Saker got us in the dressing room and said: 'Just get together and talk to guys who've got experience of playing here, pick their brains about what it takes to succeed.' It was actually a really good exercise, and we continued it back at the hotel bar. Next day we were training out on the ground and I saw Mark Waugh, who was the selector on duty. I'd known Junior a long time. He gave me my first New South Wales cap when I was 21; he'd been a commentator at probably 80 per cent of the ODIs and T20 Internationals I'd played in, and he'd seen me in plenty of BBL matches too. He'd played a lot in India, so I thought, in the spirit of the exercise, that I'd approach him and pick his brain. 'On the back of what Sakes said last night, Junior, have you got any advice for me about my game?' I asked. 'What I need to do to succeed here? Or just anything in general?'

And he said: 'Well, I've never really seen you bat.' I mean, what do you say to that? He'd picked me for the tour without apparently being able to remember my batting. Then I got dropped – presumably it was my fault we lost the previous game.

Anyway, ever since then I've felt like I had more in me. I've become a far better cricketer. I might not be as fast as I was ten years ago, but I know a lot more about my game, and I feel like I'm still improving. I'm excited that I'll have the chance to prove it.

Sunday, 6 June 2021

To London in the afternoon, and while Jorgia caught up with a friend in Paddington I went to Chelmsford to catch the end of Notts' four-day game against Essex. In fact they'd already lost so much time in the game because of rain that they called it off at tea. So I had a beer with Pete Siddle and Simon Harmer, then went for a barbecue at Ryan ten Doeschate's place in Epping, not far away. When you've played as long as I have, there's always someone to catch up with! Overnight in the Terminal Hotel at Heathrow.

Monday, 7 June 2021

Our plane leaves at 11 am, with a stop in Singapore.

Tuesday, 8 June 2021

We land in Sydney about 7.30 pm and head for the Marriott. The first message I get is from my coach at the Manchester Originals. Cricket Australia have sent out a press release with the team containing my name. Kat says congratulations, but is also wondering about The Hundred: can I make any of it? The truth is that I don't know, although by then I should be fully vaccinated. It looks like the team for the West Indies will go unchanged to Bangladesh for nine days, which leaves just a slight chance I could be back for the Originals' games on 11, 13 and 16 August, and then the finals the following week if we get there. Whatever the case, it looks like the Caribbean Premier League is out of the question now, even though they've changed its dates to eliminate the slight overlap with the restarted IPL. Exactly how much cricket I play in the next few months, however, is very much in the hands of the decision-makers about quarantine.

Wednesday, 9 June 2021

Open the blinds in our room and look out over the Harbour Bridge and the Opera House. It's home, but not as we know it: four more walls, and just our own company. Mind you, it's not as bad as my trip home from the Blast last year. I had four flights from London cancelled before I got on a fifth, which dumped me in Perth. There was nothing wrong with the hotel, the Westin, but the novelty of lovely full-length windows with a beautiful view of the city wore off pretty quickly – and I had two weeks to get through. Then, because Melbourne was in lockdown, I decided to go to Sydney, but they let me out of quarantine so late that I missed my flight and had to spend another night in a different hotel before flying east. And then I had another fortnight in New South Wales. It wasn't terrible: I spent some of the time at Moises' place, while he was at the IPL, and some with my mum in the Blue Mountains. But all in all it took me almost six weeks to get home.

Thursday, 10 June 2021

An exercise bike, bands and some weights arrive, courtesy of CA. My pre-tour training program! Then, in the dead of night, I watch Notts begin our Blast campaign – a nasty flashback. The last time we played against Worcestershire, we lost. We don't need to talk about it, do we? Needed 12 to win, had an absolute gas truck. They brought the field in at the start of the 19th over, so I had a go and got out, and we could get only nine runs off the last 11 balls.

In this game we were flying too. Chasing 152, Alex Hales and Joe Clarke put on 76 in the powerplay but we lost wickets in the sixth, seventh, eighth and tenth overs, including that of Steve Mullaney, who has taken the captaincy on. Our chase lost all momentum. We needed five from the last over but managed only four, losing Luke Fletcher then Peter Trego run out. The tied result was as good as a loss. I remember I got a bit of a Scotch addiction after the game two years ago; a few guys probably did the same after this one.

My 'other' team, the Karachi Kings, also went down as the Pakistan Super League recommenced without me in the UAE. We lost by 12 runs to the Multan Sultans. It feels like there's a lot of cricket going on without me as I kill time in yet another hotel room.

Friday, 11 June 2021

Breakfast at 5.30 am, nap in the afternoon, wake at 8 pm for dinner, watch an hour of television, fall asleep again – my body clock's a mess. But in the meantime, we got the results back from Jorgia's blood test, and we're having a girl. I suspected it. I don't know why. Maybe because all my mates have had girls recently, except Moey and Krista, who had their son, Archie, 18 months ago. I made sure to tell Moey that if Archie ever comes near my little girl, I'll have a shotgun handy.

Jorgia and I have been discussing whether she should have a Caesarean on a specified day so I can be sure of being there. Babies have not always arrived on time in Jorgia's family and I am worried about the possibility of us being apart at the crucial moment because travel is so difficult. At least Jorgia will be in Clovelly, not far from the children's hospital in Randwick, where Archie was born. But we have some challenging decisions to make.

Saturday, 12 June 2021

Another bad night for the Notts Outlaws, and for my jet lag – I woke up in the early hours of the morning, decided to watch us play the Birmingham Bears at Edgbaston, and saw us lose by 18 runs, thanks largely to my Sixers teammate Carlos Brathwaite making 44 off 18 balls and getting rid of Joe Clarke and Tom Moores.

Sunday, 13 June 2021

I've spent most of the last year in various bio-bubbles, so I can well understand why players are wrestling with whether to tour the West Indies or not. Since Marcus Stoinis pulled out, essentially giving up his place to me, Steve Smith, Daniel Sams, David Warner, Pat Cummins, Glenn Maxwell, Jhye Richardson and Kane Richardson have joined him. Steve is nursing an elbow injury, but the rest have opted out of more bio-secure travel. The selectors' hands are tied because CA has committed to supporting players who do not want to tour because of 'bubble fatigue'. I would never give up an opportunity to play for my country. Imagine if I passed up this West Indies/Bangladesh tour and as a result missed out on a T20 World Cup. It's what you play for; it's the best time in your life. Whenever it is I retire, I know I won't be telling myself I played for Australia too often.

Monday, 14 June 2021

Put my exercise bands, bike and weights to use in a Zoom workout overseen by Adam Kellett, the Aussie strength and conditioning coach, with Sean Abbott and Ben McDermott, both of whom have returned from county cricket. I enjoyed it, actually: weird as it sounds, the fact other people are involved adds to your motivation. The same applies, maybe, in the case of a phone call I had afterwards from my new Aussie skipper, Aaron Finch.

Finchy wanted to discuss how the team should respond to the West Indian push to align with the Black Lives Matter movement. The West Indies team are very keen to take the knee before our matches; they originated it in cricket in England last year, and they've kept it going since.

Actually, Finchy approached me last year after the Aussies were criticised for not taking the knee before their ODIs in England. At the time, I didn't have a particularly strong opinion. What changed my mind was a presentation that Carlos Brathwaite made at the Sydney Sixers. It was pretty powerful, starting with a quote from Martin Luther King: 'Our lives begin to end the day we become silent about things that matter.' Carlos talked about the history of taking the knee, and raising the fist. The former was developed by the San Francisco 49ers' quarterback Colin Kaepernick in September 2016, as a compromise between standing for the national anthem and sitting it out, but it also harked back to MLK's custom of taking a knee in prayer. The latter comes from the 1968 Olympics, where Tommie Smith and John Carlos held their fists aloft on the medal podium – their full gesture, Brathwaite explained to us, comprised black socks to evoke black poverty, black scarfs to portray black pride, an unzipped tracksuit for solidarity with the working class, and beads to remember victims of lynching.

He went into other subjects, too, from the history of slavery, including the compensation paid by the British government to slave owners, to the staggering disparities in the sentences levied on blacks and whites in American courts for similar offences. Afterwards, the Sixers were only too happy to endorse taking the knee, which we did for the rest of the tournament.

After my chat with Finchy today, I share Carlos' presentation on the Aussie team WhatsApp. I hope it stimulates some discussion; there's apparently going to be a meeting when the team gets together to train ahead of the T20s in Saint Lucia.

Tuesday, 15 June 2021

A second win for Notts against Durham, with my good mate Alex Hales making an unbeaten 96 from 54, and a second Zoom fitness session with Adam Kellett. The combination of the two left me feeling pretty tired.

Thursday, 17 June 2021

Another day in quarantine. What can I say?

Friday, 18 June 2021

The Aussie team is starting to gather in Brisbane for the pre-tour camp at Allan Border Field, with the exception of the New South Wales contingent, who are due to fly out tomorrow week: that's me, Moey, Josh Hazlewood, Mitchell Starc, the team manager Gavin Dovey and the team doctor Leigh Golding. But our plans have changed so often that I'll almost be surprised if it happens that way.

Saturday, 19 June 2021

My guys, the Karachi Kings, have made it through to the eliminator in the Pakistan Super League. I hardly got to know them, which was a pity, and they've drifted to the middle of the table since the tournament restarted. But I've certainly missed playing cricket these last few months while others have been.

Sunday, 20 June 2021

Permitting myself thoughts about getting together with the Australian team again, with Finchy and JL. Like with most people, I go back a fair way with the coach: he was Mickey Arthur's batting coach when I was called up for the World T20 in 2012. JL has always been intense, and at the time he had this theory that training extra-hard would help 'make the game easy'. When we gathered for the pre-tour camp in Darwin, JL had come up with a team exercise I remember well. Knowing that we were going to have to bat on these shit tips in Sri Lanka, he'd had pitches prepared that were going through the top and ragging square, and some hardline rules for our practice sessions: if you got out, you were out for good – but you were also out if you hit the ball in the air and it didn't go for six. At the end of the day, for every wicket we'd lost, the whole group would have to do five 20-metre shuttles – basically sprints between the wickets.

We all looked at each other, and everyone was thinking: 'Well, this is going to be interesting.' And it was. Over the next few hours, we lost 44 wickets. The worst thing was that the all-rounders – me, Shane Watson, Maxy, Dave Hussey – were effectively penalised for getting guys out. So we had this long practice session in the draining Top End heat and humidity, and at the end we all had to put on our full gear and do 220 run-throughs! I mean, I'd heard JL was tough, but this was next level.

Anyway, that was JL then. I do think he's mellowed, quite a bit – and I dare say a couple of years in his job would do that to you. I've enjoyed the conversations I've had with him over the last six months; he seems to have worked out that hard work isn't the solution to absolutely everything.

Monday, 21 June 2021

On our last full day in quarantine, there's some disconcerting news: a COVID cluster in Bondi of 12 cases. The New South Wales government reintroduced masks on public transport here last week, but it feels like that won't be enough. It also feels like COVID is chasing me and Jorgia around the world. CA have given us a heads-up that our plans will be subject to last-minute change. No surprises there.

Tuesday, 22 June 2021

A morning update from CA: they have brought our Brisbane flight forward to tomorrow afternoon. So it looks like Jorgia and I will be going our separate ways at once, because she's returning to Adelaide around the same time to stay with her mum. But things are changing quickly: the Bondi cluster is now 22 cases, and we know how fast these things can grow. The minute that Jorgia and I step out of the hotel this afternoon to go to stay with Moey and Krista, we'll be passing through a red zone.

Wednesday, 23 June 2021

A happy morning with Jorgia as we finally get a chance to see our new home in Clovelly – and compare it with the photos we bought it off. We're pleased. The bedrooms are a bit poky, and we're going to need those bed bases with drawers because the storage space is limited, but the living/dining area is big. Jorgia immediately started planning things, including for a bathroom renovation and new carpets.

While we're there, though, shit gets real. South Australia reimpose a hard border with New South Wales. Jorgia can get back in as she's a South Australian resident, but it's clearly not ideal. We discuss the idea of bringing the settlement date for our apartment forward so she can stay in Sydney; the vendor is happy to do so, but the bank isn't ready. In any case, she would have no furniture, because ours is all interstate and no removalists can bring stuff to New South Wales without needing to quarantine when they go back. So our parting in the afternoon is a little chaotic.

When Jorgia gets to Adelaide, she faces another 14 days' isolation. At least she'll be with her mum, but it does feel like everywhere I've led her since April has involved being locked up; and now, if I stay overseas at the end of this tour, I may not see her until the end of November. A lot has always been expected of the partners of cricketers, but this year has been a shocker.

My plans are changing too. If Queensland declares Sydney a COVID hotspot, which they're likely to do, there's no guarantee that the New South Wales–based players won't be forced into another two weeks of quarantine. So CA have deferred our flight; now it might be on Saturday, which is when it was originally scheduled.

Thursday, 24 June 2021

Time for some cricket: Moey and I drive out to Cricket NSW at Homebush for a two-person session. You don't often practise in such a way, but two all-rounders can really get the job done. We do an hour and a half – basically, each of us bowls to the other for 40 minutes, giving throwdowns, watching each other's technique and stopping for a chat every now and again. There's no time limit, no one watching and no one waiting for a net. When you work one-on-one like this, you really see how good people are, in a way that you don't in a structured squad session. Moey is amazingly talented. There's just nothing he cannot do. Slogging, sweeping, bowling yorkers, hitting yorkers: I enjoyed it all because he's such a gun.

Moey and I have known each other for almost 20 years. Back then, although we were both all-rounders, we were quite different. He was 16 and amazing – bloody quick, opening the bowling in first-grade, having always been the outstanding player in his age group. I was 20, and I'd never been that. Because he'd always been the most advanced cricketer among his peers, he'd already done a lot of captaining, and he went on getting those roles; as I've said, that never happened for me. But we got on well straightaway. We played against each other a lot in the Sheffield Shield after I moved to South Australia, then came together again at RCB in 2013.

Moey had a well-publicised mental health battle a few years ago, which resulted in him taking some time away from the game. It surprised a lot of people, although maybe it shouldn't have. He'd always been that guy in every dressing room: steady, mature, considered, making good decisions on and off the field. But he expected a lot of himself, and suffered if he didn't do well. Maybe he didn't have an outlet for those feelings because others were always looking to him for leadership. The break he took has really been the making of him. He seems to have lost his fear of failure; he's almost carefree. He's become a husband and a father, and one of the best things about staying with him these last few days has been watching him with Archie, because he's a beautiful dad. Five weeks on the road will be just as tough for him as for me.

In the afternoon, the schedule for our pre-tour camp was posted to the team WhatsApp. Things have clearly changed a lot since last I played for Australia. Turns out it was never a camp in the way I remember them, where we'd have a few hits and maybe a team dinner. Now the agenda is dominated by culture, with discussions led by Tim Ford, a leadership consultant. Sitting in a room with a crate of beer and talking shit about cricket? I'm always up for that. Talking about culture on Zoom? I'm not so sure, although I know that if they weren't doing anything it would be a poor look. I'll wait and see how it goes.

Friday, 25 June 2021

Moey and I have another session at Homebush, just as enjoyable as the first. But by the time we're finished, New South Wales is announcing that the Bondi cluster is now 65 cases, so there'll be a lockdown in four local government areas: Sydney, Randwick, Waverley and Woollahra. To stay a step ahead, I drive to Faulconbridge in the Blue Mountains, where my mother and her partner have lived for the last ten years. Everything's changing by the minute. Now the plan is that we'll fly to Brisbane on Monday. We'll fill out a border transit exemption as we won't be leaving the confines of the airport, then we'll board the charter flight bound for Saint Lucia.

After a home-cooked meal, I settle in on YouTube to watch Notts play a bizarre game against Derbyshire, which we could easily have lost, should really have won and ended up tying. We were eight for 94, and dragged ourselves to finish at nine for 137. They were five for 128 with 14 balls remaining, then lost four wickets for one run in five deliveries, which meant they needed five to win off the last ball. Matt Critchley – who could have won it for Derbyshire if he'd kept the strike a bit more – slogged one down long-on's throat, but Sol Budinger dropped it and the ball went between his legs for four. Our third tie in eight games! We're still at the top of North Group, but we should have been ahead by miles.

Saturday, 26 June 2021

Woke up to the news that Qantas have cancelled our Monday flight. While CA try to find us another, I participate remotely in the culture and values meetings of our camp-that-isn't-really-a-camp. Finchy talks, briefly. JL talks, passionate as always. There's a lot of stuff about 'making Australians proud'. I've been off the scene for a while, of course, but I don't remember anyone ever raising this as a consideration with an Australian team I was in; it's clearly a very big factor now.

Some of the discussion, I have to say, sounds a little odd to me. Michael Lloyd, the team psychologist, tells us: 'Some of you will say that that culture and values is all just a matter of being a good bloke and playing good cricket, but there's more to it than that.' I'm sitting there thinking, 'Is there? That's been enough for the last 20 years.' I didn't say anything, because I'm not sure I could offer the feedback they're after.

I do want to keep an open mind on this. Maybe the younger guys need to hear things laid out explicitly. But I've never spent much time sitting around talking about culture and values; I've always just tried to live them. And the cynic in me suspects that the national team does this just because they have the resources.

Then Tim Ford has the floor, which isn't uninteresting. He was the guy who CA brought in two years ago to advise them on the comebacks from suspension of David Warner and Steve Smith. He's clearly spoken to everyone and got plenty of feedback, so he talks about where the team has come from three years ago and where they want to get to. The consensus about practice, for example, is that it's been getting better, in the sense that guys are more able to do what they want, rather than participate in structured sessions all the time. As I said earlier, I remember training with JL was always flat-out and high-intensity. Bowlers came off their full runs, and you never got a warm-up ball; they were bouncing you in the cage straightaway.

I remember telling Broady about that a few years ago and he couldn't believe it. As far as he and Jimmy Anderson are concerned, your career contains a finite number of balls and you shouldn't waste them at training. This is why he, at 34, and Jimmy, at 38, are still going strong, where you know that someone like James Pattinson is never going to play that long. If management trust guys to know what's good for them at training, that would be a big step forward.

Sunday, 27 June 2021

The lockdown is to be extended to the Blue Mountains; looks like I'm just going to beat it out of here. I spend the day packing my gear – an old-fashioned way to prepare for what, with no wives and girlfriends, is going to be a very old-fashioned tour. That's the way it was when I started, and it has its advantages: we'll be completely dependent on each other, which I think really helps a team. In fact, if I had my way, the first two to three weeks of every tour would be players only, because it forces you to interact with one another outside of training and games. After that, I understand that players need a sense of home for the sake of their mental health and wellbeing, although that can be isolating for the single guys, who can find that there's nobody to hang out with when other team members spend their free time with their partners.

Monday, 28 June 2021

This is going to sound like an ad, but the Dreamliner, on which we left for our 16-hour direct flight to Saint Lucia this morning, is a fantastic plane. It's probably the most comfortable I've ever been on an airliner. The air seemed amazingly fresh, which apparently is a thing: it's meant to help you get over your jet lag quicker.

Tuesday, 29 June 2021

After what just seemed like a long day, we landed at 5 pm in Saint Lucia. The tropical heat washed over us and the two-hour bus ride from Hewanorra International Airport, right at the bottom of the island, was probably more tiring than the flight, winding along the coast, then between the mountains, then through Castries to our destination of Gros Islet.

Wednesday, 30 June 2021

A compulsory day of self-isolation at the Harbor Club, a Hilton on Rodney Bay: fortunately, I've had a bit of practice looking through the window at bright sunshine. Inside, though, our first team meeting felt great. JL makes a point of encouraging guys to 'use the resources' at their disposal – to tap the experience of those who've played a fair bit. I'm actually closer in age to some of the coaching staff, guys like Andrew McDonald and Dene Hills, than I am to a few of the junior players, like Josh Philippe, Nathan Ellis and Tanveer Sangha. But I'm rapt to be here. I feel like I can really make a contribution.

Pulling my gear out, in fact, I'm reminded of when I first played international cricket in 2010. My cap number is 44 – of the guys in this squad, only Moey has a lower one, 34. On my back I'll as usual be wearing 54, which I opted for back then because my preferred number, 45, had been snaffled a few months earlier by Ryan Harris. I'd played all my state cricket wearing 45 – for my birthday, on the fourth of the fifth – but Ryano had by then had some success with it so there was no shifting him.

45 is my lucky number but it was taken.

Like any cricketer, I'm superstitious. In fact, before the IPL, RCB consulted a numerologist and insisted on us wearing certain numbers. I can't remember what mine was because I said no, I had to be 54. Kyle Jamieson agreed but after a couple of matches reverted to his usual number 12. The way he's bowling at the moment, having been man of the match in the World Test Championship final, I'd imagine he's pretty happy to continue wearing it.

Thursday, 1 July 2021

Our first training session, and I go pretty hard after the long break, just to shock my body into the playing experience again, with the idea that I'll taper off as games get closer. It feels like my feet are getting in the right place, and my slogging swings feel okay. There's a terrific feeling in the group. Lots of interaction, lots of fun.

Because the weather's been poor, the nets aren't great: Zamps and Mitchell Swepson are turning it miles on these crusty surfaces. But nobody's complaining; we're all so grateful to be playing. Makes me wonder about all the culture meetings we had before coming over, because this is my idea of culture: a good, tight-knit bunch of blokes excited for what's to come. That even goes for Tropical Storm Elsa, which the Harbor Club announced it would be 'locking down' for – when you're living your life in a bubble, any break in the monotony is welcome.

Friday, 2 July 2021

Elsa turns out to be a fizzer: impressive winds, but not many houses being unroofed or anything like that; it just frustrates our training. Another slight frustration for me today too. I learn from Kat that they're going to have to replace me at the Manchester Originals for The Hundred – I just wasn't going to be available enough. So I've gone from filling in, to captaining, to not playing at all. It looks like Carlos Brathwaite will take my place. It also now seems that I'm no chance to play for Notts this season. The ECB is insisting that nobody can play in the finals who hasn't played a group game – it's a means of stopping counties from signing big names for one-off appearances at the end of the T20 Blast. So even though I've played 73 games for the county, I'm precluded from playing.

On the plus side, that means I'll be heading home to Australia after the Bangladesh leg of the tour, which will be a bonus. Jorgia, who's still in isolation in Adelaide, just had her first Zoom call with the midwife, and she's getting ready for her 4D scan next week. Bizarrely, though, there's now talk that Cricket Australia is scheduling a white-ball series against Afghanistan that will coincide with the second half of the IPL. I have no idea who will be available or how it'll work relative to the T20 World Cup. But that's the kind of year it's been.

Saturday, 3 July 2021

Training session in stinking heat after the storm, which is really tough but good. JL had set up a gruelling drill in which batting pairs had to run twos while boundary fielders tried to run them out, which had you sprinting 44 yards every 15 to 20 seconds. At one stage I was down on my haunches gasping for breath, and JL says: 'Welcome back, DC.'

I said: 'Hey, this is a walk in the park compared to the drill you had us do in Darwin that time.'

And he starts laughing, which you don't often hear. 'Yeah, that was one of my first sessions with Australia,' JL says. 'I might have gone a bit hard that day.'

Sunday, 4 July 2021

More practice, then some golf, even if there's a bit of a rigmarole involved in scoping the course out first to ensure there's nobody else on it. It's good, though, to socialise with the guys outside the confines of the hotel, and leaves me feeling more positive about the group. That's what I tell George Bailey when he texts to see how things are going. As a player, George was critical of how the selectors handled communications with players; since becoming a selector himself, he's made a point of staying in touch with everyone, getting their feedback and letting them know his thinking. We've been in regular contact since he took the job, even though I wasn't in the team at the time. He's just as he was on the field: very straightforward to deal with.

Monday, 5 July 2021

An intra-squad, 22-over-a-side practice match under lights at the Daren Sammy Cricket Ground between Australia I, led by

Aaron Finch, and Australia II, led by Matthew Wade. I play for the latter, with Moey and Josh Hazlewood. It's a pretty impressive testament to our pace bowling, with Mitchell Starc, Josh Hazlewood, Andrew Tye, Jason Behrendorff, Wes Agar, Riley Meredith and Nathan Ellis. I was seriously impressed with Ellis when I faced him playing against the Hurricanes last season: he has an action that's a tangle of arms, he bowls a yorker at good pace and his slower balls are hard to pick. He's probably closer to selection than some people think.

I came out in the tenth over to join Moey, and we batted together for half an hour or so. I got 47 off 31 balls, while Moey got 36 off 27 in a score of five for 193. I won't say the innings got a monkey off my back, but I did feel good, like I belonged. I also bowled a couple of overs for 16 when they wanted ten an over; Josh Philippe hit me for a boundary but I then bowled him a couple of dots. The ball came out well.

It was useful to get a feeling for the conditions, seeing that we're set to play five consecutive T20s here. The track we used was completely different to the crusty practice pitches we've been warming up on. The Sammy Stadium is a big ground with a lush outfield, and the ball doesn't deteriorate much; it tends to skid on and to favour changes of pace. We'll need to get our slower balls in the right spot; our Australia II guys got a bit short towards the end, and Mitch Marsh and Ashton Turner took the game away from us. So, lots to think about.

Tuesday, 6 July 2021

The West Indies, who arrived here yesterday, were out at breakfast this morning – there was a cast of thousands, with quite a few families, commentators and ex-players, like Curtly Ambrose and Richie Richardson. If I get a few rum punches under my belt, I might remind Richie that I once played against him and his London club for Lashings – one of my favourite cricket memories. They had Vasbert Drakes playing for them, while Collis King, who was just brilliant, swaggered round with a four-pound bat and a bottle of rum. I'm looking him up now. If I want to spook 24-year-old Josh Philippe a bit about our age difference, I can tell him that I played cricket against a guy who's now 70.

I've been thinking back on the practice game and what's a par score here – at the 20-over mark, Australia II were 178. I asked our analyst Dene Hills for some stats about the T20 World Cup back in 2010, when there were ten games here, of which Australia played three. Nobody made more than 200. The two highest scores were in the semi – that fantastic match where Mike Hussey hit 22 off Saeed Ajmal in the last over. The stats from the Caribbean Premier League also suggest that the team batting second wins more often: strike rates against spin in the first innings in a winning game are 136, and in a losing game 107; in the second innings, those figures are 129 and 136, respectively. The dew here doesn't seem to be a factor, and Ashton Agar was harder to get away last night than Zamps or Mitchell Swepson. I don't have a feel for it yet, but that may mean JL deviates from his old Scorchers formula of five specialist bowlers and extends his batting with a couple of all-rounders. If so, I hope to be one of them.

Wednesday, 7 July 2021

This is actually a very good team. Some great kids. Gun cricketers, obviously, but just decent, respectful young guys. No complaints about being stuck in the hotel; no complaints about COVID tests every three days; just really happy to be here.

I'd never had a chat to Ashton Turner before. Thought he was a dickhead, actually, from playing against him – he was always sledging me. Turns out he's a great bloke. He sat down next to me at breakfast and said: 'I've been dying to have a chat to you about batting.' We talked about how I'd taken on the task of batting at five and six at Notts and the Sixers, coming in around the 12th and 13th over, moving around the crease, accessing particular parts of the field; in turn I learned about him. It was a healthy cricket conversation – hopefully part of the contribution I make on this tour.

In the evening we had a second practice game, in which the chasing team won easily, so if we win the toss we'll be bowling for sure. I'll definitely be playing, batting at seven because we're slotting Mitchell Marsh in at number three, and bowling a few overs. I'd like to be a slot higher, but at this stage I'm not fussy.

Thursday, 8 July 2021

Today we sat down for that long-promised conversation about taking a knee, which the West Indies are keen to continue doing. We were led by JL and Finchy, and I was invited to say a few words, along with our psychologist Peter Clarke – he lives in Brisbane but comes from Barbados, which is where our ODIs will be held.

Peter talked about the history of his island, about how the indigenous population was virtually wiped out. The modern population is almost entirely of African descent, brought as slaves – it was a powerful way to think about colonialism. When it came to my turn, I did feel a little like a *Betoota Advocate* headline: 'Token Aboriginal Guy Asked to Say a Few Words after White People Have Given Their Views'. But the boys were really receptive. I tried to explain why Aboriginal people are passionate about the issue, a little about how they see Australia Day, a bit about my family's story – about my aunties and uncles trying to stay ahead of the welfare officers and the police in the 1950s when they were coming to take my dad away. People were very respectful. In fact, you could have heard a pin drop.

There were good questions around the group. If we kneel now, what do we do next? Do we keep kneeling to the end of time? There's a nervousness about doing the wrong thing, saying the wrong thing. To me it's about attitude as much as specific gestures. On the plane over, I'd had a go at a statement the team could release to explain our stance; it's based on a similar statement we drafted at the Sixers.

> The Australian men's cricket team stands with the West Indies cricket team in condemning racial injustice and discrimination, both at home in Australia, and throughout the World. As a team we'll continue to educate ourselves, provide support where possible and create awareness for those who are victims of racial injustice and/or discrimination in any form.
>
> We kneel alongside our West Indian friends to recognise and show our support of all those who have been victims of racial injustice and/or discrimination, past and present.

It's my view that wherever we go, unless there's a political reason we shouldn't, we should support whatever social issue the local team is behind – just like the Indians did for our barefoot circle initiative last season. So we kneel here. And if there's something Bangladesh feel strongly about – maybe it's ending child labour – then we should speak to them ahead of the series about how we can support that.

It's showing care and respect for the country we're visiting, in order to stamp out discrimination and social injustice. So that it's not seen as virtue signalling – a criticism I do understand – I think we should also be prepared to donate to the relevant cause, visit a community or do some coaching, or at the very least take the time to educate ourselves about the places we visit. If you go to someone's house, if you accept their hospitality, you fall in with their customs; I don't see that this is any different. So, yes, we'll be kneeling in solidarity with the West Indies. After that, we'll be trying to defeat them, and they us.

6

FROM THE WEST TO THE EAST

The West Indies and Bangladesh are hugely skillful sides. I really admire them. But their conditions are demanding, and I'm going to have to fight my way into the first-choice XI.

Friday, 9 July 2021

I could come up with a more delicate way to put this, but I might as well say it straight. We controlled the first T20I at the Daren Sammy Cricket Ground, for nine-tenths of the game. Then we fucked it up.

Early on, after we won the toss, Josh was unplayable: the ball was holding in the top and bouncing. West Indies were one for 11 after four, and Chris Gayle needed eight balls to get off the mark. Then Lendl Simmons hit a huge six off Ashton

Agar with the wind, which was blowing hard. The wind became increasingly influential in the game, especially when Andre Russell came to the wicket.

No international team hits the ball as hard as the West Indies – you can't even really replicate it at training – and no West Indian hits it harder than Russell. He has muscles on his muscles, and he can destroy you in 20 balls if you let him, which we did. Moey dropped him at midwicket early on; I had a chance to get him running around the boundary, but my relayed throw didn't quite make it to Ashton Agar, who Russell then hit for massive consecutive sixes. Russell ended up with 51 off 28 balls, and Dwayne Bravo hit Josh's last ball for six to take them to six for 145.

I bowled the ninth and 18th overs, mainly from around the wicket, and they came out well. I conceded a boundary when Josh Hazlewood and Josh Philippe let one run between them on the straight boundary; otherwise, the round-the-wicket angle, which I started using during the power surge overs in the BBL last season, worked well. And the total looked very gettable when we were two for 53 off five overs, with Mitch striking the ball with authority and the pitch skidding on nicely.

Then I think we got a bit caught up in our own analysis. JL has been talking tactically about being really positive at the beginning of the over. It's a good plan. If you're a bowler and your first two balls get smashed, you're under the pump the next four and more likely to give some width or miss your length. But sometimes batters get trapped in that thinking, and forget to play normally. Moises, Josh Philippe and Ben McDermott all got out playing the plan rather than the situation, and when I came out to bat with Mitch at five for 117, I was thinking, 'Let's just knock this on the head straightaway.'

The West Indies then went straight to a death overs formation – bowling wide outside the off stump to a six/three field, with a long-on, a deep midwicket and a 45 in the ring. I decided to try to sweep everything because there was so much space to leg. But Obed McCoy's slower ball is bloody good. It spins out the back of the hand so it dips, and his length is perfect – he lands right on the crease. Mitch now got a bit confused too. Rather than smash one down the ground from Hayden Walsh, he blocked back a return catch, and we lost Ashton Agar in the next over.

That left me with the tail, and I decided I had to be positive. 'If Walsh throws it up,' I thought, 'I'm going to hit down the ground.' Unfortunately, with 21 needed, I shanked it. Could I have blocked a few more? Probably. But I think I'd have played the same way nine times out of ten. Anyway, we fell short, having lost six for 19, the kind of collapse that can happen in T20 cricket – which is not to say it should, but it does. We did a lot right in the game, especially considering how long it had been since we'd last played, while the West Indies have just had some good, tough cricket against South Africa. So losing was not a calamity, but it's still a disappointment.

Saturday, 10 July 2021

The morning was patriotic. We cheered ourselves up by watching Ash Barty in the women's final at Wimbledon: I saw the second half of the second set, all of the third and the presentations – which were lump-in-the-throat stuff, when she went to the coaches' box like Pat Cash and mentioned Evonne in the presentation. I know nothing about tennis, but she was massively impressive: in that third set she was so calculating, keeping the ball in play against Plíšková with that little sliced backhand and waiting to pounce with the forehand. Calculating: that was what we needed to be in the evening. We weren't.

Momentum is definitely a factor in T20, within games and from game to game. The West Indies took confidence from the first match; we were carrying some baggage. I suggested to Finchy that he hold Hazlewood back, and that Mitch Marsh and I could do the donkey work from the bottom end in the first six, but he stuck with the plan. Ashton Agar bowled well, but slightly twinged a hamstring, and Shimron Hetmyer and Dwayne Bravo put on 100 in ten overs.

I was given overs 16 and 20, when Dwayne Bravo and Andre Russell were established, which went well until the last delivery. With Andre, you need to be different every ball or he'll line you up. In hindsight, I should have bowled a wide leg-cutter going away from him, a fast bouncer over his left shoulder or a slower ball. I went for a second consecutive yorker, which was just too low-percentage. I didn't miss by much, and with a new batter it would probably have been fine. But Andre smashed it miles to finish with 24 off eight balls.

The wind proved a real factor again. Eleven of their 13 sixes in these two games have been wind-assisted, and fielding when the ball goes in the air has been really hard. I ran 20 metres at long-off to catch Bravo's lofted drive, only for it to get carried in the wind and hit my hands harder than I expected. Zamps then missed Bravo's top edge off me in the last over at deep fine leg as it swirled away from him. We still should have taken both. When we batted – and we were two for 23 after four overs, needing 11 an over – the West Indies' bowlers used the wind superbly. They basically shut half the ground down, bowling wide outside off at one end and into our pads at the other. The pitch spun more but bounced less than the day before, and Walsh's leg-spin was very effective because it was going down as it reached the batsmen. When I came in, we needed 86 from five overs. Moey was caught at cow corner two balls later, and Ashton got run out two balls after that – there'd have been an easy single but for my forgetting about his hamstring. Bravo bowled me off my pads in the 18th over, and we ended up losing by 56 runs.

Sunday, 11 July 2021

It's true what they say, that winners have parties and losers have meetings. We watched the first half of the UEFA Euro soccer final and then adjourned for our review, but we could hear the hotel going nuts as we discussed why someone bowled a slower ball in the 17th over or whatever. I did enjoy Jimmy Neesham's tweet: 'Why is it the penalty shootout and not just whoever made the most passes wins?'

The meeting wasn't too bad. Everyone got their say, and the tone was constructive. We bossed the first game but failed to win; they bossed the second and won. The margins are quite narrow. Mitchell Starc has gone for 89 off eight overs so far, but he's bowling very fast, and it's really a matter of a fraction of a length: his yorker is not *quite* landing, and that's all it takes. My concern is that I'm not sure what we're learning. T20 is so role-specific that batting Josh Philippe and Ben McDermott out of position does not make sense; they're top three bats in the BBL, but here they're at four and six respectively. Five-day cricket is more flexible, but even then you wouldn't pick Marcus Harris to bat at four in a Test. There'll be some forced changes for the next game, with Ben having done a quad: we'll take in an extra seamer, probably Riley Meredith, and a new batter, probably Ashton Turner. But it feels like we need a more general rethink.

Monday, 12 July 2021

Sometimes in T20 you can end up a bit haunted by your last game, and it felt that way tonight. At our reviews after game two, guys had talked about taking responsibility, but it was as though we got caught up in that through the middle. We'd tried to mix it up by bringing in Alex Carey as a left-hander to disrupt Hayden Walsh, but that didn't come off, and after Finchy got out for 30 off 31, we added just 61 in the last 8.1 overs.

Six for 141 wasn't really enough for our bowling plan, where Finchy threw everything at getting them out. We'd bowled defensively in the first game and kept them to 140. Now we had fielders in catching positions and guys bowling attacking lengths, and Chris Gayle took us to the cleaners: he hit 67 off 38 overs with seven sixes. His partnership with Nicholas Pooran took the West Indies to victory with 5.1 overs to spare. Riley Meredith bowled fast but leaked 48 off 3.5 overs; I didn't bowl, and my contribution to the match was one not out off one ball.

I did achieve at least one thing during the day, which was to acquire a new home. Despite a few last-minute hiccups, settlement proceeded on our apartment in Clovelly. But now Jorgia can't get to it, the COVID situation having deteriorated so badly that the New South Wales borders have been closed again, and she's marooned in Adelaide with her mum. If it's not one thing these days, it's another.

Tuesday, 13 July 2021

Andrew McDonald led a good discussion today: we went around the room, with everyone agreeing that we got it wrong last night, were too aggressive; that we should take a leaf out of the West Indies' book and bowl more defensively. For all my reservations about meetings, I think Ronny and Michael Di Venuto lead these ones well: having coached teams successfully in their own right, they know to keep things simple and short.

Again, though, I think we're making things too complex. I now understand that this tour is a bit of a fact-finding mission. I don't agree with it – I think that, two months out from a World Cup, you should know your best XI and be playing blokes where they're going to play. But I do understand the ideas. It's just that we seem to be getting in our own way.

Wednesday, 14 July 2021

An amazing finish tonight, which we ended up on the right side of at last, but which depended on a freak circumstance. On another windy night, we hit ten sixes, they hit 11, and the ground authorities basically ran out of suitable balls. For the last over of the match, with the West Indies needing 11 runs and Andre Russell at the wicket, Mitchell Starc had a ball that was an absolute rag: at least 30 overs old and really soft. He bowled four pinpoint yorkers, getting every ball to tail in at Russell's back heel, and Andre couldn't do anything about it.

Earlier we'd made a great start, Finchy and Mitch Marsh putting on 114 in 57 balls. We then lost our way against Hayden Walsh again, losing five for 40 in the next 34 balls, so that when Mitch Starc joined me at number eight we had three overs to go, with only Zamps, Riley and Jason Behrendorff to come. Anyway, I managed to slog 22 not out off 14, and we did okay to get to six for 189, although Evin Lewis and Lendl

Simmons then blitzed us in the powerplay, racing to none for 56 off four.

The fourth over was mine, which was a bit of a surprise as I usually bowl in the middle overs, and I vanished for 23. We actually had a good plan: for me to bowl off-cutters across Lewis, get him off strike, then bowl at Simmons' hip with two leg-side catchers. Unfortunately, my cutters were called wides, and I then couldn't get Lewis off strike, which was disappointing – even more so when it proved to be my only over. Still, Zamps and Mitch Marsh got five for 44 from their eight, and in the end we did just enough to scrape a win, even after Fabian Allen smacked Riley for four sixes in the penultimate over to give us a scare.

Thursday, 15 July 2021

One of those days. When I'm on the massage table I get a message from JL: 'Sorry, mate, give me a call when you're finished.' So when I catch up with him, he tells I'm not playing the last game and asks if I'm okay with that.

'Honestly?' I say. 'Well, I'm pretty pissed off. I didn't come halfway around the world to sit on the bench.'

JL says: 'Look, sorry. It's just the make-up of the side. When I was with the Scorchers, we did some work with our analyst, and he was adamant that teams with five bowlers win more often than teams with six batsmen.'

I like JL a lot, but I just sat there thinking: 'Well, how many games has your analyst won? Doesn't it depend on who the six batsmen and five bowlers are? How can the analyst adjust for the different way your top order play when a guy who should be at number ten is coming in at number seven?' When JL enjoyed success with the Scorchers, it was in a domestic competition with a super-hot attack: Johnson, Behrendorff, Tye, Richardson, Hogg. I just don't think it's possible to generalise from that. Anyway, all I can report is my observation from the last few years that teams do best with all-rounders batting all the way down, so guys can play with freedom and you have all varieties of bowling. As I pointed out, our best bowler in the last match was Mitchell Marsh, the sixth bowler we used.

Then JL says: 'I agree about all-rounders in the one-dayers. That's my philosophy. So how do you feel about playing in the one-dayers?'

I said: 'Well, obviously I'd rather play than not play.'

He said: 'That's good, because we're seriously considering playing you in Barbados.'

I didn't say anything, but I thought: 'That's great – except I haven't played any 50-over cricket for four years.'

I shouldn't make this sound antagonistic. It was a perfectly reasonable cricket conversation in which there was a difference of views. And it turned into an interesting dialogue, because JL asked my opinion of the next generation of leaders in Australian cricket. There aren't many, to be honest, but I think probably the standout is Mitchell Marsh. He's 29, playing really good cricket, and he's developed the smarts to go with it. We're tough on all-rounders in Australia. Remember how we used to treat Shane Watson, who was an absolute gun?

The other thing JL raised was the possibility that if I don't make the squad of 15 for the T20 World Cup, I could come as a reserve player with an additional focus on mentoring younger players. We have some outstanding coaches on this tour, and it would be fun to work with them. But will I want to go to the UAE and not play when Jorgia is in the final stages of her pregnancy? I haven't been a coach before. But neither have I been a father.

Friday, 16 July 2021

It was, for the first time, a still night at the Sammy Stadium; our XI also had an unfamiliar look: one specialist bat (Finchy), two all-rounders (Moey, Marsh), three keepers (Philippe, Wadey and Carey), two spinners (Zamps and Swepson) and three pace bowlers (Josh, Behrendorff and Tye). Yes, we had five specialist bowlers. But we also had two of our bigger hitters, Mitch and Moey, at three and four, and Wadey and Carey as finishers. Wadey can bat anywhere, but he hasn't batted down the list for a long time; Alex opens in the Big Bash League.

Mitch and Tye prevented the West Indies from setting us more than 200, and we were two for 93 off nine, but then Finchy was brilliantly caught off Walsh, Fabian Allen diving full stretch at long-off and grabbing the ball in his left hand. Wadey came in two balls later, but with Tye and Swepson at seven and eight he was in no position to take any chances, even though the required run rate was already ten. Our last-wicket pair took 15 off the final eight balls to narrow the margin to 16 runs, but we'd long since fallen out of contention. Except for that rag of a ball in Wednesday night's game, we could easily have been beaten 5–0. It's been a very disappointing week.

Saturday, 17 July 2021

Another day, another charter flight. The West Indies off-spinner Kevin Sinclair slept in and missed the bus, which meant that both teams and the media had to wait for him on the tarmac for an hour. After we landed at Grantley Adams International Airport in Barbados, a bus took us to the terminal, where we filled out our forms to say we didn't have COVID, then we took another coach to the Courtyard Marriott in Bridgetown for 24 hours of isolation. Out my window, a beautiful view of the beach. Wonder if I'll be allowed to go there? Probably not.

Sunday, 18 July 2021

Training at Kensington Oval ahead of Tuesday's one-day international. Finchy sits it out with a knee injury – he's actually looking a bit doubtful for the series – and our session isn't great anyway. We practise on the edge of the square, where the surface is pretty poor – slow and poppy. I faced the flicker and Mitchell Swepson, and it was seaming and spinning. The whole square looked the same, so 230 will be a winning score here.

Monday, 19 July 2021

It's amazing how little you can get done when there's so much spare time. Catch up with the latest on COVID news on your iPad and half your day is gone. Moey, who's in the next room to mine, got so bored today that he decided to cut his own hair, which he did pretty badly, and then he had a go at mine, which he did a bit better. In the meantime, there is just the chance I'll play tomorrow – JL says it's between me and Matthew Wade to bat seven, because they're going to stick with Josh Philippe as opener, while Finchy will be replaced by Ben McDermott.

That would actually be fun. The only 50-over cricket I've played in the last four years was for the University of New South Wales early last season, and after so much T20 it was fascinating to get back to: you have so much time, there's real ebb and flow. Only England has really brought a T20 flourish to 50-over cricket. Nobody else has, and they haven't really had a chance to because guys play so little 50-over cricket at domestic level.

Tuesday, 20 July 2021

The selectors stick with Wadey, to give him more exposure in the position he'll probably occupy for the T20 World Cup, so I'm looking on as Alex Carey leads us. It's actually a

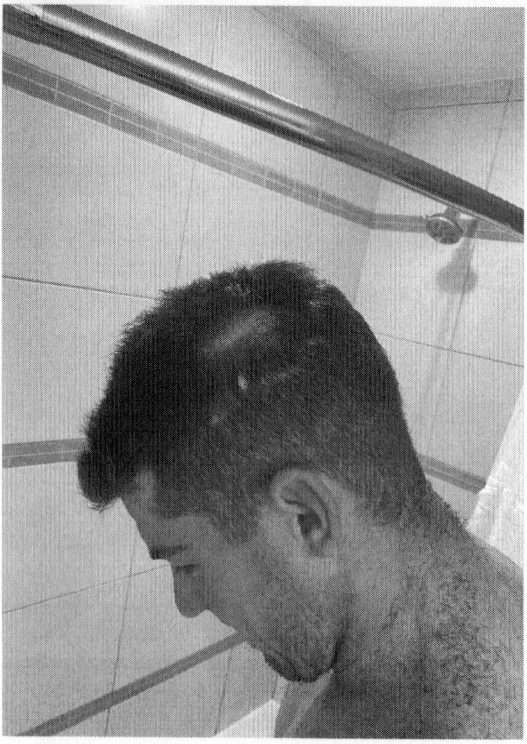

Isolation breeds strange haircuts. Moey's didn't go so well.

really good performance, on a poor surface where it's almost impossible to drive down the ground. Their fast bowlers are a bit short and don't attack the stumps enough, which allows us to grind out 230. Then Mitchell Starc opens with a fantastic spell, and they're too far gone at six for 27 in the eighth over to come back. A satisfying win.

Wednesday, 21 July 2021

Time seems to be standing still here, but it's passing at home. Jorgia, finally out of isolation with her mum in the Adelaide Hills, had another scan today, which went well. But the COVID outbreak in New South Wales has spread, first to Victoria, then to South Australia, pushing all three states into lockdown – so there goes our chance of getting my stuff in Melbourne and Jorgia's in Adelaide moved to our place in Clovelly. Removalists have been blamed for the spread of infection, so nothing's going anywhere.

Jodie Hawkins, our old general manager at the Sixers, messaged today to see how Moises, Josh Philippe and I were getting on. So I sat down to calculate how many days I've spent locked down in hotel rooms since leaving Australia to start the Pakistan Super League. And – what do you know? – this is my hundredth. The flight from Barbados is my 13th plane journey in that time too. I'm used to hotel rooms and to travelling, and I might even have done slightly less than in a usual year because we moved around so little during the IPL.

But there's more ahead, because RCB advised me today that they expect us in the UAE in late August ahead of a week's isolation and a week's training. I'd be lying if I said that the grind of our current situation, where there's no option but to hang around the hotel, isn't starting to pall – I'm at that point where home is starting to look pretty good, even if I am flying into a lockdown. At least then I'd be able to sort out stuff like getting the utilities turned on in our new place.

Thursday, 22 July 2021

Well, going home might be closer than I imagined. As I sit here tonight in my hotel room, this tour and our tour of Bangladesh are in the balance, the second one-day international having today been postponed. We'd had a cap presentation for Riley Meredith on the event of his ODI debut, we'd had the toss and we were out on the ground warming up when suddenly the word went round: everyone off. So we traipsed off and found our doc, Leigh Golding, waiting for us in the dressing room to explain that the West Indies' team manager, Rawl Lewis, had returned a positive test – four days after returning a negative one, and despite being fully vaccinated. Apparently, Rawl had only taken the test because he was leaving the team bubble to attend to a family crisis.

I don't really know Rawl, although I have met him: after the first one-day international, the teams and support staff all shook each other's hands. The doc said that was likely not a problem – he'd be more worried if we'd shared an enclosed space with him, like a lift, because of the possibility of aerosol transmission of the virus.

But the game was off, and we returned to the Courtyard Marriott and dispersed to our rooms. At about 6 pm there was another briefing, this time on Zoom: we were to be tested, and would have to isolate until the results come back tomorrow. The problem is that even if we're negative, we're all close contacts, and so could be infectious for the next ten days, which rules out the rest of this tour and most of Bangladesh. A few scenarios were discussed, including returning to Australia and basing ourselves in Adelaide, where the hotel is part of the ground, so we could train in isolation.

Leigh advised us 'not to speculate', but it's hard not to. At the very least, the third ODI, scheduled for Saturday, is looking very doubtful.

Friday, 23 July 2021

Passed the time waiting for my COVID test result by watching some of The Hundred, which I'd passed up the opportunity to play in order to be here. The team I'd been slated to represent, the Manchester Originals, went down to the Oval Invincibles, although it was good to see my Sixers teammate Carlos Brathwaite and my Notts teammate Calvin Harrison almost get their team over the line with a stand of 53 in 32 balls.

Calvin is an interesting one. He played for Hampshire last year, then opened the batting against Notts for Oxford at the start of this season and made a hundred, although he's actually a leg-spinner. He had a hit with me, Alex Hales, Samit Patel and a few others when we were warming up for the Vitality Blast, and I was really impressed: he's quick through the air and has a good wrong 'un, which makes him perfect for T20. Notts picked him up for the Blast, where he bowled really well, and I recommended him to Kat when the Originals lost Shadab Khan.

Sunil Narine was turning it miles. I guess we should be thankful he's in England and not here.

Saturday, 24 July 2021

No positive tests, so the delayed second ODI proceeds, although we have to leave out Josh Hazlewood, who after 36 hours in a hotel room has got a niggle in his calf. It's a wonder that sort of thing hasn't happened more often, given how regularly we usually active men have been made to stay cooped up. The West Indies bowl better on a pitch that's that much poorer and we're bowled out for 187. Mitchell Starc is rhythmic and quick, and we have them five for 72 in response, but Moises and Wadey both drop Nicholas Pooran, whose sixth-wicket partnership of 93 with Jason Holder decides the match.

Sunday, 25 July 2021

Although we've been prohibited from golf, we are finally allowed to visit the beach. It's funny. On the coverage, the commentators have these sections where they promote

Barbados as a tourist destination – the sun, the sea, the luxury, the cuisine, the natural wonders. We won't see any of them. We certainly won't get to Harbour Lights, the beachfront bar and nightclub on Bay Street that's a favourite hangout for cricketers. Nor will we be seeing Finchy again on this tour. He flies home today, where he'll have to spend two weeks in quarantine before a surgeon can look at his knee.

When I go into the team room to drop my washing off, I bump into JL and Alex Carey, who are talking about whatever a coach and a stand-in captain talk about.

'It's easy,' I say. 'You want to win this last game? Just pick me.'

JL starts laughing. But maybe they will.

Monday, 26 July 2021

They do. So after a seven-year break, I return to one-day international cricket – and I have what's kind of a perfect game. I don't bat, I don't bowl and I field just three balls – but we win the match, and therefore the series, on a shocking pitch, two-paced and unpredictable. I actually spend most of the West Indies' innings standing at slip next to Alex Carey, who's getting a lot of advice about what to do from various senior players – Wadey, Moises, Mitch Marsh and Ashton Turner are all experienced captains. My advice to him is simply to trust his own instincts, and more often than not he does.

When Ashton had bowled his eighth over, I said I thought we should bowl Starcy and Zamps out. Worst-case scenario,

I'd bowl 48 and 50. But we got the last wicket in the 46th over, and were chasing 153. We kept sending out lefties – Alex, then Wadey, then Ashton Agar – to deal with the leggie Hayden Walsh and the left-arm orthodox Akeal Hosein, which worked really well. It was actually very hard to bat in the first 15 to 20 overs, when the seam was still hard and pronounced – the ball was gripping big, and turning a metre. Later in the innings it got a lot easier.

A bunch of West Indians came in afterwards, including Phil Simmons, Jason Holder and their fielding coach, Trevor Penney, who a few of the guys know. I go back to early Redbacks days with Kieron Pollard, and we had a long talk with Mitchell Marsh. Mitch was picking Kieron's brain about playing spin, and Kieron was saying that if he can't step and hit, he plays back. He's so big and strong, and his levers are so long, that he can do that, although he'd struggled here because he didn't feel he could trust the bounce. Hayden Walsh is a real character. He asked Alex where he lived, and Alex said: 'Just a suburb in Adelaide, you wouldn't have heard of it.'

And Hayden goes: 'I would. I played third-grade for Sturt in 2012.' The things you learn over a beer ...

Tuesday, 27 July 2021

Probably the best day of the tour – bloody awesome, actually. Our psychologist Peter Clarke had organised for us to celebrate our series win on a catamaran for a few hours, and Zamps, who took over from Wadey as the song master for the white-

Celebrating a one-day international series victory in style, at sea.

ball teams a couple of years ago, led us out on the water as the sun set. Later we had a few more drinks on the beach, with the speaker playing some tunes. A few of the guys, a bit pissed and a bit courageous, were begging Pete to let them kick on in town. 'Come on, doc, surely we can go to Harbour Lights? We'll be safer there than in Bangladesh!'

Wednesday, 28 July 2021

We fly out of Grantley Adams on the Qantas charter in the afternoon. Quite a cool process – very rock star – coming through the back entrance of the airport, although we did have to have our backpacks searched. So we set off on another 16-hour journey, nonstop, flying east over Spain – a quiet trip, with a few of the guys a bit subdued after the big night last night.

Thursday, 29 July 2021

I've only played in Bangladesh once before, which was in the World T20 in 2014. It can be a shock. You think India's crowded until you get here. I can remember the airport when we arrived – it was just a sea of people. I also remember the stat I read afterwards: the country has 170 million people, in an area the size of Victoria.

Arrive at the Intercontinental in Dhaka – like a lot of hotels in South Asia, it's nice but not quite finished. Still, we've taken over a wing, and we have our own staff, team room and kitchen, so the setup is good. Some guys feel concerned about

COVID, although that's more from those who didn't play in the PSL or IPL this year – those of us who did are used to bio-bubbles now and feel pretty safe in them.

I actually feel better for being here. It knocked me round a bit being left out of the last T20 – there's nothing worse than looking on in a game where you feel you could have made a difference. From a financial point of view, being left out also made it harder for me to obtain a contractual upgrade, as the points system in use allocates one point for a T20 and two points for an ODI – so potentially the game was worth $300,000 to me, which means a lot when you've just taken out a big mortgage and the bank's asking you where your income's coming from. But winning the ODI series lifted my spirits, and I reminded myself that money isn't why you take these opportunities. This might be my last chance to play in a global tournament.

Friday, 30 July 2021

Another day's isolation, another day looking out the window – which isn't encouraging if you glance at the overcast skies. It's monsoon season and there's a 70 per cent chance of rain. There's also meant to be a lockdown here, which started after Eid, but you'd hardly know: there seem to be plenty of people on the streets. Which makes it like Sydney, from what I'm told.

Mushfiqur Rahim will not be permitted to re-enter Bangladesh's bio-bubble after leaving it, which will not make the locals happy; that's due to a Cricket Australia directive that had nothing to do with the players. They will still have some good cricketers. Shakib Al Hasan is a world-class all-rounder; Mahmudullah is very experienced. My likeliest match-up will be Mustafizur ul Rahman, so I'll spend some time watching his variations in the next few days, to see how many slower balls he has and how to pick them. They're talking about 190 being an average recent score at the Shere Bangla National Stadium, which would make for a pleasant change after the poor pitches in Barbados.

Saturday, 31 July 2021

Who will play here? I think I'm a good chance. We had no spare batters on the bench the other day because Ben McDermott is recovering from an ankle injury he suffered running into the boundary rope. They'll probably pick something close to the team in the last ODI: two quicks (Mitch Marsh and me), two spinners and Ashton Turner. They might rest Starcy, while Riley Meredith has a sore side, so it's possible they'll call up Nathan Ellis, one of the reserves, who has been activated.

Who's going to captain us? With Finch gone home, the nominal T20 vice-captain is Matthew Wade, although there's also a case for giving Alex Carey more experience. He's an impressive guy. Ripping bloke, and pretty much what you see is what you get: a natural leader who just needs a few more games to build confidence in his tactical intuitions.

Sunday, 1 August 2021

A bit of a breakthrough in life admin at our new place: we can get an exemption from the prohibition on interstate removals, because it's from storage to house rather than house to house. Jorgia is also finally getting vaccinated, which is a relief in the present climate.

Our first day's training is really enjoyable too. Forty-five minutes with Michael Di Venuto, who's an outstanding batting coach, tactically and technically, and so quick to work out how to communicate with people. Also spent some time thinking about how to play Mustafizur, who's the real wildcard in the Bangladesh pack, with all his variations and his incredible wrist. I contacted my old Notts teammate Brendan Taylor, who suggested staying leg-side of the ball and playing for the slower delivery, because he seldom bowls the quicker one. Sounds like good advice, assuming the pitches allow it.

Monday, 2 August 2021

The signs aren't good, frankly. The pitches here when last I played weren't bad. This one looks unprepared, ideal for bowlers who can spin and cut the ball. There's no way anyone will be making 180–190 here, which makes me wonder whether there's much point playing Mitchell Starc and Josh Hazlewood. I think there'd be some upside in Nathan Ellis, whose yorkers and slower balls are seriously impressive. Although maybe I should be thinking about my own place.

Tuesday, 3 August 2021

It turns out that there isn't a spot for me: the team goes round on the WhatsApp in the morning and I'm not part of it. So for me it's another game on the bench, and a hard one to watch. The competition could hardly have been more different to what we just experienced in the Caribbean. There we were playing the West Indies, who smash it on a medium-sized ground in a gale; here the nights are still, the ground is huge, the rope has been pushed right back and boundaries are very hard to come by.

We bowled really well to keep Bangladesh to 33 in the powerplay, and only a few late blows from Afif Hossain got them to seven for 131. But then each of Shakib, Mahedi Hasan and Nasum Ahmed got wickets with their first deliveries, and only Mitch Marsh batted more than 25 balls. It was a tough task to adapt but we really should have done better.

Because of COVID, we eat after we return from games rather than at the ground, so there was food on at the Intercontinental when we got back. As I was heading for the lift, JL walked past and said: 'Make sure to be ready tomorrow.' So maybe I'll get my chance.

Wednesday, 4 August 2021

Or not. The team goes round on the WhatsApp and again I'm not in it – in fact, it's unchanged. I was picked on my record, but now, it seems, people have forgotten about it. 'This isn't working,' I thought. 'I reckon I've got to plead my case.' The Notts analyst sends me some numbers from my last five years of T20: I've played more games than any two other players in our squad, and nobody has a better bowling strike rate in the death overs.

For what they're worth, I flick the stats on to JL, with a comment: 'All I'm after is a decent go at it. If I fuck it up, so be it, but I think what I've achieved in my career, both individually and from a contribution to my team's success perspective, so far deserves an opportunity to prove I can do the job and win games of cricket for Australia.'

Nothing much comes back: 'These are excellent domestic numbers mate. Thanks for sharing. See you on the bus.'

We made a better fist of things tonight: we were two for 88 entering the 15th, with Mitch and Moey going well – and 120 can be a winning score here, if you bowl well. But then we lost three in four overs, with the guys having lots of trouble with Mustafizur: 46 of his 48 balls in the two matches have been slower balls, which on this surface are exceptionally difficult to handle. He bowled Josh Philippe around his legs with one that dipped after bouncing; he got one to absolutely take off and glove Ashton Agar. We had them five for 67 in the 12th, but then Afif Hossain got a few away, adding an unbeaten 56 in 44 balls with Nurul Hasan.

So having never lost to Bangladesh in T20 cricket, we've now lost to them twice in 24 hours.

Thursday, 5 August 2021

A bit of soul-searching going on in the camp today. It feels like we've been arrogant here – that we've turned up thinking we're better cricketers and will just blow Bangladesh away. T20 doesn't work like that. They've shown us how to play these conditions: lots of spin, lots of pace off the ball, deep batting. We've gone with a keeper, five batters and five specialist bowlers, including three pacemen. Even if we were playing well, which we aren't, we'd struggle with that combination.

At a meeting today, there was discussion about a proposed white-ball series in Oman against Afghanistan at the same time as the second half of the IPL. Would I go if selected? If it was the squad for the T20 World Cup essentially warming up, sure. Otherwise, I'd rather play IPL, quite frankly. Even if you're not being picked, you're practising against the best players in the world, and better for it.

I don't regret coming on this tour, because I know I'd have regretted not having a go. Playing for my country has always been my biggest motivation. But I'd be lying if I said I wasn't disappointed with how it's turned out.

Friday, 6 August 2021

I've played 600 games of competitive cricket and never have I faced such challenging batting conditions as tonight. In the penultimate over of tonight's game, there was just the slight chance that if I got hold of one, we could fluke a win in the last over. Instead, Mustafizur bowled me four dots, and if he bowled me the same four balls again I probably wouldn't do much better. On the same crumbling pitch and with the same huge boundaries as the second game, 100 was a reasonable score. Back in the day, Boof Lehmann used to have very simple KPIs for T20 cricket: hit 20 boundaries and bowl 50 dots, and you would win more often than not. Those goals aren't much use on a surface like this: tonight the teams hit 23 boundaries between them.

Again, although we left Mitch Starc out to give Nathan Ellis his first cap, we probably just offered a bit too much pace on the ball – even if Nathan, amazingly, picked up a hat-trick with the last three balls of Bangladesh's innings. They made 127, which was 20 too many. I bowled the 12th, for four runs, and the 16th, for five runs – off-cutters to the left-handers, leg-cutters to the right. Old tricks, really – I learned to bowl cutters on flat decks at the Adelaide Oval when I played 50-odd games for South Australia, and I used to love bowling them on the pitches Victoria rolled out in Alice Springs. Tonight I built up enough pressure that we actually got a run-out in each over. But we let through a couple of expensive overs and, in games like these, one over, even one boundary, can make all the difference. It takes away the double-bluff you might use in other circumstances – where you set the field for a full ball and bowl it short, or for a slower one and really let it go. You can take no chances. It's just a grind.

Shakib and Nasum were very tight, but Mustafizur was incredible: he bowled four overs for nine, including a powerplay over that went for just three. He's basically a medium-pace Murali, with an incredible wrist. One ball would bounce, one would turn, then on the same lengths they would grub and skid. With the monsoon around, the outfield is soaking the ball, so it becomes heavier and heavier. Although we'd kept wickets in hand, we left our run till it was hardest to score: after 17 overs, we were three for 94, but needed 35 off the last 18 balls when the rate had been about a run a ball all night. I came in when Mitch Marsh got out, and we ended up needing 22 from the last over. I got a height no-ball, but I was crouching so low to get under it that it flew past my shoulder. Alex could then only get a single off the free hit, and we fell ten runs short.

I was pleased for the Bangladesh guys. COVID meant that we couldn't even shake hands with them, but it was clear how much the series mattered to them. On the field, there was some good banter between the teams. They got into me a bit when I was batting against Mustafizur, and I got chatting to their keeper, Nurul Hasan. I was going: 'How do you bat against this guy in the nets? Because I can't get a bat on him. Got any tips?' And he was joking back to me. They're a good team that plays smart cricket. I watched them in their celebratory huddle and they were ecstatic. We were like any team that's gone down 0–3. JL texted afterwards to say well bowled, but I was pretty dark on myself.

Saturday, 7 August 2021

At times in this diary, I've consoled myself that in T20 there's always another game. But it hasn't always been true: I got left out in the IPL, then got left out in the West Indies. But tonight I got another chance, and made the best of it.

The day didn't start so well. I wasn't present when it happened, but apparently there was a bit of a scene at breakfast when our manager, Gav Dovey, had a crack at the reporter from Cricket.com.au, who had posted a video to CA's website of the Bangladesh guys celebrating after their win. JL seems to have joined in. I'm disappointed by that. The reporter is a great young guy whom all the boys like. He finds himself in a very tough position, reporting for Cricket Australia on a series that Australia has lost so conclusively. In the warm-ups at the ground later, I saw JL talking to the reporter near the boundary rope, obviously trying to sort out their differences. I respect that the reporter, comparatively junior, stood his ground.

By that stage, I knew I had a new role for the night, because Wadey had told me on the bus that I should be ready to bat number three. In the event, Bangladesh decided to bat first, and we did well to hold them to nine for 104, with Mitchell Swepson taking three for 12 in a great four overs in the middle – including Mahmudullah with a beautiful googly. As I came off, I checked with JL what he wanted, and he said: 'Yep, you'll bat first drop if Wadey gets out first.' So I ran off to get my pads on, which was a good move, as I was in to face the fifth ball of the innings. I slogged it for a couple, then I slapped the next ball over cover for four, and it made sense to keep going.

I've actually felt in good shape all tour, so when Shakib came on for the fourth over I backed myself to take him on – and I hit five of the next six deliveries for six. I came down to the first one, slog-swept the next two, drove over mid-on and pulled over midwicket. We were one for 45 after four overs – almost halfway there. We still almost stuffed it up, though. I smacked my 15th ball to point to get out for 39, poor Moey got run out at the non-striker's end off Shakib's hand, and before we knew it we were six for 65. Fortunately, Ashton Agar slog-swept a beautiful six off Nasum, then a couple of other boundaries, and was out with us only needing six to win.

'You've got big fucking nuts,' JL said to me after the game. 'You did just what the team needed.'

But it wasn't courage so much as common sense. As tough as batting was, it would only get tougher, so up front was the time to take the game on, when the field was up and the ball hard. Anyway, I know not everything works in T20, but this did, which is a good feeling.

Sunday, 8 August 2021

Winning doesn't change that we're still 1–3 down in the series, and we've struggled, again, against slow bowling on an overseas tour. Australian cricket has a funny attitude to

A message from the coach.

playing on pitches that spin. I remember a Sheffield Shield match I played back in February 2015 for Victoria against New South Wales at Robertson Oval in Wagga Wagga, where the pitch spun from the get-go; no team totalled 250, and we faced Nathan Lyon and Steve O'Keefe nonstop. Although we lost, it was a good game, really tight, and a great learning experience for all the batsmen. But Robertson Oval hasn't hosted a first-class match since, probably because people get hung up on the idea that the Shield is a place for guys to make big hundreds on flat pitches, when it should actually be about exposing them to a variety of conditions. And so when young blokes come to Bangladesh, they've never seen anything like it. And they probably reason that they won't see those conditions again anytime soon, so they have little incentive to adapt.

I'm not sure our training has been quite right either. We've had Ronny and Diva and Pete Clarke, who's quite good on the wanger, throwing down all this seam-up stuff, and in the middle we've probably had a total of two overs of proper pace. Although that's also partly because of having no net bowlers, who in their own conditions would also have helped our adaptation to these pitches.

Monday, 9 August 2021

We certainly didn't adapt tonight in the fifth T20I, although it was really our bowling that let us down. The pitch was so poor that we shouldn't have let Bangladesh make 100, let alone eight for 122. I bowled out for the first time since the PSL, overs seven, nine, 15 and 19, and took two for 17. But when they threw up me to open the batting, my third ball from Nasum skidded through; Nasum then got Mitch Marsh as well. Wadey hit a couple of sixes, Ben McDermott another, and we were two for 37 after seven. It took just 40 more deliveries to bowl us out completely. I'm told it was Australia's shortest international innings: 13.4 overs, all out for 62. It certainly felt like it. The whole air of hurry was reflected in the fact that we were already packed and ready to leave the country. From Shere Bangla it was straight to Hazrat Shahjalal International Airport, where we walked across the tarmac to board our charter flight. When we took off at about 12.30 am, I can't say that anyone was sorry.

7

ABNORMAL NORMALITY

As I planned my year, I'd set this time in 2021 to be playing in the Vitality Blast and The Hundred. Instead, I'm back in Australia, first in a quarantine hotel, then acclimatising to a new city and moving into a new home as I contemplate becoming a new father. Plus, our coach is under pressure. A lot of pressure.

Tuesday, 10 August 2021

We land in Adelaide around 2 pm and we're whisked to the Sebel Playford. I'd heard we were going to be staying at the Oval Hotel so we could train at the cricket ground, but apparently the South Australian government changed their mind, which is going to make it a pretty long two weeks. One bonus: I have a tiny balcony. My only view is of city rooftops, but for the first time this year I have a hotel room with fresh air.

Jorgia, she's a good egg. She left a care parcel at reception for me, with nice cheeses and bread and other delicacies which she bought at the market; she'd left parcels for Moey and Zamps too. And today she stood in the laneway and waved up to me, like the reverse of the balcony scene in *Romeo and Juliet*. I felt like tying my sheets together and climbing down.

Also caught up with another long-term partner, my manager, Cade Brown. I met Cade, who's an accountant by training and worked many years at PwC, when he was playing at University of NSW: he'd come up from Canberra where he'd been very successful with the Comets to have a crack at first-class cricket. It so happened that was the year I was looking at my first Blues contract, and he offered to have a look. We've carried on in a similarly informal way, and he now advises few other guys, like Chris Tremain and Tom Rogers, and women's pace bowler Maitlan Brown. For him it's mainly a sideline to his work as a partner of a professional services firm called Callida Consulting. Over the years I haven't really needed much more than someone to look at my contracts; I've stayed in my lane.

Wednesday, 11 August 2021

Long chat to George Bailey today. I think they're going to settle on a squad for the T20 World Cup in the next 24 hours, so guys can start planning for their next few months. They can pick 15 squad members and an unlimited number of reserves, but it sounds like they're reluctant to send Test guys over to Dubai who might end up sitting on the bench – Marnus Labuschagne and Nathan Lyon and the like. I told him that I'm really keen to be part of the 15, but less keen to go as a reserve. Being a net bowler while Jorgia is in the last month of her pregnancy holds no appeal for me at all. She got her second vaccine shot this morning, and she came to see me again, this time waving from the corresponding level of the multistorey carpark opposite my room. It feels like we should be getting ready to be parents.

In the afternoon, there was some chat on the WhatsApp about journalists looking into the story about Gav, JL and the Cricket.com.au reporter. I got some messages from other reporters, which I ignored; there's nothing I can add, although if it came to it, I would support the guy from Cricket.com.au. He has to have the freedom to report what he sees. The context, of course, is of a team and a management bitterly disappointed by the outcome of the two recent series, and also, after six weeks together, maybe a bit sick of each other's company. A story was published this evening that will no doubt cause some discussion, partly because there's not much else to occupy us at the moment.

Thursday, 12 August 2021

There's an uneasy feeling about the camp at the moment, what with us all being in isolation, with no outlet, no direct

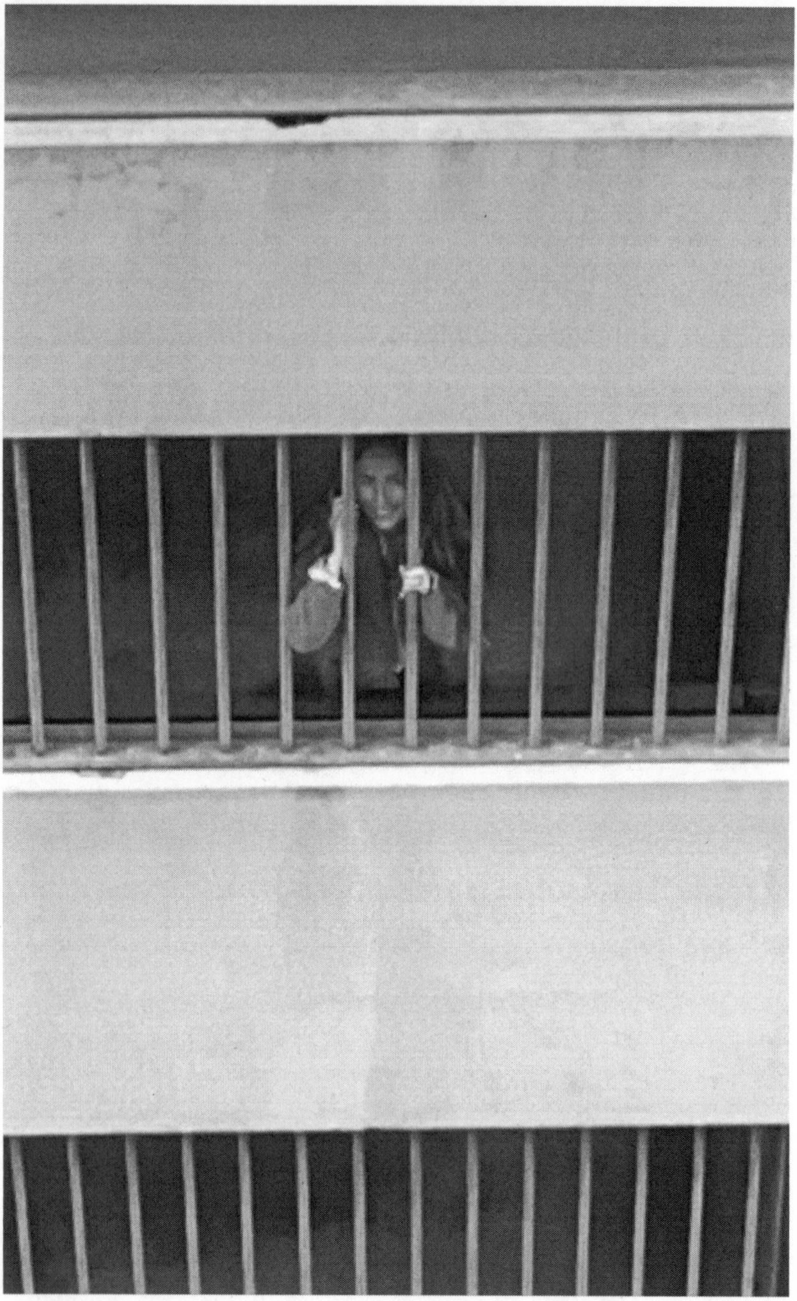

Looking down on Jorgia, looking up at me, across Victoria St, Adelaide.

interaction, coming off some bad defeats, with a selection in process and the coach under public scrutiny. From what I saw in the West Indies and Bangladesh, I'm not sure the set-up is working well. I understood JL's desire to experiment, but I think it started inhibiting players. I might as well repeat my philosophy of T20, which is that everyone needs confidence. You need guys to learn specialist roles. You need deep batting so those at the top can play with freedom. You need simple messages delivered with absolute clarity. JL likes to get into technical stuff with batting, and he knows a lot. I mean, the man was a gun. But was this tour the time to be looking at players' swings and foot placement? Especially young guys who weren't secure in their place in the team, and who were always being asked to bat in different slots.

Sometimes, I should say, JL's technical curiosity is really fascinating. During the reviews for the fourth T20I in Bangladesh, he showed footage of my sixes and said: 'Look at that. In each shot, he dips his head. All the great players dip their heads.' It was an interesting observation, although I'd want a bit more proof before going along with the idea. It did kick off a bit of a running gag. At the breakfast buffet? Make sure to dip your head. Barista made you a bad coffee? Obviously didn't dip his head. I did wonder, as I have a few times, about the wisdom of giving guys another thing to think about when they already have so much going on.

Friday, 13 August 2021

There was actually talk today that JL might not be going to the T20 World Cup, which was pretty alarming and turned out to be a false rumour. The team hasn't been announced, which is adding to the unease. But we're not at the coach changing time yet, surely.

There's also a lack of clarity around the IPL. I had a message today on WhatsApp from Mike Hesson at RCB: 'Still in limbo from the BCCI for UAE but trying to put some plans in place for travel. What day did you have in mind for travelling back? Still need to do six days' quarantine, even though you're fully vaccinated. So far the overseas guys we know that are going are arriving between the 5th and the 8th of September.'

Gee, I thought, the first game's on 23 September. Do I really need to train for ten days? I messaged back: 'I've spent enough time in bubbles and locked down in the last 12 months. I need a break.'

His reply was sympathetic. 'Understand. Certainly challenging times. How about we get tickets for the 9th? Makes sure you'll get a bit of time at home as you won't need too much time to acclimatise.'

But that's still five days out of quarantine. Do I need five whole days to prepare for a game I may not even play in?

The other thing is that I still haven't been paid for the first half of the IPL. There were supposed to be payments on 15 April, 15 May and 15 June. Other guys have apparently been paid, but so far I haven't received anything. RCB first claimed they hadn't received my bank details, then that they'd fixed my bank details and had a bounce-back – the usual excuses. It's not providing me with a huge incentive to race back for training that I'm not sure I need and that I certainly don't want.

Saturday, 14 August 2021

In addition to trying to sort out my payments with RCB, my manager, Cade, texts regularly to check on how I'm doing in quarantine. I'm fine, really, and I'm used to it. But apart from a couple of games of golf in Saint Lucia and the hours we spent on the catamaran in Barbados, I haven't been outside to do anything but play cricket in two months. I haven't been to the shops, let alone visited a friend or family. You don't get out of the hotel often in India in normal times, but at least you know you can. I remember at Delhi three years ago, there was a Nando's just a short tuktuk ride away from the hotel, and we used to go there for lunch. Word would get around, of course, and there'd suddenly be dozens of people waving at us through the window, but it was otherwise just a nice, pretty normal thing to do. Now that even something as simple as that is not an option, it can be hard. We're also increasingly conscious of how our families are getting on without us. I've just learned that Mike Hesson rather than Kat will be coaching us in the back half of the IPL. The reason is a combination of Kat's long period away from home, and also the lockdown in Sydney, where his kids are doing home school.

There's been a funny story in Adelaide last few days: some guy crept out of hotel quarantine at the Grand Chancellor, went to Macca's, got hammered at the Duke of York, then got caught trying to get back into the hotel at 6 am. For me this has been the strictest quarantine of the year. Not only are we not allowed to train, we're not even allowed to send our laundry out, so I'm washing my clothes in the bath and hanging them on the furniture. Not that I mind. But I do understand the hankering for some Macca's.

Sunday, 15 August 2021

While we stew in our hotel rooms, we've been offered some activities to take part in if we're interested. There are, for instance, daily Zoom fitness sessions. I've opted out of those. There was a funny story last week about the Manly Sea Eagles in their bubble on the Sunshine Coast, how they'd had to introduce a rule that their coach, Des Hasler, was barred from talking to them about footy on their days off. He was so desperate to talk that he started playing cards with the players in order to start footy conversations, but they warned him off that too. I totally understand that. Partly, I think, because sport has become so complex and touring parties have grown so big, there's always something to do, always some meeting to attend, a schedule to follow, an app to fill out with data. Any chance you get to push back against that, in my opinion, is one you should take.

We've also been offered sessions with psychologists, including Peter Clarke, who's still with us. This has never been my go. I've always been nervous about where the content of a conversation like that might end up; for personal matters, frankly, I have my friends and family. I did actually have a chat today with Peter's colleague Matthew Berg, which I quite enjoyed – we talked about my sleep patterns and went through a few reflections about the tour. But that will do me.

Monday, 16 August 2021

The rumours about JL won't go away unfortunately. His former teammates Adam Gilchrist and Mark Taylor have come out in the last few days and lent him their support, as well as expressing disapproval about players talking to journalists. Like most players, I'm pretty guarded about journalists – and there are some that you know to be particularly cautious about. But it's not the only way word gets out. Players chat to their managers, state coaches, state teammates, family and friends – journalists talk to those people too. And I don't think anyone should be surprised about that. We were badly beaten in a format in which we're about to play a World Cup, and as much as I respect JL, I do think some of that went to coaching. This is well above my pay grade – I'm not a senior player and nobody's going to ask me my view – but if I was asked, I'd say we have things to work on, and there's no harm being honest about that.

The voluntary fitness sessions continued today. In fact, a rowing machine turned up, which I carefully assembled and then used to hang my washing on. I posted a photograph on the team WhatsApp with the caption: 'Gee these clothes lines are hard to assemble.' Got a couple of laughs anyway. But if I wanted to row, I'd be a rower. I'm a cricketer.

Tuesday, 17 August 2021

Maybe that rowing machine made me feel guilty, as I clicked on the Zoom link to do a fitness session today. Seems like I haven't been the only guy taking some time out, as there were only four guys involved. George then called, saying that they'd like me to be a reserve player in the squad if I'm up for it – although he'd understand if I wanted to opt out. But having given this a bit more thought, and having also discussed it with Jorgia, I reckon I should go. I will be in the UAE anyway. And I will be tantalisingly close to what was always my goal, which was to play for Australia in a big tournament. There's also the fact that I can say yes now and change my mind later if I have to; I can't do that if I say no.

So Jorgia and I have to hope that the bump stays there, as it didn't with her sisters, until I get back, because the worst thing that could happen is that I miss the birth of my daughter for the sake of being a net bowler. There wouldn't even be any point in my flying home in an emergency, because I'd have to serve two weeks of quarantine. But the chance to play in a World Cup is one I think I'd regret not taking.

Wednesday, 18 August 2021

A story was published today in the *Sydney Morning Herald* about the 'volatile, high-stress environment' JL creates in the team; it concluded with an unnamed player quoted as saying: 'It becomes draining and affects everything.' I know it's not me! I wasn't surprised by the content, though I was slightly surprised at the gossip-column-ish air. But it will add to the groundswell of negativity around JL; it might even lead Cricket Australia to the conclusion that he needs a break before the Ashes and should skip the T20 World Cup. I honestly don't know, and I try not to hold views on things I can't influence. But it's tough being marooned in this hotel with so much time to think and so little certainty.

Later in the afternoon, we hear that Cricket Australia has released a statement of support for JL, stating that he has 'done an incredible job in raising the culture, values and behaviours of the Australian men's team since he took on the role in 2018', that he has 'restored public faith in the national team which is a side all Australians can be incredibly proud of' and that he is 'contracted as Head Coach through to the middle of next year with the focus now on a successful T20 World Cup campaign followed by the home Ashes defence'. I don't know quite what to make of it, but I'm not sure it's a great sign: how many footy coaches have had the 'full support of the board' until the instant they haven't? Still later, word goes round that there is to be a meeting between representatives of the players and of the board in the evening, although I don't know who and I don't know why, which is also unsettling.

The day's one piece of good news is that the team has been issued exemptions to train tomorrow at Adelaide Oval. I don't know how that's happened, and it does seem weird that after all the effort expended on keeping us apart, tomorrow we're going to be travelling together on a bus, sharing nets, using the same balls and so on. But I'm not about to complain.

Thursday, 19 August 2021

George announces the World Cup squad at 11 am: Aaron Finch (c), Ashton Agar, Pat Cummins (vc), Josh Hazlewood, Josh Inglis, Mitchell Marsh, Glenn Maxwell, Kane Richardson, Steve Smith, Mitchell Starc, Marcus Stoinis, Mitchell Swepson, Matthew Wade, David Warner and Adam Zampa. I'm one of the reserves, along with Nathan Ellis and Daniel Sams. That means no places for Ashton Turner, Josh Philippe, Andrew Tye, Riley Meredith, Ben McDermott, Jason Behrendorff, Wes Agar and my friend Moises Henriques.

JL rings to commiserate on my not being part of the 15 and to welcome me to the 18. But the superseded team members get on the bus at 1.50 pm anyway, which is a slightly strange feeling. Also strange is that JL spends a lot of his time walking laps and talking one to one, notably with Wadey, Zamps and a few of the other senior guys. It's tempting to read all sorts of things into people's behaviour at the moment, but I just try to get on with training and enjoy the sunny day.

Friday, 20 August 2021

The squad has effectively divided into two groups. Because we're going to the IPL, I'm with Josh, Moises and Nathan Ellis, who's just been picked up by the Punjab Kings; Mitchell Starc's joined us too. We're in T20 mode, fine-tuning our skills with the white ball. Over the other side there's Philippe, Turner, Carey and McDermott with a red ball, getting ready for their Shield stuff. Zamps is with them, because RCB have bought out his contract and replaced him with the Sri Lankan Wanindu Hasaranga. Wadey's having a rest. He's just come down to throw a few balls. The air is relaxed and productive, and almost – if not quite – normal.

Saturday, 21 August 2021

Another one of those rites of passage I'm not around for: today Jorgia oversaw us moving into our new place in Clovelly. Before she left Adelaide, she was kind enough to drop me in a sandwich press, which introduced some welcome variety to my diet.

I trained at Adelaide Oval with my group. Moey and I commented on how fascinating it is to be back on good decks again. After finding it so hard in Bangladesh, we were both hitting the ball beautifully. It was also interesting being in the nets alongside JL after the week he's had. He was working with Carey and Philippe, and you could hear the enthusiasm in his voice as he talked technique with them. He loves it so much.

JL's been pretty good the last couple of days, like he's making a big effort to take on board the criticism he's received. It's probably the first time he's heard this stuff direct. He wouldn't have got it from the West Australians; there was a push earlier this year, but that had the consultant Tim Ford as an intermediary; this time he's had it straight. He will know how hard it is for a player to come back at a coach like that, especially a powerful one with selection responsibilities, and say that things aren't working as they should. If he takes it the right way, I think this last week could really help him develop.

Sunday, 22 August 2021

There was footy on at Adelaide Oval today so no training. I notice that RCB have recruited the West Australian Tim David, who's had a big week, playing in the winning team in The Hundred and getting picked up in the Caribbean Premier League as well. He's replaced Finn Allen in our squad. I was pretty impressed when he played for the Hurricanes in the Big Bash League last season. He's a powerful hitter and a useful bowler – more competition for my spot! He also ups the quota of Aussies, Dushmantha Chameera and George Garton having come in for Daniel Sams and Kane Richardson.

Monday, 23 August 2021

Jorgia's in Sydney unpacking all our stuff, taking the glasses and plates and cutlery out of the wrapping paper. When she went to the shops for a click and collect, she told me, people were everywhere – all the cafes were open, hardly anybody in masks. Very different to where I am, especially when rain interrupts our training at Adelaide Oval. I do the fitness session and finally give the rowing machine a workout. Tomorrow it can go back to being a clothes line.

Tuesday, 24 August 2021

We landed in Australia at 1 pm on 10 August, so in theory we should be out of quarantine from that time today. But that would be too simple! South Australia requires you to stay until midnight of the day a fortnight from your arrival, so we have an extra day's training at Adelaide Oval and a bonus night at the Playford. Someone who seems more relaxed for that is JL, who's continued his one-to-ones while walking laps – today he went around with a few others. I think he's taken the feedback on board; it obviously made a difference coming directly from the players rather than through a consultant. Apparently one of the things he's said is that he'd be disappointed, having received this criticism, not to have the opportunity to set it right. Needless to say, everyone wishes him well, as nobody wants him to lose his job. The most ridiculous thing said about this fuss in the last few weeks is that 'player power' was trying to get rid of the coach. Players were simply trying to make their concerns known, but nobody seemed to be listening.

Wednesday, 25 August 2021

Our Sydney-bound plane leaves 9.50 am, and Jorgia, looking a good deal bigger than the last time we were together, is there to welcome me to our new home. The television is on the floor and our dining table is the outdoor setting with a tablecloth on it, but I can go to a shop for the first time in three months, and also accompany Jorgia on an appointment with the midwife. She's getting a lot of 'movement'. The baby's so busy that the midwife cannot get a heartbeat, and finally gives up. Reckon from all the activity we can assume the baby's fine.

Thursday, 26 August 2021

This is a great spot. I can cross the road to a cafe; Moises, Pat Cummins and Sean Abbott are all within a ten-minute walk. Rang Phil Jacques to ask if I could join the Blues' training next week, and he said fine, so I'll be able to keep my loads up until I go. The only downside is that I have to apply for an exemption to get to Homebush. And despite so many of us living so close together, we each have to travel independently.

Overnight there was a bit of disappointment. Notts Outlaws, having topped the North Group in the Vitality Blast playing great T20, bottled their quarter final on a tired wicket, going from one for 66 in the eighth over, chasing 125, to lose by two runs. I'll be getting in touch with Mick Newell and Peter Moores in the next few weeks to talk about next year, and we'll now definitely have something to aim for. I'll be looking to take the family – which is something I need to get used to saying. It won't be 'bring your missus' anymore. After December, it will be 'take your family'.

Friday, 27 August 2021

RCB has finally paid me for the first half of the IPL, so we're go for the second half. My departure date from Sydney will be 11 September. So on the twentieth anniversary of 9/11, I'll be boarding an international flight to the Middle East. Good job I'm not superstitious.

Saturday, 28 August 2021

A day at home. Abnormally normal.

Sunday, 29 August 2021

An email from George today covering off on my selection for the T20 World Cup – the kind of thoughtful thing he does. It takes up the conversation I had with JL about acting as a kind of mentor, in addition to being a travelling reserve: 'Whilst knowing you still harbour the desire to play and contribute on-field to the team, we know you're looking at coaching opportunities post-playing and hope that this trip will enable you to combine the best of those ultimate worlds.'

I've had a lot of time to consider the future while travelling this year. Perhaps because the playing opportunities have been limited recently, I still have the hunger to play. Although I'm 38, I think I've at least another two years in me. Brad Hogg and Brad Hodge were both playing good cricket in their 40s; I'd like to think I could do the same, and I'm certainly fit enough. This season will be the second year of my contract with the Sydney Sixers. Cade has been talking to Greg Shipperd about extending it, although ultimately it'll be up to Cricket New South Wales's head of high performance, Michael Klinger – who as coach of the Renegades took an extension for me off the table! As a freelance player, I appreciate the value of multi-year deals. They provide a basis on which you build everything else. After that, yes, I would like to coach. I've been lucky enough to have had some fantastic coaches, from Shippy to Peter Moores, and I've learned from all of them. I value experience; I like working with young players. I hope that will provide the basis for sound coaching skills. But not yet, not yet.

Monday, 30 August 2021

Little traffic on the road on the way to training at 8 am – and huge lines at the nearby vaccination centre – but training at Homebush was pretty normal. The wickets were a bit fresh, but it was great to be around both senior players and good kids. They split the group into two, and in my group, along with Moises, were Patty Cummins, Josh Hazlewood and Dan Sams, as well as Olly Davies, Lachy Hearne and a couple of young quicks. There's another white-ball session on Friday; I think I'll skip the red-ball session on Wednesday. No point confusing myself if I don't have to!

Tuesday, 31 August 2021

A normal day, which still feels so abnormal, or at least unfamiliar. Jorgia finding bargains on Facebook Marketplace: cots, change tables, a Snoo 'smart bassinet'. How brilliant is a Snoo? What a great idea. Out for a walk, because the weather's superb. It feels like everyone in Sydney thinks that lockdown just means you don't have to go to work. Unlimited exercise. Golf courses still open. Huge crowds for takeaway coffee.

Also an obstetrician's appointment, which, for some reason, I was not allowed to attend. Jorgia is determined to schedule a C-section on 4 December, seven days before her due date, so that I can play my first Sixers game the day after. But apparently we have to wait until the pregnancy is 35 weeks before we can apply for that. I'm relieved to learn that I can actually attend the birth.

Wednesday, 1 September 2021

Nesting. Jorgia bought nappies today. When I sounded incredulous, she insisted: 'We've got to plan ahead.' My mum is doing the same, and has bought us a pram – an UPPAbaby Vista. It's her first grandchild, and already being spoiled!

Thursday, 2 September 2021

On our walk today we ran into Sean Abbott and his partner, Brier, who is due on 20 December. That's two Sixers players who'll be doing like their skipper this season: not hanging round at training and looking to wind up team meetings in order to get home.

Friday, 3 September 2021

A white-ball session with the Blues in the nets at Homebush today. It's going to be a confusing early part of the season, what with the national players and the IPL players not around, and a bit of an asterisk on Sheffield Shield performances because they're not against full-strength opponents. Meanwhile, the number five spot in the Test team is up for grabs; Moey and Mitchell Marsh are probably the frontrunners, but their red-ball opportunities are going to be limited. On top of that, COVID. Around the older Blues, there's definitely a feeling of deja vu. Everyone had assumed that the bubbles of last season would be a one-off. Now it's like: do we really have to go through this again? And if you're not in the first-choice XI, I can't see grade cricket starting much before Christmas.

Saturday, 4 September 2021

Rest day today. One of the beauties of freelancing is that you do as much or as little as you feel you need. Particularly from a bowling point of view, I pretty much know how much I have to do to feel like I'm landing it where I want. With batting, it's important to have a mix of sessions: some in which you have to work, when batting conditions are tough and it's important to get off strike, and others where you just aim to feel good, so that when you get a ball in the slot you'll hit it for six more or less every time. Simple priorities, really, but playing only T20 enables you to concentrate on them.

Sunday, 5 September 2021

A centre-wicket white-ball session at Blacktown, which is in the middle of nowhere, nearly an hour away on the M2. I remember going out there for a practice match with Victoria a few years ago and seeing signs saying 'Beware of snakes'. The surface today was pretty ordinary, too, although, as I told the boys, it was still better than Bangladesh – I don't think I'll ever complain about an Australian pitch again after that experience.

Moey and I had a death batting session against one of the young quicks, which was good for us and good for him. Chatting afterwards to assistant coach Shawn Bradstreet, we talked about how one of the big steps up for players from grade cricket is getting used to the tightened margin for error. In grade cricket, if you miss your yorker, half the time guys will just shank it. Bowl the wrong length to Andre Russell and they'll need to get a new ball.

Monday, 6 September 2021

Speaking of Andre – in a way, anyway – this morning I had a great message from my Sixers mate Carlos Brathwaite. He's been flying in the Caribbean Premier League, and got 58 off 40 for the Jamaica Tallawahs last night against the

Trinbago Knight Riders. Carlos is a ripping bloke, but when he arrived last summer he was going through a stage of having lost his swing. He's massive, but he wasn't getting the power and the connection he wanted. I watched him for a while and I could see that he wasn't using his levers as well as he could: he wasn't extending his arms like a golfer or a baseballer, and he wasn't using his legs to drive from the ground and rise with the ball. I thought of how Andre hits a six: he starts so low, then uncoils. So I started working with Carlos, first of all giving him some really slow throwdowns, then gradually picking up the pace. His message today included highlights of the sixes he's been hitting in Saint Lucia, so that was really satisfying.

Tuesday, 7 September 2021

Out in the morning to look at cars with Jorgia, basically to accommodate a baby seat. It seems like parenthood involves resizing your entire life, because we're not in the market for a Corolla. A couple of hours in the car later, driving to and from a centre-wicket session at Blacktown. It's been great in the last week or so to be back with the Blues – my first state team 15 years ago, and now my home base again. Warner and Smith are missing, but otherwise all the senior players have been present. Moey and I will probably have one more session ourselves at Homebush, just for a feel-good slog, as we've probably done enough proper batting. Then, next week, a new bubble.

Wednesday, 8 September 2021

JL rings in the evening – just a general catch-up, where we talk mostly about his golf swing. He's in a relaxed mood. I think it's been good for everyone to spend some time apart. Only in hindsight do I see how claustrophobic our tour was, and the pressure everyone was under.

Thursday, 9 September 2021

A story from Sydney lockdown, via Moises, whose brother is a copper. Early one morning, the police visited the place of a guy who'd tested positive, to check if he was isolating. He was home, all good. Then they go back in the afternoon – and, guess what, he's not there. So they ring him and say: 'Where are you?' And he goes: 'Aw, I'm just taking the bins out.' And they go: 'Mate, we're at your house.' Turns out he was at the shops. That's so Sydney.

Friday, 10 September 2021

Out for a stroll in Clovelly in the morning, and on social media I see that Bondi is absolutely packed. One thing I would say, though, is that the beach is one place you can absolutely guarantee social distancing. If anyone comes anywhere near you, it's like, hey, get out of my personal space. In the afternoon, one last session with the Blues at Homebush. The Blues had been due to leave today to start quarantining in Howard Springs before proceeding to their state bubble, but their opening game, which had been scheduled for 29

September at the Junction Oval, has been delayed because of the latest lockdown in Melbourne. I doubt it's the last fixture that'll be delayed this season either.

Saturday, 11 September 2021

A tough day. Partings always are. Jorgia and I have had such a great couple of weeks. We'd just started settling into our new house, just got used to domestic life together again, buying baby stuff, exploring the local neighbourhood, the coffee shops, the supermarket. It's a new city for Jorgia, and she's pregnant for the first time, so it's really challenging for her. Now I'm off again to my default setting of life in hotels, training and playing.

Sunday, 12 September 2021

RCB had a driver holding a sign for me when I landed. They're obviously a bit better organised than the Punjab Kings, because there was nobody to meet Moises, so I took him along for the ride. The JA Lake View Hotel is about 45 minutes from Dubai; it's another 45 to Abu Dhabi. Back to my normal abnormal life.

One upside of being in the JA Lake View is apparently that the Australian team will be staying here for the T20 World Cup, so I won't face a further period of isolation at the end of the IPL. In the meantime, it's like a lot of the hotels I've stayed in this year: full of great facilities I can't use. Outside my window is a beach and a golf course under a blazing sun, but my only option in this room is an exercise bike – which I won't be needing, as I don't need to do my own washing here.

I see that three English guys, Jonny Bairstow, Chris Woakes and Dawid Malan, have opted out of the IPL today, and I wouldn't be surprised if a few more who are down for the World Cup do the same: three months is a very long time in biosecurity, particularly if you've already done your fair share this year.

Monday, 13 September 2021

Very quiet at the JA Lake View. Not everyone is around yet. I chatted to Maxy this morning; I've been in touch with Kyle Jamieson on the RCB WhatsApp; through my window this afternoon, I saw AB de Villiers and his kids by the pool. Tim David certainly won't be here, because I watched him playing for the Saint Lucia Kings in the Caribbean Premier League last night – the fact that he's still there might actually make it tough for him to be available for our first game, against KKR in a week's time. In the afternoon there was a Microsoft Teams meeting for the Australian T20 World Cup squad run by Brian McFayden, who's going to be our team manager.

Tuesday, 14 September 2021

I have a new coach to get to know: Mike Hesson. He's a low-key type who, when he was coach of New Zealand, was a very good foil for a stronger personality in Brendon McCullum. Hopefully he'll form the same kind of bond with

Virat. It's notable that Hess was not a first-class cricketer himself. I'm probably old-fashioned in that at times I've seen this as a disadvantage. For sure you can make up for it in other ways, and Hess's record with the Black Caps speaks for itself. But players have an instinctive respect for those who they know have succeeded on big stages. The year I had at Delhi with Ricky Ponting was outstanding. His knowledge is so complete, his communication skills are so good – plus, he's Ricky Ponting!

At the same time, I have to concede that Ricky is something of an exception, as not many great players go on to be successful coaches. You'd put Mahela Jayawardene and Stephen Fleming up there, but it's not enough to put a great player in the coach's role and expect great results. I always remember a conversation with Dan Harris at South Australia about what it was like to be coached by Greg Chappell. Greg had great relationships with Darren Lehmann and Greg Blewett and Matthew Elliott – the really talented players. But he struggled to relate to those who weren't so good, to young players and fringe players.

What people don't expect with Ricky is how approachable he is, how down-to-earth, and how, like the best motivators, he can make you feel like the best player in the world – which you're not, but he was, and maybe that's a reason it works.

8

A CHALLENGE TOO FAR

RCB starts the second half of IPL14 among the favourites, but nothing is predictable about T20. In the UAE, everyone is a threat, and one bad game can set you back a long way – collectively and personally.

Wednesday, 15 September 2021

The Caribbean Premier League wound up today with the final between the Saint Lucia Kings and the St Kitts & Nevis Patriots, so pretty soon we'll be at full strength and it will be matter of whittling the squad down for the XI to play our first game, against KKR in Abu Dhabi on Monday. One thing I've learned that's potentially an issue is that AB de Villiers' back is playing up, so Mohammed Azharuddeen will probably be wicketkeeping instead – that's effectively a place for an all-rounder gone, which isn't good for my selection prospects.

Interestingly, AB was telling me that he and his father got COVID when he went back to South Africa. His father, who's a doctor, had had his jabs and was pretty fine; AB hadn't got around to getting vaccinated, so it absolutely ironed him out. He's a super-fit elite athlete, so imagine how hard COVID hits others. Several of our Indian players have been affected too: Yuzi Chahal lost seven kilos, and there was nothing of him before. Definitely to be avoided.

Thursday, 16 September 2021

Funny story coming out of the County Championship today: a blue at Essex over an alleged 'drinking culture', with former captain Ronnie Irani criticising current players for what Cricinfo described as 'complacent and unhelpful habits such as a propensity to relax over a few drinks', which is 'not conducive to an elite sporting environment'. They really are determined to make cricket joyless. Drinking used to be pretty standard in first-class cricket back in the day; the expression used to be 'five and drive'. In fact, it's that as much as anything else that has curbed it: nobody wants to lose their licence after a breath test, so everyone today is responsible.

Usually, England is more sensible about these things, with a bit more respect for old-fashioned customs. I see that Darren Stevens, a great fella who I've played some golf with, is playing in another final at the weekend: the Vitality Blast.

I posted a message on his Instagram today: 'Old blokes win shit.' Because they do.

Friday, 17 September 2021

Out of isolation in the afternoon, meaning we could head to Dubai International Cricket Stadium for some centre-wicket scenarios in the evening – which I probably didn't need, but it was good to catch up with the squad after a week of my own company, and to meet the new boys. Wanindu Hasaranga's leg-spin and batting were really impressive, and Dushmantha Chameera has clearly got some wheels. The guys have now arrived from the Caribbean Premier League, having done a bubble-to-bubble transfer so they don't have to serve an isolation period. The only one of us not here is George Garton, because the English season is running so late this year.

Saturday, 18 September 2021

Celebrated ending iso by hitting a hundred balls on the driving range, then a long training: 25 minutes of soccer, then a demanding fielding session, then half an hour bowling in the nets, followed by half an hour batting – during all of which the temperature was nudging 40. Back in the day it was a custom to talk about 'hardworking players'. That doesn't make much sense now – working hard is mandatory, the minimum, the price of entry. But being an all-rounder is still the toughest job. You're doing a third more skill work than a specialist batter or bowler, and on the subcontinent or in the Gulf you have to plan the allocation of your effort – it's so damned hot that whichever of batting or bowling you do second will be impaired by tiredness. It's important to do that, because you have to be able to execute your skills while fatigued. But after six days of not much, I was cooked.

Later on there was a get-together at the JA Lake for the squad, hosted by Rajesh Menon, a vice-president from Diageo who looks after RCB. The franchise does stuff like this really well: they make a real point of congratulating everyone on their successes. Rajesh welcomed everyone individually, talked about what everyone had been doing since March. He congratulated me on getting back into the Aussie team, and on my impending fatherhood. There was sad news too. One of our logistics people was missing because his one-year-old daughter had died; we'll be wearing black armbands in our first game in her honour.

Sunday, 19 September 2021

A round of golf today, early, to elude the heat, then a message to my mate Darren Stevens, who's won another trophy with the Spitfires. He's an amazing cricketer – and why wouldn't he be? There can hardly be a situation he hasn't faced. How lucky are Kent's youngsters to have him around? I look back on how much I learned as a teenager from Jungles Robson in fourth grade at University of New South Wales. Older players among younger players – that's exactly how it should be. Because old blokes win shit.

Well, they can if they play. Mike Hesson's told me I won't start against KKR, which isn't unexpected: in fact, I prefer to be told now, rather than five minutes before the start, and/or after being told I'm playing. With Washington Sundar injured, there's also a good rationale for picking Shahbaz Ahmed as a left-hander when we struggled against left-arm orthodox in our two defeats back in March. When part two of the IPL opens in the evening, CSK beat the Mumbai Indians to go top of the table; we need a win to stay in touch with the leaders.

Monday, 20 September 2021

In the team meeting before we headed to the Sheikh Zayed Cricket Stadium in Abu Dhabi, Virat announced that he would be standing down as RCB's captain at the end of the tournament; he's also given up the Indian T20 captaincy. It surprised me, but I wasn't shocked. He's getting older, he's got a family so he's a bit more jealous of his time, and I think he genuinely wants to stay fresh for Test cricket. He wants T20 to be more fun, and presumably to have fewer extra responsibilities.

We didn't get it right in the evening. The selection was unexpected. In place of AB as keeper, we chose not Azharuddeen but KS Bharat, and slotted him in at three ahead of Rajat Patidar; we also picked Sachin Baby, a specialist batter, as a left-hander ahead of Shahbaz. But our main mistake was at the toss. The pitch wasn't bad, but it got dewy later on, and the ball skidded on during their chase. Mind you, we should have set a lot more than 94 after being one for 41 with one delivery of the powerplay left. Andre Russell got Bharat and AB in the same over, then Chakravarthy got Maxy and Hasaranga in consecutive balls and we just melted away.

Tuesday, 21 September 2021

Needless to say, there's a lot of media comment about Virat's decision yesterday, including that his captaincy record is no better than average: in fact, RCB under his leadership have lost more games than they've won (66 losses versus 60 wins). That seems remarkable, given that in every game he leads, Virat has the services of the best batter in the world: himself. But what it shows, I think, is that bowling wins IPLs. RCB have had all the best batters: Dravid, KP, Gayle, Watson, plus the current trio of Virat, AB and Maxy. But they've never had the bowling to go with it, in the way that, say, Mumbai had Malinga, and now have Bumrah. RCB really need to build something around Siraj and Saini and Yuzi Chahal. Instead, I think they tend to get hung up on match-ups, which makes for very volatile selections. Two or three changes to the XI in every game is too disruptive. The cricketers here are so good, and the quality of the cricket in the IPL so high – higher than a lot of international cricket, quite frankly. So wouldn't it make more sense to just trust guys to adapt their skills and experience to whatever situation they find themselves in?

I also got to wondering who in due course might succeed Virat as captain. Among the Indians, I don't think there's anyone with the tactical nous or presence in the room to be a captain; there's certainly nobody on par with Dhoni or Rohit. My tip would be Maxy – and not just because I play golf with him most days! There's no nominated vice-captain at the franchise, but he's the nearest thing to it. They love him at the Stars: he's a guy who thrives on responsibility, and I reckon he's probably playing the best cricket of his career. It could be the making of him.

Wednesday, 22 September 2021

After training at Abu Dhabi today, I learn that Marcus Stoinis, for whom I'm understudy in the T20 World Cup, has broken down in Delhi's game in Dubai. I knew he'd strained his back during preseason training with Western Australia, but this is apparently a hamstring. I'm tempted to text him to commiserate, but it might seem a bit like I'm trying to get his spot!

Thursday, 23 September 2021

Golf today with Maxy. We start early, around 7 am, to avoid the worst heat of the day. There are some keen golfers in the squad – George Garton and Tim David have their clubs here, and AB plays when his family lets him. It's good to get out there, but we're restricted to our own company.

I've been trying to catch up with a friend of Andy Lee, who I play golf with back home, but the tightness of the biosecurity regime precludes it. There are very few cases in the UAE now. But the franchises are paranoid – understandably, after what happened earlier this year. There was some alarm earlier this week when T Natarajan tested positive before the Delhi versus Sunrisers game. It's possible that the positive test might have been virus shedding, as it was with the West Indies manager when we were in the Caribbean. But we'll probably never know.

Friday, 24 September 2021

A big crowd for our game against the Chennai Super Kings, which was old, and a dust storm before the start, which was new, although not that unusual – the wind comes off the desert here, and you do occasionally begin in a haze, which can in turn affect the dew. Again, the selection was confusing. They wanted to play Navdeep Saini, so the overseas bowler, Kyle Jamieson, missed out, which meant Tim David came in to lengthen the batting; I guess they'd been watching him making runs in the Royal London Cup and the Caribbean Premier League. Nothing against Tim, but it did feel a bit weird to be sitting on the bench with Jamo – $3.5 million of the salary cap, filling up the Hydralytes. And it was downright disappointing to be none for 111 after 13 overs, then in 19 balls to lose five for 16 and finish on six for 156. Still, it should have been enough – the pitch was slow, gripping. But the bowlers were too full, allowed too many step hits, and CSK passed us with almost two overs to spare. Because RCB faded away towards the end of last year's IPL, it's our seventh consecutive defeat in the UAE.

Saturday, 25 September 2021

Generally in the IPL there's always someone going worse than you, and at the moment that's the Sunrisers. Tonight they failed to chase 125 against the Punjab Kings, with David Warner picking up a second low score since he arrived. With his coach, Tom Moody, having left him out earlier this year, Davey's probably only playing because Jonny Bairstow withdrew, and I'm not sure Moody will give him another chance – they haven't always seen eye to eye on things. I know that Davey can be a divisive figure, but personally I've always found him excellent. We go back to underage cricket in New South Wales, and we debuted for the state in one-day cricket around the same time; he's captained me for Australia and been awesome. He's a bit like Maxy in thriving on responsibility; what happened a couple of years ago in Cape Town, unfortunately, has put a ceiling on that.

Sunday, 26 September 2021

I'd had a hint of it yesterday, but it was a good feeling when the team for today's match against the Mumbai Indians in Dubai went round on the WhatsApp at 10.30 am and I was in it, to bat number six and bowl. There's only so many drinks you can run, and Jamo and Shahbaz felt the same way.

In the end, we were hardly needed, so brilliantly did Maxy bat – and on a challenging pitch that tested everyone, even Virat. The captain hit three fours and three sixes in 51 off 42, but when he came off said: 'The pitch is slowing up. It's hard to get it away.' But Maxy hit six fours and three sixes, almost all of them reverse, smashing the spinners towards the short boundary – incredible.

What do you do when someone plays like that? I have no answer, actually: he's done it to me and I still haven't figured out a strategy. You'll put someone out to cover the switch hit and he'll just hit it to wherever the bloke's come from. You simply have to get him out early. Maxy and AB falling in the penultimate over hurt us, so we had scoreless batsmen facing Trent Boult and Jasprit Bumrah in the last two and only managed nine runs. But we were happy with six for 165.

I was a bit surprised to bowl in the powerplay. Jamo bowled overs one and three, Siraj overs two and four; they didn't get a wicket, and then I was thrown the ball for over number five. That's something we try to avoid at Notts – a fresh bowler against set batters in overs five and six. Unfortunately, I started with a rank half-volley, which Quinton de Kock drilled over my head; he then cut me off fifth stump for four. I came around the wicket and tightened up after that, but Shahbaz made a mess of a regulation stop at square leg off the last ball to give Rohit a third boundary. After six overs they were none for 56, but things turned our way when Maxy got

Rohit off the last ball of the tenth. By then the ball was getting softer and the seam had lost its sharpness.

In our last match we were umming and ahhing about who to bowl in the 15th because Kieron Pollard and Hardik Pandya were in: should we go back to Jamo, or Harshal, or bowl Chahal out? I said: 'Give it to me, and I'll bowl around the wicket to the big side.' Maxy and Adam Griffith agreed, and I bowled a good over for six runs, by the end of which they needed 60 off four. Harshal Patel then picked up a hat-trick: Hardik caught, Pollard bowled, Rahul Chahar lbw to a low full-toss. And we were home, for back-to-back wins.

Monday, 27 September 2021

Started the day playing golf with Maxy. He doesn't hit reverse on the course, although he did have to hit one left-handed at one stage when a ball went behind a tree. After that, an interesting call from Finchy, following Scott Morrison's announcement yesterday about the borders reopening. The plan had been for the Australian team returning from the UAE to travel on a charter back to Brisbane, then serve two weeks in quarantine before returning to our home states – but if the borders are genuinely open, then in theory there's nothing to prevent me from flying commercial to Sydney and quarantining at home with Jorgia.

Reviews later in the day. I'm convinced we should try to burn either the first or second overs, maybe with Maxy or Shahbaz; it limits consecutive overs, avoids introducing a new bowler in overs five or six, and gives you a bit more flexibility later on. But I can't persuade anyone, so we'll continue on the way we have been – and I guess we have been winning.

Tuesday, 28 September 2021

Some comments today around Steve Smith playing his first game of this second leg of the IPL for the Delhi Capitals, as a stand-in opener against KKR. Delhi's top order is as strong as anyone's in the league – Shikhar Dhawan, Prithvi Shaw, Shreyas Iyer, Rishabh Pant, Shimron Hetmyer – which gives them the luxury of picking both Anrich Nortje and Kagiso Rabada as overseas quicks. Somehow, Smith has never broken through as a T20 batter: he seems to bat in second gear a lot of the time, despite being really powerful and a very hard guy to set a field for. Mitch Marsh left us with a real problem for the T20 World Cup by succeeding on the recent white-ball tour of the West Indies and Bangladesh: now who bats at number three? It's funny but I've always felt that Steve would be an ideal finisher; I can see him providing death bowlers with a lot of problems. But somehow, as far as Australians are concerned, number six is not where 'batsmen' bat – indicative, I think, of our stereotyped thinking in T20.

Wednesday, 29 September 2021

A solid win today against the Rajasthan Royals. We left out Jamo for George Garton, just to give us a left-arm option and allow us to hold back Yuzi Chahal until their dangerous right-handers in the middle order, Sanju Samson and Liam Livingstone, came in. Their openers, Evin Lewis and Yashasvi Jaiswal, got off to a flier and were well set when I came on to bowl overs seven and nine, but I managed to make an impact. I kept Lewis, who took me down in the West Indies, to three off four balls, and would have had him caught off a mishook had we had a mid-on in place. Jaiswal hit my slower ball for a beautiful six, but I had him caught at mid-off the next ball to break their opening partnership. Yuzi then bowled beautifully, quick through the air and into the pitch, to get Livingston and also Mahipal Lomror, and Shahbaz got Samson and Rahul Tewatia with his little tweakers before Harshal Patel wiped out the tail. We ended up only needing 150 on a really good pitch, and Maxy hurried us to a win by taking 22 off the 17th over from Morris, ending up with an unbeaten 50 from 30 balls.

Thursday, 30 September 2021

I'm keen to take advantage of the impending border opening in Australia, so I sounded out the logistics guy at Cricket Australia about flying direct to Sydney after the T20 World Cup: given the choice between two weeks in a quarantine hotel and two weeks with my pregnant partner … well, do I really have to say more?

Friday, 1 October 2021

Training day at Dubai. It's funny. I've played more games than I've scored runs in this IPL, but I can honestly say that I've hardly hit the ball better. I also feel fantastic. When I arrived for the isolation three weeks ago, I was feeling a bit sloppy, so I decided to give up meat for a while. The weight's just slipped off me since: I've gone from 93 kilos to 87. Obviously I'm sweating a lot because it's so damn hot, but the change in diet is having no impact on my energy levels. If anything, I feel fitter than ever.

Unlike some other guys, I tend to avoid the gym. I've never found it to be beneficial – the only outside training I think helps my cricket is running. I had an interesting conversation about this a few years ago with Dale Steyn. At the time, the strength and conditioning guys were all about bowlers needing explosive power, which meant turning them into gym brutes. Dale thought this was completely wrong: bowling was about endurance, he said. It wasn't about the capacity to bowl a few fast balls in a spell; it was about being as fast in your fourth spell as your first. So he would just run, for miles – it was awesome. I'd been resistant to running early in my career because it made me sore afterwards. But since taking running seriously, I've suffered no soreness, in the legs or the joints. I think it will add years to my career.

Saturday, 2 October 2021

Heard back from our tour manager, Brian McFadyen, about flying commercially direct to Sydney after the T20 World Cup. The answer, annoyingly, is no: the intention is to get the whole team, as well as the overseas BBL players and the English touring party, together in this hotel on the Gold Coast, and CA are claiming they can't make any changes to that plan because they don't know what the Queensland government might do. As Brendan Drew at the Australian Cricketers' Association said when I discussed it with him, CA are completely indifferent to the human dimension of problems; to them, everything is an operational issue.

I'm having very strong second thoughts about my place as a reserve for the T20 World Cup squad. I said yes when George asked because I knew I could always say no later if circumstances changed. But if I'm signing up to spend a month as a net bowler and then another fortnight in a hotel while Jorgia is going through the last stages of her pregnancy alone in a new city ... how much do I really want that? I took a long time getting to sleep as I turned this over in my mind.

Sunday, 3 October 2021

A good win against the Punjab Kings. I was only going to bat three in the powerplay, but when we got off to a reasonable start Virat said bugger it, I should come in anyway and throw the bat, because it looked like it was going to get harder to score as the innings went deeper. I ended up coming in when Virat got out in the tenth over – to none other than Moises, from whom, of course, I've faced a million balls this year, on tour, at Homebush, at the SCG. He then proceeded to get me out. I threw the kitchen

Some days he's my rival, some days he's my teammate, he's always my friend: Moises Henriques.

EXIDE
muthoot
FINCORP

sink at my first delivery and smashed it to Shahrukh Khan at point, who was actually running in so hard to stop the single that he almost shelled it. So there you go: a first-ball nought, although I consoled myself that if I hadn't done my job, I had at least not *not* done my job. The worst thing you can do in these circumstances is make three off nine balls that would otherwise have been available to other players. The priority in T20 is to do whatever it is you do quickly. And it was better to have Maxy batting than me, in fact: he made 57 off 33 with three fours and four sixes, quite overshadowing AB in a 38-ball partnership of 73 for the fourth wicket. The Punjab Kings went to yorkers too early in the death overs, and Maxy took a toll of Mohammed Shami and Arshdeep Singh.

I bowled the eighth over, and gave away 11, which was more annoying than getting out, frankly. In hindsight, we misread the conditions slightly, thinking slower balls would be more effective than they were, so we ended up overdoing them: rather than bowling four slower balls and two quicker ones, we should probably have gone for five quicker ones and one slower one. Hard length was coming through waist-high, not chest-high, and was hard to hit to leg; slower stuff you could wait on, which Agarwal did to me twice, with a pull shot and paddle sweep.

It was Yuzi Chahal who did it for us again. Like a lot of spinners in T20, occasionally he'll go looking for a wicket and toss one up, but batters in IPL pounce on that and just don't miss. So now we've got him bowling quicker and more back of a length, and he got Nicholas Pooran first, then Agarwal and Sarfaraz Khan off consecutive balls. When I caught Aiden Markram off George Garton at long-off, Moey came in and hit a beautiful six, but he was batting too low and we came away comfortable winners and comfortable qualifiers. It's the first time in a decade, in fact, that RCB has made it through to the IPL finals with games to spare.

Monday, 4 October 2021

It's disappointing to have had a batting opportunity last night and not to have taken it. But I've been buoyed by the attitude of those around me. We're playing well: our top order are making runs; our key bowlers are taking wickets; management seem to regard runs from six, seven and eight as a bonus. If we come off, fine; if we don't, it's not a problem. They apparently like my competitiveness – which they seem to regard as unusual, but I think of as just normal!

The thing about T20 batting is that games abound. When I started in first-class cricket, it seemed like you had to make every innings count. Theoretically, there were 20 digs in a season. In probably five games there'd be no second innings, so that's 15. You'd probably have two hits on green wickets, which are a bit of a lottery; you might get two bad decisions and be run out once. That's ten real opportunities, so you had to cash in. In T20 the opportunities are both more frequent and more constrained. There's always another game but, especially down the order, only every so often will everything be ideal. In the meantime, you just have to trust your preparation and your process.

There's one thing I will take out of yesterday's game, which I discussed with Griff at the reviews today: ensuring that I'm operating at a variety of paces. Even on a slow pitch, you need to be able to hit 135 km/h, so that the change of pace remains a genuine surprise; you also need gears, in a way, so you can bowl in the range 120–125 km/h and 100–105 km/h, which have slightly different trajectories. I didn't quite execute last night. My last delivery to Agarwal, in particular, I didn't get in quite the right place: I was too straight when I should have been outside off, which made it too easy for him to get the ball through the four fielders on the leg-side.

Later on, there was a bit of bonding. The RCB management have been putting on some group activities for us here: a table tennis tournament, pool volleyball, karaoke (not my forte). This evening it was golf, under lights, with a few beers, followed by a buffet dinner on the rooftop with a few cocktails, followed by a few more cocktails. I ended up having a long and wide-ranging conversation with Virat. There really is nobody quite like him. It started with me talking about how I haven't been eating meat since I got here, which led him to explain something of his approach. Virat's obviously hugely talented, but what singles him out is how ruthlessly he pursues perfection – he's obsessed with working harder than everybody else. He talked about all the aspects of his training regime, his diet, his sleep. He's top of the pops for a reason, not just because he has a great cover drive.

Tuesday, 5 October 2021

Definitely feeling a bit rough this morning, especially as I've hardly touched alcohol since I got here. Woke up at 8 am, thought I had plenty of time, went back to sleep, and before I knew it there was a knock on my door. It was noon and I was required for a player appearance with our sponsors Muthoot Fincorp, a financial services company from Kerala. Not my finest hour.

Sweated it all out at training later, where I worked on those variations I'd discussed with Griff: full pace, three-quarters pace and half pace. When you're running in, you can lose it all a bit. You're constantly changing your grip – stock ball, slower ball, cutter, thumb on, thumb off – because the good batters are watching your hand. You need to think about how it's leaving your hand too.

I also had a great batting session with Sanjay Bangar. It's surprising how tiny little changes can make a difference even at my age. Sanjay suggested that rather than leaning forward and holding my hands under my left hip as the bowler approaches, relying on my wrists, I try holding them back near my right hip – which just leaves the bat slightly less to do. I tried it and really liked it. I felt comfortable and I was hitting the ball as cleanly as I have for a while, so it's definitely something I'll persevere with against the Sunrisers tomorrow night, where I've been told I will bat at number three again.

Wednesday, 6 October 2021

Everything was set up for this game. Sunrisers are bottom of the IPL. A win would provide us with a top-two finish and we would play in the Qualifier on Sunday, rather than the Eliminator on Monday. I also went in feeling great. I was chatting before the game to Brad Haddin, who's Trevor Bayliss's assistant coach at the Sunrisers, and he commented that it looked like I was really enjoying my cricket. I said I was. He told me they'd discussed where to bowl to me in their meeting, and that he'd said: 'If it's his day, just forget about it.' So that gave me a lift.

When I came on to bowl after Virat sent them in, I ran in fast and hit the pitch hard. I cramped Priyam Garg for room and he top-edged the ball to AB in the deep. I bowled tight to Jason Roy, who was flying – then, ironically, got him out with the worst ball I bowled. As I let it go, I thought, oh no, that's in the slot; but he absolutely smashed it back at me and I couldn't get out of the way. I've got a huge bruise on my leg where it hit me, but then it bounced up into my hands. Off the last ball of the innings, I caught Jason Holder at long-off too.

Unfortunately, we butchered our chase of their seven for 141. I was in quickly when Virat was lbw in the first over. Then Siddharth Kaul bowled me a split-finger slower ball that swung a mile late in the flight; I closed the face too early and ... straight up the chute to mid-off. Which just shows: even with the best preparation, nothing in T20 is guaranteed. We were two for 27 with two balls of the powerplay to go, and although Bharat hit these for four and six, he then swiftly nicked off.

We still had Maxy, and his good form continued: he blasted his way to 40 off 25. But the pitch was poor and slowing up. Dev Padikkal got behind the asking rate, in his panic ran out Maxy, then got out for 41 off 52. There was a bit of criticism afterwards of Dev for losing his way in those middle overs, although I thought he showed a bit of character in continuing to battle the way he did. Makes me think of something Mike Hussey used to say of those periods in your innings where you're struggling: hang in there because, as much as you're struggling, it will be harder for the next bloke. Dev's mistake wasn't batting slowly; it was getting out.

In the end, the Sunrisers were smart. They made sure to keep AB off strike in the last five, and we needed 13 off the final over. AB hit a six off Bhuvi Kumar, but otherwise Kumar's full and wide bowling paid off, and we went down by four runs.

Afterwards the presentations: I won Upstox Most Valuable Asset of the Match and VIVO Perfect Catch of the Match, which required me to stand behind two of those oversized cheques. But my smiles were for the camera. It's a downer to have missed out on the double chance, because you worry that you're going to pay the price.

Thursday, 7 October 2021

After last night's game I ended up chatting for a while to Jason Roy and Tom Curran from the Sunrisers. They were both saying how great The Hundred had been – how brilliant it had been to play in front of crowds, and how life in the United Kingdom has pretty much returned to normal. Nobody sweats on case numbers anymore; people are going to restaurants, pubs and cafes. They can't believe our lockdowns in Australia. Nor can I, really.

This morning as we played golf I got talking to Maxy. Since my disappointing conversation with Brian McFadyen on Saturday, I've been carrying around the sense that I'm not where I should be – that although I'm not a parent yet, I should be with my daughter-to-be and her mother. Jorgia has been a trooper about it, and completely supported my playing, despite me leaving her not just preparing for motherhood but also setting up our new home. Why am I getting ready to be a net bowler for a month and then to spend another fortnight in quarantine? I've only had 16 nights in my own bed since July 2020.

Maxy is a thoughtful and sensitive guy. He said he'd suspected there was something on my mind, and that he knew how it felt to be playing cricket when you weren't quite completely involved. He talked about his decision to take a mental health break from the game two years ago – how the minute he made the decision, he knew it was the right one. He'd immediately felt the pall over him lift.

That was it, really. When I got back to my hotel room, I called Jorgia to see what she thought about me pulling out of the T20 World Cup squad. She would be fine, she insisted; I shouldn't do it on her account; she would support me whatever I decided. When I told her I had decided, though, I could tell she was relieved, and I was relieved too. Maxy was right. The instant I heard myself articulating it, I knew I had made the right decision.

Friday, 8 October 2021

Today's final round robin game was, on paper, a dead rubber, but it didn't feel like it. The Delhi Capitals were top of the table, ten wins and three losses. They're coached by Ricky Ponting, led by Rishabh Pant, and so strong in batting that they can leave out Steve Smith. With the ball they have Kagiso Rabada, Anrich Nortje and Avesh Khan all bowling in the 140s. It was incredibly hot at Dubai International Stadium, with no breeze to speak of – it reminded me of our game in Mumbai against CSK, where AB reckons he saw four balls coming down the pitch at him. And so today I was amazed that Virat sent Delhi in. Then again, he also tried out the plan I've been advocating, of burning the odd over in the powerplay: Maxy bowled three of the overs, Mohammed Siraj and George Garton the rest.

Delhi made a great start, Shikar Dhawan and Prithvi Shaw taking them to none for 88 off their first ten. The very next ball, though, Harshal Patel bowled a slower one, and Dhawan absolutely nailed it, almost vertically. I found myself under it at mid-off. It didn't disappear completely, which sometimes happens at Sharjah, where the lights are older and lower, but it got ... well, very, very small. Anyway, then it started coming down. For a catch like that I just try to relax, position myself early and keep my elbows loose. I catch underhand cup-style, rather than overhand – some people think of that as an English style, but I regard it as a Sydney thing. It's Victorians who put their arms up, a la Aussie Rules; in New South Wales we catch the cricket ball as we'd receive a rugby ball. Anyway, in it went – a lovely feeling and a big wicket.

Shimron Hetmyer later put away two length balls of mine, but I also had Rishabh Pant caught behind with one that bounced a bit more, and I caught Shreyas Iyer. In fact, we were very good in the field, and the importance of out cricket was further underlined when we chased their five for 164. We lost Virat and Dev early, followed by AB in the tenth over. Then, in the 14th over, Delhi dropped Maxy twice: Iyer missed him in the deep, Ravi Ashwin was slow diving at third man. Neither was difficult. It was almost like they spooked themselves; they were trying to catch not the ball but the man, knowing how well Maxy has been batting.

In the end, however, our matchwinner was Srikar Bharat. He made 70 in one of our practice games back in April and it was clear he was a very good player. I know he was in India's squad in England too. But until you see a guy on the big stage, you never know. Well, now I do. He zoomed to 50 off 37, five balls slower than Maxy. Nortje bowled a superb penultimate over, giving away only four runs, and leaving us with 15 to win, which condensed to five from the last ball. Avesh proceeded to bowl a full-toss that Bharat smashed into the stands. Sometimes you see these Indian domestic players and their talent just blows you away. Imagine a guy coming in as a substitute keeper in the BBL. He'd probably be a first-grader. Bharat's international class already.

Maxy was just cooked. His shirt had gone totally dark from sweat, and he was on his haunches in the showers, completely dehydrated. It's a little exasperating to be playing the Eliminator rather than the Qualifier, but the mood afterwards was buoyant. We were actually laughing with Virat on the bus, saying it was his fault: if he hadn't batted first against KKR, and we hadn't been bowled out for 92, our net run rate wouldn't have suffered so badly. It would be great to win this for him. I always knew he was a great player, but as a man he has really grown in my estimation during this IPL.

Saturday, 9 October 2021

I rang Finchy and explained my decision regarding the T20 World Cup. By coincidence, he's actually a new dad himself, with his daughter born just a month back. Before that, he said, he mightn't have understood where I was coming from. Now he did. I'm grateful to him. The next bit is the hard part, though, as there are, almost literally, no flights home. At the moment, New South Wales has a cap of 750 people per week – basically 100 people a day, who are arriving on ten flights. I spoke to RCB and they said yeah, of course, we'll sort it out, we'll do whatever you need – nothing is ever a hassle for them (unlike CA, unfortunately). But the earliest I can get back into Australia right now is 26 October – and that's only to Brisbane, so there's not a lot of point.

Sunday, 10 October 2021

I had a chat today with George Bailey, who's keen for me to stay with the squad, given that I have to hang around in the UAE anyway. If I wait until 1 November, when New South Wales reopens, I can walk in my front door and quarantine at home, which is a great deal more appealing than more isolation in Queensland. That would take me halfway through the T20 World Cup. But do I want another three weeks of bubble life? I suppose I could suck it up, but I really feel like I'm at the end now. I'll think about it overnight, but I reckon I already know my decision.

Later in the day, the Chennai Super Kings squeeze past the Delhi Capitals in the First Qualifier at Dubai, thanks to a stand of 110 between Ruturaj Gaikwad and Robin Uthappa. I think that's good for us: after consecutive defeats, Delhi have lost some of their early invincibility. If we can get through the Eliminator against KKR tomorrow, I would fancy us in the Second Qualifier. And in finals anything can happen.

Monday, 11 October 2021

Cricket contains as many bad days as good, and this was one. RCB have missed out again, and I was part of it. I went for three sixes in my only over, the 12th, which might have been the difference between us progressing and not. It's a bitterly disappointing conclusion to a campaign that promised so much.

Virat chose to bat, and we had a solid 53-run powerplay for the loss of only Dev, but the runs dried up when Eoin Morgan threw the ball to Sunil Narine. We managed only 60 in the next 11 overs: he bowled Virat and AB, then deceived Maxy, as our batting got a bit frantic on another slow pitch. We ended up with seven for 138, but probably left 15 or 20 runs out there. For instance, there were two lbws given in our innings that were then overturned – but we lost the leg byes we took, and first Maxy and then I missed out being on strike. I was then wastefully run out trying for a second on a misfield, where we never should have crossed, with two balls left.

I came on with KKR three for 80, with Narine having just come to the crease. He's dangerous because he's not a specialist batter and doesn't mind risking everything straightaway. If it's in the slot, it goes; if he's out first ball, it doesn't matter: thus he has a T20 average of 15 but a strike rate of 145. In our bowling meeting before the game, we'd agreed to bounce Narine as soon as he came in. There were also stats on lengths in the middle overs at Sharjah which suggested poorer economy rates when the ball is full, and Harshal had already got Venkatesh Iyer with a bouncer.

So when Nitin Rana took a single off my second ball, I gave Narine a short one first up from around the wicket: maybe he was expecting it because he hung back and hooked, and it took a top edge over fine leg. Next ball I bowled length but he also anticipated that and cleared the leg boundary again – it's only 60 metres, and pretty hard to protect. I conceded a wide going for the tramlines, then bowled a slower one, which he miscued one-handed down the ground just over AB's head at long-off – another six.

It was one of those overs that changes the balance of a game: KKR's required rate went from almost seven an over to less than five. You walk away thinking about what you could have done differently. The bouncer could have been higher; maybe I should have been over the wicket ... anyway, from that point we were chasing the game. Siraj got Narine and Dinesh Kartik in the 18th over, which gave us a shout. I was thrown the ball for the last over to defend seven runs, but a quick single with two balls left won it for KKR.

I might have won a lot of tournaments, but I've lost a lot too, and the feeling is always the same. The dressing room was very flat in the immediate aftermath as we replayed events in our minds, then, as it inevitably does, conversations started and the esky came out. Mike Hesson got us in a circle and spoke about the disappointment of losing; then he congratulated Harshal, Yuzi and Maxy on their seasons, and paid tribute to Virat's captaincy. Virat offered some gracious words, and AB chimed in.

I still have the nagging sense that we shouldn't have been here – that if we'd finished off the Sunrisers, which we would have, had AB faced more than 12 of the last 33 balls, we'd have bypassed the Eliminator. But that's cricket. It's not about what might have been but what is.

Tuesday, 12 October 2021

When you turn your phone back on after a game, it's like plugging back into the world. You have to address all those things you've been putting on hold, which for me included the T20 World Cup. This was it: I was out. 'Sorry mate I can't do it,' I texted George. 'My head's already at home with Jorgia. I've had a gut full of bubbles and the way I'm going I'll be no use to you blokes anyway. I need a break.' He texted back straightaway, very understanding, which I appreciated under the circumstances.

Then as I was looking at my phone, I realised I had a lot of notifications, which was strange because I'd turned them off for my mentions. What had happened, in fact, was that a whole bunch of RCB 'fans' had followed a comment I'd made on one of Jorgia's Instagram posts and just started nailing me, and then going at Jorgia too. I've dealt with this before and I can block it out. That doesn't make it right but I can deal with it. But going at Jorgia – that's a different level. She had 400 comments on her post. She had about 2000 private messages, almost all of them pop-up accounts with one follower and no posts, set up simply for the pleasure of abuse, much of it vicious, graphic and misogynistic.

I'm generally very private with my public social media profile – I keep my family and friends away from it, keeping it for cricket and sponsors' stuff. In fact a few months ago Jorgia got a bit upset with me, saying I hadn't posted anything about her on my social media, and that was probably what I was thinking about when I posted on her Instagram. But that was all it took to flush out the trolls of social media. Privacy is really hard to get back once you've conceded it. In the last 24 hours, my follower count has grown from 70,000 to 92,000; Jorgia's has gone from 7000 to 13,000. It's fair to say that they weren't there to wish us well.

I screen-dumped some of the trolls' work with a comment: 'Check out the comments on my partner's Instagram post. I didn't have a great game tonight, but that's sport. Please leave her out of it.' That's been seen by 591,000 people. Then I posted: 'Now they're making fake accounts and they're in Jorgia's DMs. Stay classy people.' That's been seen by 555,000 people. And then I shared one of the vile messages she received: 'I will hit and rape you so bad that the child inside you shall also lose virginity.' That one's been seen by 413,000 people. The mob even attacked a guy called Daniel Christensen, who had to identify himself as a German actor based in the Algarve.

I have to say that many people were very supportive. Maxy sprang to my defence on social media, and both RCB and KKR posted stuff hashtagged #SayNoToOnlineAbuse. Every player has suffered it at some time; everyone knows it could be them next time. But it did put an extra dampener on what was a pretty damp day anyway. We had a final function in the evening, where RCB showed a nice video of our season, and made sure to acknowledge everyone involved in the campaign. But those nights are always slightly awkward. You understand the need for them, but everyone's ready to go home – even if I can't actually get there.

9

COUNTDOWN TO PARENTHOOD

The IPL is over, but travel is a challenge and borders are shut. As I watch Australia take on all-comers in the T20 World Cup, I'm readying myself for life to change – a long way from who is about to change it.

Wednesday, 13 October 2021

Freedom! But not. In fact, given that neither Moises nor I can get back to Australia except via a fortnight in a quarantine hotel in Brisbane, we've decided to stay in the UAE for a while. I made the 40-minute drive from the JA Lake to where Moey's staying, the Intercontinental at Festival City. We'll stay together until we can fly direct to Sydney and quarantine at home.

I had a final commitment with Australia, which was a Zoom request from JL. I confess I was slightly dreading this. I know how passionate JL is about representing his country; I wasn't sure how he'd take my decision. But I have to say he was awesome. He started off by saying: 'You're the most positive guy in cricket I know. If you say you need a break, you really need one.' I should have known, really. JL has always talked about his family life being an absolute priority. It was great to find out that he really means it. By one o'clock I was on the golf course with Moises, feeling a helluva lot lighter.

In the evening, Delhi went out to KKR in the Second Qualifier, plagued by the same slow Sharjah pitch that frustrated us. KKR, who've scrapped their way through, having lost Pat Cummins and Ben Stokes, will now play CSK in Saturday's final.

Thursday, 14 October 2021

The last RCB teammate I saw yesterday was Kyle Jamieson, who had the room next door. It was his first IPL and he told me how tough he'd found it, mentally as well as physically. I said that they're always tough. You're always cooped up, you're constantly being watched, you're always under pressure, and it's a ruthless format in which you can't always make an impact. We've got this expression for when someone's feeling that way: 'He's got his undies on his head.' Because it gets to you – the lack of privacy, the lack of freedom, not being able simply to walk outside without being scrutinised. It's more intense than international cricket. Jorgia wasn't getting abusive DMs when I missed out with the bat in a T20 in Bangladesh. It's a relief to be out; it would have been a relief had we gone all the way.

Thursday, 14 October 2021

Maxy turns 33 today, which is a bit of a shock – he's always taking the piss out of me for being old, so it's a surprise to find that the difference is only five years! He's had an amazing tournament: with bat and ball, in the field and in the camp. Virat really relies on him. Finchy will in the T20 World Cup, too, if he's smart – nobody knows this format better than Maxy, or thrives more on responsibility.

Friday, 15 October 2021

So CSK are champions; they beat KKR in the final, comfortably. Feels like another confirmation of my long-running thesis that old blokes win shit. There's just so much experience, whether it's Dhoni, or Jadeja, or Raina, or Faf, or Rayudu. I played with Deepak Chahar and Shardul Thakur at the Pune Warriors when they were just kids, and they've really kicked on. Ruturaj Gaikwad didn't make runs against us but he's clearly a gun, taking out the Orange Cap with 635 runs. I think the split season worked in their favour – or maybe it's truer to say they made it work: they were super sharp from the get-go in the UAE; we, frankly, weren't.

I was glad to see Harshal awarded the Purple Cap for his 32 wickets. It feels to me like we're building something at RCB that's a bit like CSK. They've got over the idea of basing everything on Virat and AB. Along with Harshal, Mohammed Siraj and Yuzi Chahal could be the core of an attack that lasts us years. But for losing to the Sunrisers and missing out on the double chance, we might well have made it this year.

Saturday, 16 October 2021

Life in our gilded prison: cafes for breakfast, shops we can walk into, golf whenever we want … but we're still a long way from home. At least we're learning a bit about the stuff usually taken care of for us on tour and during tournaments. Washmen, a laundry app, will accept as much washing as you can fit into an oversized bag, and return it fresh and crisp the next day for 30 dirham – about $8.

After a bit of spitballing, Moey and I have decided to waste the next bit of time in Portugal, which is an eight-hour flight away, and about 15 degrees cooler.

Sunday, 17 October 2021

Having bought our tickets, we found out as we were checking in that while you can fly directly, Portugal isn't allowing entry by visitors direct from the UAE. So we hastily cancelled that flight, bought tickets to Milan, caught a connection to Lisbon and walked through Delgado airport without so much as a passport stamp. A long day, a few more frequent flier points, a bit less sleep and a welcome drop in temperature.

Monday, 18 October 2021

Welcome to the Algarve, on the south coast of Portugal. Among other things, it's the home of Daniel Christensen, my actor near-namesake, who took some social media pummelling on my behalf last week! The town of Vilamoura surrounds a huge marina and it has more golf courses than you can shake a club at – and they're where Moises and I plan to spend most of our next few days. I noticed in passing that the Aussies have won their World Cup warm-up match against New Zealand, but that already seems a long way away.

Tuesday, 19 October 2021

It feels amazing to have escaped the bubble conditions of the last year. Life here is virtually normal – or at least the way I remember normal to have been. Nobody is wearing masks, the cafes and restaurants are full, the golf is fantastic. We hit a few kerbs in our rent-a-car as we adjusted to driving on the right-hand side of the road – it was strange even to be driving after so long having been driven around. Jorgia told me about the restrictions still in place in Australia, which just seem ridiculous by comparison.

Wednesday, 20 October 2021

We've been joined for a few days by a good friend of mine from Sweden, and my former Notts teammate Michael Lumb, who also played with Moises at the Sixers. There are five golf courses in Vilamoura, and seven more in what's called the

Golden Triangle. We'll never have a chance to play them all, but we'll give it a go.

Thursday, 21 October 2021

Michael, who is now a manager at Phoenix Management Group, was 37 when he retired from cricket due to a long-term ankle injury – younger than me, a bit older than Moises. This made the two of us reflect a bit on why we keep going. We agreed that one of the main reasons was the possibility of getting better. Moey mentioned a technical change he'd made during the IPL to help him play later and hit harder. He said it had occurred to him that while you're encouraged to get into position early in first-class cricket to cope with late movement, in T20 it can be wiser not to commit so soon. If you wait that tiny bit longer, you're not so static and you can accentuate your bat speed; it sounds a little like the adjustment I made with Sanjay Bangar. It's exciting still to be learning at this stage of our careers. We're not marking time; we're still exploring.

Friday, 22 October 2021

Also, in the meantime, exploring golf.

Saturday, 23 October 2021

Australia get past South Africa in their first game of the T20 World Cup. I'm pleased for Marcus Stoinis, who is playing as the extra all-rounder, and disappointed for Ashton Agar, who's been our best T20 bowler this year but missed out for the extra pace bowler. Still, I think Pat Cummins should be playing. His off-cutter is very effective because he's so quick, and he has three seasons of IPL experience to draw on. Kane Richardson relies more on a deep-in-the-hand knuckle ball, which is less effective on slow wickets.

It's strange to see South Africa without AB and Faf du Plessis, who would strengthen the team immeasurably. I had a brief chat with AB about this during the IPL, and he just said that the selectors weren't prepared to let him pick and choose events, even at 37. I think they're mad not to select him. Were the Australians mad not to select me? I'm not really missing it, to be honest. And I'm happy to leave the net bowling to Daniel Sams and Nathan Ellis.

Sunday, 24 October 2021

I can't help watching some of the India–Pakistan match, which turns into a ten-wicket romp for Pakistan. Looked like the dew came in, as it did in Dubai during the IPL, which made chasing a lot easier. Anyway, a favourite going down early is probably just what the tournament needs. It's also good to see Sri Lanka, with my RCB teammates Hasaranga and Chameera, getting the better of Bangladesh.

Monday, 25 October 2021

As I'm packing for my return to the UAE, I notice a souvenir of my IPL: a new Vivo mobile phone, which I received when my caught-and-bowled against the Sunrisers was deemed the Perfect Catch of the Match. Dad will be getting that for Christmas, given that he seems to break a phone every fortnight.

Tuesday, 26 October 2021

A four-hour drive, with Moises at the wheel, back to Delgado for our 2.15 pm flight to the UAE. No test to get on board. Everyone just getting on with things. It's been impossible to explain to anyone in Portugal what's still happening in Australia, and it's hard to explain to Jorgia what it's like here.

By the time we arrive at the Taj in Dubai, the news headlines are full of the story about Quinton de Kock having declined to take a knee alongside his teammates before South Africa's game against the West Indies. I don't know Quinton, and I don't know what the circumstances were, but it seems a puzzling decision.

Wednesday, 27 October 2021

From what we can tell, it sounds as though Cricket South Africa sprang a requirement that all players must take a knee as the team were en route to the ground. Quinton felt like he was being pushed around and said no. The accusations of racism are certainly premature. Of course, I'm in favour of taking a knee, but I'm also an optimist. I think it's great that people are thinking and writing and talking about the need to fight racism, whether they agree with me or not. If it keeps the issue alive, I'm all for it.

After golf, Moises and I had dinner with Pat Farhart, who was the physio with New South Wales when I started out and has since worked all over the world, including with India. Pat is an absolute guru, and highly sought-after. He was Delhi's physio during the IPL and has since been loitering in the UAE, where his brother lives, awaiting the 1 November deadline. Everyone's counting the days down now.

Thursday, 28 October 2021

Jorgia was at Pilates today – she goes twice a day, being a bit of an overachiever – and the baby 'dropped'. Right there. While she was sitting there. In front of everyone. Our daughter's head literally dropped in Jorgia's pelvis and engaged with her pelvic bones. This is our first rodeo, of course, so the 'before' and 'after' photos left us both a bit amazed.

Apparently, this usually happens about two weeks before the birth, so it seems our little girl is coming early. Guess she can't wait to be home. I know how she feels.

Friday, 29 October 2021

A good win for the Aussies today against Sri Lanka, but I still feel at peace with my decision to opt out of the T20 World Cup. Nobody's been injured, and it can be tough anyway when you're a reserve player who is basically advantaged by someone else's misfortune. My place as a net bowler ended up being taken for a few weeks by Ben Dwarshuis, who stayed around after his stint with the Delhi Capitals because, like

Moises, Pat and me, he preferred to return to his home in Sydney rather than muck around with a quarantine hotel in Brisbane.

Saturday, 30 October 2021

To Expo 2020, which is located between Dubai and Abu Dhabi. As a designer, Jorgia was envious, and although architecture doesn't really float my boat, it was pretty cool. Each country exhibitor has a building, and they must have spent hundreds of millions on the structures and the content. The Australian building was a bit underwhelming: yes, there was Vegemite, there were lamingtons, there was a Melbourne barista. The Star Dreaming Gallery, a planetarium explaining Indigenous astronomy, wasn't bad. But it did feel a bit like a school science excursion to Questacon.

Sunday, 31 October 2021

Shocking day for the Aussies today, monstered by England by eight wickets. Again we went back to five special bowlers, leaving out Mitchell Marsh, which left us a batter short when we lost David Warner and Steve Smith early, then Maxy got out cheaply. Despite having neither Ben Stokes nor Jofra Archer, England look a very good combination. India, by contrast, look a bit off their game: Virat was visibly unhappy after their defeat by New Zealand.

Nicer to tune in to the Sixers playing the Scorchers in the Women's Big Bash League match. For the first time, the

Sixers were wearing a shirt with Indigenous motifs – I was involved in Jordan Ardler's design with Ash Gardner, who I know from our England tour in 2018, and it looks excellent. It was particularly great to see the shirt in the field in the week that the Quinton de Kock story has had so much airtime. If you look around, there are always good things happening in cricket.

Monday, 1 November 2021

Back to Sydney with Moises – the same flight as Pat Farhart and Ben Dwarshuis, as it happens. All goes smoothly until we land. The seatbelt sign goes off, everyone gets up, retrieves their bags from the overhead locker – but when the door opens, there's an announcement on the PA that we all have to sit back down and wait. It's a very long five minutes, and hearts sink as a health department official comes on board wearing full scrubs. Oh no ... what is it? Someone aboard has tested positive? Do we all have to go into quarantine? Has a new lockdown has been called while we were in the air?

Turns out the official is just giving us the necessary info about what to do in case of symptoms, how quickly we have to get tested and so on. Our relief is overwhelming, and it's fantastic to re-enter Australia through an airport where there are shops open and people waiting and reunions taking place – including, of course, my reunion with Jorgia. Thanks to COVID and cricket, we've only spent 17 days together out of the last 131. Can you believe that?

As we were walking out, Pat said to one of the policemen there: 'I just want to make sure – can I actually take this mask off? Can we actually, really just leave?'

Huge smiles all round when the policeman said yes.

Tuesday, 2 November 2021

Back in our old new home again, which Jorgia has revolutionised in my absence – you get used to that as a cricketer! The bookshelves look amazing. The furniture is perfect. Jorgia has nannied a lot so she knows all the babyproofing tricks. The new dining table, for instance, is round – no sharp corners for our daughter to bump her head on. Whoever lived here before us can only have had a bar fridge, so I've just taken some of the cabinetry out to fit our fridge. Would like to get new doors on the kitchen cupboards, but carpenters and joiners don't seem too keen for work at the moment. At any rate, I now have the time to do it myself.

I heard on the grapevine that Peter Moores might be going to coach the Karachi Kings in the Pakistan Super League, and soon after I got a call from the boss at the Kings asking if I was available next season. I put two and two together and texted Peter: 'Assuming this is not a coincidence!'

In fact, he told me, it was. 'Haven't even looked at the squad list yet but are you interested?' he wrote back.

Hmm. Looks like the PSL will overlap slightly with the finals of the BBL, so that's a factor. But obviously it weighs most heavily on my mind that by then I'll have been a father for all of eight weeks, and who knows how I'll feel? Anyway, there's no need to make a decision immediately. In the meantime, I'm looking forward to a bit of nothing.

Wednesday, 3 November 2021

Golf: I've now played rounds in three continents in just over a week. Moises has gone back to training to prepare for a Shield match; I'm going to wait until Monday. India, meanwhile, have collared Afghanistan in Abu Dhabi to give themselves a chance at a semi-final berth. This is turning into a fascinating World Cup.

Thursday, 4 November 2021

Having dropped our search while I was away, we went car hunting today and decided to go the full Tesla. Just one of the small ones, but the test drive was amazing. Although it means a wait of eight to 12 weeks, I do like the idea of an electric car. It's also a safety improvement on what I'm driving at the moment: a Volkswagen Amarok, which is a good car, but has no airbags in the back seat. In future, of course, I'll be driving for three.

Friday, 5 November 2021

The boys have got themselves back into the running in the T20 World Cup with a big win against Bangladesh – who, of course, had the better of us not long ago. We now have Maxy, Davey and Cummo in the team, of course, but the biggest difference was the pitch. Mustafizur Rahman, whose pace-off stuff was virtually unplayable in Bangladesh, looked a completely different proposition on a flat deck where he couldn't bowl so many slow balls. Finchy took him for 32 off two overs as we chased down their score of 76 in the powerplay plus two balls. Great to see Zamps get five-for, and Mitchell Marsh back in the XI where he belongs – we exchanged messages after the game, agreeing that it was nice to put Bangladesh back in their box after they smashed us in Dhaka.

Saturday, 6 November 2021

The first members of England's tour party have arrived in Brisbane and headed for the Gold Coast Mercure. We were there last year during the BBL: it's next to a golf course, so looks a bit more luxurious than it actually is.

More strange news from England overnight: Michael Vaughan has been stood down from his BBC show because of remarks he's said to have made to some Yorkshire teammates of Asian heritage before a game in 2009: '[There are] too many of you lot, we need to do something about it.' He denies it: 'I have nothing to hide. The "you lot" comment never happened. Anyone trying to recollect words said 10 years ago will be fallible but I am adamant those words were not used.'

Even if he did say it, I feel a bit uncomfortable condemning someone for something they said in a very different context quite a while ago. Have I experienced casual racism in my career? Sure. But I think it's been said out of ignorance rather than malice, and maybe a bit of not knowing how to act. The most annoying examples of it have been unintentional, even oblivious. When I was first picked to play for Australia in February 2010, a journalist asked me: 'When did you find out you were Aboriginal?' That irked me: the assumption was that because of my pale skin, my heritage must have been a mystery to me. Of course, I've known it all my life, and it's been a source of pride. But I can see now that the inquiry was made innocently – the journalist would never have understood what it meant to me. I was probably a little sensitive at the time too. I wanted to be asked about my cricket. I wanted it understood that that's what I was there for.

I think we understand those attitudes better today, which is why it feels like we should be capable of drawing a line now. Everyone has said stupid things in the past. Just as we'd hope to be pardoned for ours, I think we should be capable of excusing those of others.

Sunday, 7 November 2021

Just as Bangladesh was a completely different proposition on a flat wicket, so were the West Indies. We beat them comfortably; as I watched on television at home, I was actually surprised at how poor they were.

Monday, 8 November 2021

Off to Blues training, which is fun – a lot of kids there because the XI has been playing Victoria. I tell Dave Freedman, the chairman of selectors, that I'm available if he wants me to play in the Marsh Cup, pointing out that I was in the last Australian one-day international team – without batting or bowling, of course, but I did what was necessary!

Tuesday, 9 November 2021

An obstetrician's appointment for Jorgia, which again I'm not allowed to attend. But because Jorgia's keen for everyone she knows to get a booster shot against whooping cough, Dr John Orchard, the Sixers' team doctor, who lives about five minutes away, came over and gave me mine. He says that the season is going to be what we'll loosely call a 'semi-bubble' – masks, social distancing, any restaurant meals will have to be outside, et cetera. Not ideal, but by the standards of this year quite survivable.

Wednesday, 10 November 2021

Today might prove to be one of the more significant days of my life, let alone my career. It's now about twelve months ago since I sat down with Shippy, and he asked me if I'd ever seriously considered coaching. The answer was 'Not really' but, as I've mentioned a few times in this diary, I have since. Today it came a little closer to reality.

The Sixers have agreed to my contract extension for the 2022–23 season, with Shippy pushing hard for me to succeed him in 2023–24. You never know, do you? Maybe I'll have another couple of great seasons and want to keep going, but I may have had enough in two years, in which case it would be great to follow in the footsteps of someone I greatly admire.

Thursday, 11 November 2021

Wake to the news that New Zealand have beaten England, handicapped by the absence of the injured Jason Roy and Tymal Mills, in the first semi-final. That's knockout cricket – our turn is coming up. With Australia to play Pakistan for the other spot in the final, Cricket Australia today affirmed their commitment to touring that country next March and April – the first time we will have been there since 1998. There's some wriggle room in the announcement. 'We will work over the next three months, we're going to be doing a [reconnaissance] over to Pakistan,' says CA's CEO, Nick Hockley. 'We will be working with all the relevant agencies to do our due diligence to make sure security programs are in place.'

Would I go? Of course. It's a great country, with great people and great cricket. The Pakistan Super League is full of talented players – there are two guys at every franchise who bowl 145 km/h, others who are absolutely smashing it. I may not return to the Kings next year simply for family reasons, but all the Aussies I played with loved the experience.

Friday, 12 November 2021

Up early to watch the Aussies win their semi against Babar Azam's previously unbeaten team, with Stoin and Wadey putting on 81 in 40 balls for the sixth wicket – another vindication of the four-bowler formula for which the players were advocating in Bangladesh and the West Indies. Also, as I keep saying, experience counts. From the moment Finchy won the toss, the team always seemed to have something in reserve.

Saturday, 13 November 2021

Greg Shipperd turns 65. On the Sixers' WhatsApp group, Steve O'Keefe circulates some pics of Shippy during his playing career, with jet-black hair and a dubious moustache. These days he's got the Mr Clean look.

In and around some golf, I chat to George Bailey about what the Aussies might do in the final. New Zealand's Devon Conway, a leftie, is injured, so there might be a case for picking Agar, but only at the expense of a pace bowler. You wouldn't tamper with the batting after the brilliance of yesterday's chase.

Sunday, 14 November 2021

I played for UNSW today against UTS North Sydney on their number two ground. I took three for 15 and a couple of catches as we bowled them out for 110. Then we were three for 37, but I got 40 off 31 balls, with three fours and two sixes, to stabilise the innings. There's a nice casual feeling to the game after the sheep stations we've been playing for in the IPL. Matthew Gilkes played today, although we were missing Chris Tremain, who was preparing for a second XI game. Captain

Brandon McLean, whose younger brother Hayden opens the bowling, came in to help secure a five-wicket victory.

Monday, 15 November 2021

Although I don't set the alarm for the T20 World Cup final, I wake up halfway through the New Zealand innings to watch Kane Williamson play brilliantly, but it's as if we've already done enough. Without Conway, and with Mitch Santner batting at seven, New Zealand are just a bit restrained, and set four for 176. The Australians are then awesome with the bat. Davey makes a half-century off 34 balls, then Mitch makes a half-century off 32.

Afterwards, the boys are pretty happy, as I can tell from the text traffic. Am I sorry to be missing it? This bit, for sure. There's nothing better than celebrating success with teammates. But would I have sacrificed this time at home? No way. I've loved it.

Tuesday, 16 November 2021

Change of plans this morning. I'd been planning to come to Melbourne for 24 hours, pick up some bats from Kookaburra and play some golf with a mate. He rings me first thing: his wife has COVID, meaning they have 14 days' isolation ahead of them; much like the Aussie boys winging their way home today, the Test guys heading for their way station on the Gold Coast. Yes, a trophy would have been great. But if I'm honest, I did not have another 14 days in me. So I'm off to Blues training instead: I bowled eight overs, really pushing myself because I felt so good. After so much time inside, it's better to be outside.

Wednesday, 17 November 2021

Could hardly swing a club at Bonnie Doon today after my long stint in the nets yesterday, but a round of golf put another 12 kilometres in the legs. All part of the conditioning process!

George, meanwhile, has named his 15-member squad for the first two Tests, with few surprises: Tim Paine (c), Pat Cummins (vc), Cameron Green, Josh Hazlewood, Marcus Harris, Travis Head, Usman Khawaja, Marnus Labuschagne, Nathan Lyon, Michael Neser, Jhye Richardson, Steve Smith, Mitchell Starc, Mitchell Swepson, David Warner. If Harris opens, which I expect, that leaves Khawaja and Head duking it out for number five, with the former, I hope, getting the nod. Both of them have made a great start to the season, but the bowler always thinks he's a chance with Head. Khawaja's record in Australia is awesome – his average is 56. I go back a long way with him, to early days in first grade in Sydney. Mind you, whoever they select, it means we'll have three lefties in our top five against Stuart Broad – an interesting prospect.

The interesting omission is Will Pucovski, who sustained another concussion at training a month ago, and seems to be taking longer and longer to come back from them. I played in Will's debut Shield game at the MCG in February 2017, and he was obviously a gun, but even then it was a concern. He dived in the infield and the ball took a bad bounce on the edge of the square and struck him. Really it just winged him, but he was judged unable to bat in the second innings. This injury is, I think, his tenth concussion. I remember a conversation I had with a doctor about concussion – how repeated impacts are increasingly worse. The second time you're hit, it's not twice as bad but ten times as bad. That's consistent with what has been happening with Will, and in a game with a hard ball that flies around at 140–150 km/h, that's got to be a worry.

Thursday, 18 November 2021

Woke today to news of the testimony of Azeem Rafiq about his time at Yorkshire, where he alleges he ran a regular gauntlet of racist language during his career, including the habit of calling cricketers with Asian backgrounds 'Pakis', and nicknaming them 'Steve' and 'Kevin'. My mate Alex Hales got a mention for reputedly calling his dog Kevin 'because it was black'. I can confirm it is: a bloody great Doberman. But about the origins of the name, I have no idea.

I played against Azeem – he was a decent off-spinner – but have not met him. I also never played at Yorkshire, so I can't comment on the atmosphere he describes. But I can see how it would happen. That English idea of 'banter', it's gotta go – this idea that you can be as offensive as you like towards someone and then excuse yourself: 'Oh, it was just banter.' I've never liked it. There'll be a lot of dressing rooms right now whose occupants will be thinking about how they interact.

All this seems to underline why our taking a knee is so important. I know it annoys a lot of older fans. Their attitudes aren't going to change, I get that. But I think with kids it's important to reinforce constantly that any kind of discrimination is unacceptable, and you can't do that often enough.

Friday, 19 November 2021

They talk about always remembering where you were when you first heard a significant piece of news. Moises, Kurtis Patterson, Chris Tremain and I were in the clubhouse at Bonnie Doon, where we're members, having finished a round of golf, when we read the news that Tim Paine had resigned the Australian captaincy. It had been revealed in the *Daily Telegraph* that he had exchanged flirtatious texts with a staff member at Cricket Tasmania in November 2017, including sending her a dick pic. We'd missed the 2.30 pm press conference where he read his statement, so I started watching it online ... then I stopped, because, quite frankly, it made me uncomfortable.

I go back a long way with Tim, to our academy days 20 years ago. He was also my skipper at the Hobart Hurricanes at the time this incident occurred. He's always been a really solid guy, a strong character in any dressing room, and I've always enjoyed his company. He definitely comes across as a leader. He's done nothing illegal; apparently all this was investigated in 2018. Tim has also done a fantastic job over the last three and a half years, rebuilding the reputation of the Australian cricket team. But ever since 'Sandpapergate', Cricket Australia seems to have been on edge about anything to do with image. They could have acted at any time during Tim's captaincy, but it seems they've only done so now that there's been a tabloid exposé.

Saturday, 20 November 2021

The Sheffield Shield match goes ahead at North Sydney Oval despite Will Sutherland having tested positive for COVID. There must be a reason the rest of the team and the hundred-odd other people on the plane are not required to isolate as close contacts, but it would hurt my head too much to try to understand it.

Sunday, 21 November 2021

Our Uni match was washed out today, which is a shame as, after my aborted trip to Melbourne last week, my new bats have arrived from Kookaburra bearing new stickers designed by Emma MacNeill. The Indigenous motifs are now in earthier shades, orange, brown and yellow, which are even more to my liking. It's the First Nations Round in the Women's Big Bash League this weekend; some of the Sixers boys have already expressed interest in using the bats during the male version of the same round, which will be held between 8 and 14 January.

The bats themselves are interesting too. The bat maker has experimented with a knob-shaped enlargement on the end of the handle as a kind of counterweight, shaving a bit off the bottom so that it remains at 2 pounds and 12 ounces – in theory, it should enable you to swing harder. I quite like this idea of experimenting with the shape. When I was with Screaming Cat, Julian Millichamp led the vogue for oval handles down towards the splice – he felt it prevented the bat from turning in your hand. There was a similar principle behind those Squirrel Cricket grips which Mark O'Neill was selling a few years ago and which Daniel Hughes still uses. I actually found them a bit restrictive – they prevented me from manoeuvring the ball where I wanted. But anything that makes you feel more comfortable or seems to offer a slight advantage is worth trying.

Monday, 22 November 2021

As everyone comes to terms with the exit of Tim Paine, attention is now turning to who his successor will be. Pat Cummins is a great bloke, a tremendous cricketer and everything about him screams Australian captain, but if it were my call, I'd revert to Steve Smith. If he was good enough to do the job in 2018, and given that he has served his term of suspension, then surely he deserves the chance – otherwise his was effectively a lifetime ban. Of course, it's not my call, and it will probably go to Pat, but I do worry about him having too much on his plate, especially given the pressure on the man in the role now, with the last two incumbents having departed in tears.

I just had a beer with Shippy and with Cam White, who's in town, which turned into an interesting discussion. Shippy thinks there should be a seventh Sheffield Shield team; Cam and I don't, pointing to the pretty ordinary standard of the Cricket Australia XI in the Marsh Cup a few years ago. Yes, there are good young cricketers out there, but they're not good enough yet.

Tuesday, 23 November 2021

Golf at Bonnie Doon today with David Gallop, the former CEO of the NRL and the FFA, who also happens to be a stalwart of the UNSW Cricket Club.

Somewhat to my surprise, I've found a second-hand Tesla on Carsales in Melbourne – that certainly beats waiting 12 weeks for our order to come through.

Wednesday, 24 November 2021

Putting my 'freedom' to work. Get on an early plane to Melbourne, a cab from the airport, meet the Tesla owner, transfer the cash, sign the papers and by 10 am I'm on the road home with an estimated journey time of nine hours and 30 minutes. The guy I bought it from hadn't plugged it in overnight, so the car is telling me I'll have to stop to recharge in Euroa for 40 minutes, then in Gundagai for 25 minutes, then in Goulburn for 20 minutes. In fact, it's pretty much driving itself.

While I'm on the road, Jorgia tells me that we have a date for the C-section: Monday, 6 December, the day after the Sixers's opening game of the BBL, at home against the Stars.

We'd been hoping for the day before. But, unlike cricketers, doctors don't work weekends.

Thursday, 25 November 2021

Back to training at the SCG with the Blues guys, who won their Marsh Cup match yesterday against the Vics. Four overs of stock balls, then four overs of slower balls and yorkers, then a bit of a pause for reflection: it's seven years today since Phil Hughes sustained his lethal head blow here, playing for South Australia against his former Blues teammates. A lot has been written about that day, but not so much about what ensued.

Like everything else, the Shield match we Vics were playing against Western Australia at the MCG that afternoon was abandoned. What I remember most, though, was trying to get back into cricket and being, frankly, shit-scared. My first game back – on 6 December 2014, a week after Phil's death, and three days after his funeral – was a premier cricket fixture for the Monash Tigers against Dandenong, who had James Pattinson, on a goat track at Central Reserve North.

Nobody wanted to be there. Cameron White and I were batting, and I think Patto was as worried about hitting us as we were of being hit: we were standing a foot outside leg and just slogging. Then we went to Perth for the rematch against WA. We warmed up by bouncing the ball at each other in the nets and it all seemed okay, then I hit Tom Beaton in the head with a bouncer and it was just full-on panic for the next ten minutes – sweating, heart racing, the lot. Having got a duck in the first innings, I came out in the second, slogged at everything and got a run-a-ball hundred. It was probably getting into the Big Bash League afterwards that helped us – there's no malice to a T20 bouncer, it's just a variation. But I don't think any cricketer will forget the weeks after Phil died. It was mass trauma.

Friday, 26 November 2021

There's a bit of trauma round at present, of course, of a different kind, but still awful. In the morning it's announced by Tim Paine's manager that he's taking an 'indefinite break' from cricket; in the afternoon, Pat Cummins and Steve Smith are unveiled as captain and vice-captain respectively. I'm happy for Pat. He's a great guy and he'll do an outstanding job. But shouldn't accepting the Australian captaincy be a great moment in a player's career? As it was for Tim, Pat is stepping into a dead man's shoes.

Saturday, 27 November 2021

Decided to skip UNSW's T20 against Randwick Petersham for a weekend with Jorgia. I'll be missing her enough this season without taking on any discretionary games. She's been diligently preparing for motherhood – taking classes, reading books, googling stuff. Nobody except a doctor could know more than she does about the first six weeks of a baby's life. We even have a Christmas tree. I haven't had one since I was a kid. Now I have a home, and there'll shortly be three of us.

Sunday, 28 November 2021

I'm glad Jorgia is having the C-section now, as it means she'll have the support of a hospital and the luxury of a private room for a bit longer, with me coming and going in succeeding weeks. I'm actually wondering whether I'll feel all right about heading off to play cricket. Will I want to? Or will I just want to sit there cradling our little girl? David Gallop doesn't think so. When his wife had their son, Tom, he tells me, David played cricket that afternoon. Maybe that's why Tom played cricket at UNSW and is now on the committee at Easts – positive early influences!

Monday, 29 November 2021

La Niña is making her presence felt on the eastern seaboard, absolutely chucking it down. Also, I see, perfect weather in Perth, which is, of course, off limits to cricket. You've got to think that the WACA would have a case for compensation against the state government. No BBL games for consecutive seasons. That's a lot of gate money to be missing out on.

Our practice match against the Hurricanes at North Sydney Oval is a washout. Indoor training instead – a poor substitute, but the best we can do. As the players of both sides commune, there's a bit of talk around about an interesting bit of player management from Cricket Australia. Blokes like Sean Abbott, Nic Maddinson and Scott Boland are having a month away from home, missing a Sheffield Shield match, a Marsh Cup match and their first three or four BBL matches in order to play a game against the England Lions, which they presumably thought might give them a shot at the Test squad – until the Test squad was named on day four of their quarantine.

CA's stipulations around our second BBL game, against the Hurricanes in Launceston next week, are causing some head-scratching too. We're basically not allowed indoors while we're there. We can't go into shopping centres; we can't catch Ubers. But we're flying commercially both ways. I sure hope there are no COVID cases on the plane ...

Tuesday, 30 November 2021

Take the Tesla for a spin to Goulburn to see my dad and his dog, having not seen them for twelve months. On the way I get a text from Mike Hesson saying that I haven't been retained by RCB, for which the deadline was yesterday. Hardly surprising, of course, although it's interesting to see who has been retained by the eight franchises: a total of 27 players, eight of them internationals. RCB has kept Virat, Maxy and Mohammed Siraj, which I think is a good move – Siraj is going to be the key to their attack in years to come. I'm surprised we let go Yuzi Chahal, who seemed pretty fundamental too, but then Harshal Patel has gone despite winning the purple cap, and Devdutt Padikkal too.

Others retained include the inevitable names like Dhoni, Rohit, Bumrah, Narine, Andre Russell and Kieron Pollard. But some of the talent available in the next auction will be amazing: David Warner, Faf du Plessis, Trent Boult, Rashid Khan, KL Rahul, Shikhar Dhawan, Ravi Ashwin, Hardik Pandya, Ishan Kishan, Shubman Gill, Ben Stokes, Joffra Archer, Deepak Chahar, Shreyas Iyer. Shreyas just made a century on his Test debut, but Delhi decided to keep Prithvi Shaw ahead of him. That's a surprise, but also a sign of how ruthless the competition is for places.

Wednesday, 1 December, 2021

A week from the First Test, and both squads are assembled in Brisbane, with the exception of Tim Paine's replacement, which will be either Alex Carey or Josh Inglis. It is going to be very tough for England. As if Australian conditions weren't hard enough, virtually their whole preparation has been swallowed up by La Niña, while half the Aussies have been at the T20 World Cup and the other half playing Sheffield Shield cricket. I don't know why countries agree to itineraries like this. It gives them virtually no chance of being competitive.

Thursday, 2 December 2021

The full Sixers squad assembled at last, complete with our three visiting Englishmen, for back-to-back practice matches at the SCG against the Thunder: Moises Henriques, Jackson Bird, Tom Curran, Ben Dwarshuis, Jack Edwards, Mickey Edwards, Daniel Hughes, Chris Jordan, Hayden Kerr, Nathan Lyon, Ben Manenti, Stephen O'Keefe, Josh Philippe, Lloyd Pope, Jordan Silk, James Vince and myself. Only Sean Abbott is missing, quarantining on the Gold Coast for the Australia A v. Lions game.

We play our full-strength side in the morning, then give some of our reserves a go in the afternoon. We lose both matches – but if you're looking for omens, they beat us last year in a warm-up and we ended up winning the tournament. Moises gets 70, I picked up an unbeaten 20 at the end. For the Thunder, Sam Billings smacked them everywhere. They will be a fair unit this summer.

Friday, 3 December 2021

Spent the day at home preparing for Jorgia's C-section on Monday. We're second on the surgical list. Amazing to think that I'll play on Sunday as one of a couple, and finish Wednesday as a member of a family.

Alex Carey is confirmed in the Ashes squad as Tim Paine's replacement. I'm glad for him. Not only is he a really good bloke, he's also served his apprenticeship and done everything asked of him. Fellow cricketers value that. The media like bolters; players prefer orderly progressions, the paying of dues, the accumulation of experience. Alex is 30, and has awaited his opportunities patiently. Josh Inglis is 26 – he'll get his chance.

Saturday, 4 December 2021

A training session for the Sixers today in the nets at the SCG, starting at 10 am. Another little milestone ticked off: my last cricket practice before fatherhood. Jorgia and the team manager have swapped numbers just in case things run ahead of schedule and she goes into labour.

Our likely XI: Moises (c), me, Vince, Josh Philippe, Jordan Silk, Dan Hughes, Tom Curran, Chris Jordan, Steve O'Keefe, maybe Ben Manenti to turn the ball the other way, and possibly Sean Abbott, who I've heard might be released from quarantine in Queensland. Into the squad we've also brought the South Australian left-armer Nick Winter to cover for Nathan Lyon's absence with Australia, and the Tasmanian all-rounder Lawrence Neil-Smith to stand in while Jackson Bird, his state teammate, recovers from a lower-leg injury. Nick has been on the list at the Strikers, Renegades and Hurricanes; Lawrence was with us for the preseason last year and looked good. The overseas and interstate players, who also include Lloyd Pope, are all at the Adina, which is a good set-up – it'll ensure nobody gets lost or lonely in this long season.

You never quite know what you're going to get with our first-up opponents, the Stars, but in Maxy, Stoin and Zamps they have three T20 World Cup winners.

Sunday, 5 December 2021

All in all, a great start to our season. It looked like we hadn't missed a beat, while the Stars – for whom Nic Maddinson was unavailable, and Billy Stanlake, Nathan Coulter-Nile and Liam Hatcher are all injured – looked a bit undermanned, especially when Stoin withdrew at the last minute. We ended up going with Hayden Kerr rather than Manenti.

Josh Philippe and James Vince batted into the tenth over, and Josh looked in great nick, reaching 50 off 33 balls, including a massive six onto the roof of the Ladies' Stand. The difference, though, was probably Moises, who, after giving himself a sighter, powered to a 29-ball half-century, finishing with an unbeaten 76 from 38 in our total of four for 213. Steve O'Keefe then took four for 14: we got my Notts teammate Joe Clarke out early, then Maxy, and there was not much else.

In their line-up was the teenage pace bowler Sam Elliott, whose dad, Matt, I played against. Matt was in the crowd. It must be an amazing thing to watch your child grow up and play cricket. I wonder if I'll have the same experience. At the end, I caught Brody Couch in the ring off Tom Curran to complete our win – important, although not as important as the next thing I'll hold.

10

CRICKET, COVID AND CHAOS

In the 2021–22 Big Bash League, the Sydney Sixers are out for a three-peat against strong competition. But an even bigger threat may be in the air we're breathing, as the Omicron menace sweeps Australia.

Monday, 6 December 2021

Let me get this down accurately before I forget – it already feels like a bit of a dream! Arrived at the Royal Women's at 6.45 am to meet the anaesthetist. I waited in another room while Jorgia had 'the block' (her epidural), then the surgeon talked us through the procedure. I wanted to be down the business end, but the surgeon explained that I had to sit up top on a stool, because Jorgia's bottom half was screened off with a curtain. I understood better why when the surgeon raised the scalpel and the curtain was stained with a little mist of blood. Jorgia said it felt like they were kneading her belly until the baby's head was visible, and then – hey presto! – she was out. We were wheeled in at 9.38 am to get the block; Harper Clementine Christian was born at 10.11 am, weighing 3.7 kilograms – or 8 pounds, 3 ounces in the old money, which makes her a big girl.

About half an hour later, Jorgia and Harper joined me in our postnatal suite. Suddenly there are three of us, and soon enough there's a load in the nappy – the black tar one they always tell you about. I'm proud to say I tackled it on my own and got through it.

Tuesday, 7 December 2021

All's well at the Royal Women's. Harper is not quite attaching yet, but there's so much help for us. The suite is just awesome. The midwives seem to know all our questions before we ask them, and they're full of advice. I'm at home in the evening when Harper makes her first television appearance. Our Instagram post about the birth got noticed by the Big Bash League, and was mentioned on the coverage of the Scorchers–Heat game.

I just got some unexpected Ashes news too. Stuart Broad rang to offer congratulations, and he let slip that he's not playing the First Test. 'Are you fucking kidding?' I say. Broady tries not to sound pissed off, but it's pretty clear that he's ...

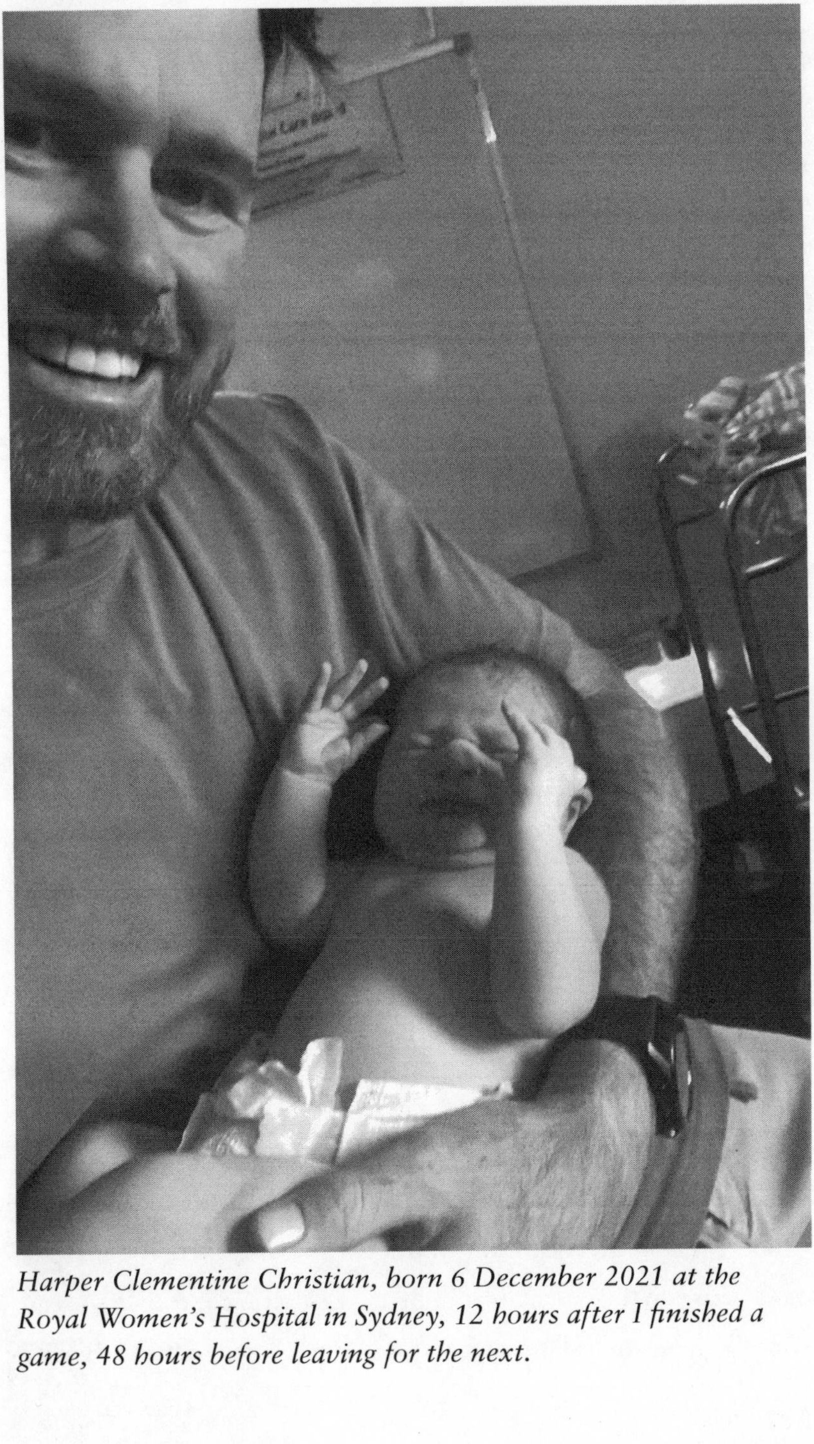

Harper Clementine Christian, born 6 December 2021 at the Royal Women's Hospital in Sydney, 12 hours after I finished a game, 48 hours before leaving for the next.

well, surprised. It seems like they want to keep him and James Anderson fresh for Adelaide. The series hasn't even started and already England are doing strange things.

Wednesday, 8 December 2021

I took off for Tasmania about 9 am to allow for all the quarantine nonsense, and it was a hard game to get up for: it was cold, there were just 3000 people there, and we struggled on a pretty poor pitch and the funny-shaped ground with its deep pockets and slow outfield. Nathan Ellis got Josh, Tim David had Vince stumped, we lost Dan Hughes and Jordan Silk in three balls, I miscued a leg-break from Sandeep Lamichhane, and Jordan Cox took a nice catch at mid-on. Fortunately we bat deep, and Tom Curran helped Moises put on 62 for the sixth wicket: our captain was outstanding again, making 73 off 48 to get us to nine for 144, when we knew that anything over 140 was defendable. The Hurricanes's opening pair of Wadey and Darcy Short are guns, but we held them in check. I bowled the last over of the powerplay for two runs. Darcy ended up with 21 off 36.

The fielding, frankly, was a bit incredible. Silky, who is almost worth picking simply for his patrolling of the boundary, denied Peter Handscomb a six with a huge leap and a one-handed swat; next over I ran back and caught David off Kerr at mid-on. Handscomb hit me for two sixes and a four to the short side in the 16th over, but it was already too late, and Tom Curran ended up with three for 27 to go with his 27 runs. It was a battling victory – apparently we were rated a 22 per cent chance at the halfway point – but we're good at winning ugly.

There was nothing to do afterwards thanks to our quarantine restrictions, of course, except catch up with the First Test, where England folded for 147. They did what Queensland got into the habit of doing in the Shield for many years, batting first when the pitch was a bit soft, banking on it being quicker and bouncier on the second and third days – the only trouble was that they were facing Starc, Hazlewood and Cummins, not a state attack.

So a pretty forgettable visit to Tasmania, all told. And while I can't say that I was distracted during the game, once we were done I felt a powerful homing instinct: when you know your daughter is waiting, that's a pretty solid incentive to get back.

Thursday, 9 December 2021

Headed to the Royal Women's on landing, where the doctors said that Jorgia could leave if she wanted, and naturally she did. We did a little bathing class, packed our bags and headed for the Clovelly Hotel for lunch and a beer or two, with a few of the Sixers boys in attendance and the Test match on the television, David Warner and Marnus Labuschagne putting on a big partnership. Sean Abbott, whose partner Brier is having her waters broken on Monday, came along, so I was able to talk him through what to expect. Now that I'm a veteran!

Then we have our first night at home. Harper gets a bit grisly around 11 pm, which leads to her sleeping on Jorgia's chest. Definitely more to learn.

Friday, 10 December 2021

Late-night transfer: Harper ends up on my chest for four hours, which is pretty cool, and I'd have been happy to carry on had I not been committed to being at the unveiling of the Sixers's Indigenous kit, which we'll wear for our next match, against the Hurricanes. I presented the shirts to our squad members and had some photos taken by Phil Hillyard standing on top of the ornate grandstand while the national and the Indigenous flags fluttered above. (I feel obliged to mention that I was wearing a safety harness!)

I love Jordan Ardler's design. It features the sand goanna totem of Ash Gardner's Muruwari mob, while the three rivers represent my Wiradjuri heritage – the rivers flow into a large circle signifying the SCG, which itself rests on Gadigal land. The Indigenous round is not until 8 January, but the Sixers have always been proactive in this area. We also foreshadowed our plans to hold a barefoot circle before every game on new country this season.

In the afternoon, Mum arrives with her partner, Rod, to meet her new granddaughter. In the evening, the Strikers see off the Renegades, with Wes Agar, Ashton's brother, who was with us on the white-ball tour this year, bowling really well through the middle to get Sammy Harper, Jake Fraser-

McGurk and James Pattinson. With Pete Siddle captaining, and Rashid Khan, George Garton and Franky Worrall also in the attack, the Strikers look a good unit.

Saturday, 11 December 2021

The Hurricanes look good too. They were too strong for us tonight – or at any rate Matthew Wade was: he took five fours off Tom Curran in the second over, reached his 50 in the fourth over, and was out in the 12th over for 93. Whenever he's in that kind of mood, he's a very intimidating player to bowl to. If you pitch it up, you'll get belted. If you pitch short, he'll pull or cut you. He gets this look in his eyes, and all his weight and momentum is coming at you. You just feel there's nowhere safe to bowl.

I got off lightly, going for 15 in my first three overs, bowling a lot of slower balls – then I went for 21 in my last, with Caleb Jewell and Darcy Short hitting me for sixes. Darcy shanked a lot of balls, but got going towards the end, which has got him into the tournament after a slow start. Annoying to have lost, but better at this end of the BBL than the other.

Sunday, 12 December 2021

Watch the Stars, who were so ordinary against us, clinch a second consecutive win against the Thunder, with Stoinis and Coulter-Nile back, and two huge pick-ups in Qais Ahmad and Andre Russell. Any team containing Dre Russ and Maxy, who make quickfire 40s in the chase, will be a real threat.

Monday, 13 December 2021

Jorgia takes Harper to the Early Learning Centre for her measurements; I'm not allowed to go because, of course, COVID, even though I do a rapid antigen test every day as part of my arrangement with the Sixers. Harper's birth weight is down about 300 grams, and her sleep is being interrupted by very mild jaundice, but otherwise we're flying. The midwife has recommended tummy time because Harper's already quite strong and can lift her head. That's our girl.

The evening brings news of another father at the Sixers: Sean Abbott's partner, Brier, gave birth to Ella Florence at 7.04 pm. He'll miss this week's rematch against the Stars in Melbourne, which leaves us a little below strength, as we've also had a couple of setbacks with injury. Ben Manenti has stress fractures in his neck and Tom Curran a hot spot in his back – a great shame, because both had been bowling really well.

Tuesday, 14 December 2021

On the plane to Melbourne, the news headlines are all about Omicron, the new viral variant that is causing a huge spike in COVID cases. The borders have only just reopened – they couldn't close again, could they? I wouldn't mind, though, if Cricket Australia just decided to play all BBL matches in Sydney. The thought of another bubble gives me a headache.

On arrival, I head to the Channel Seven studio in South Melbourne, where I'm making my debut as a commentator, after I accepted a longstanding invitation from executive producer Chris Jones to call the Hurricanes–Scorchers game with Brad Hodge and Jason Richardson. I've enjoyed my interactions with Seven over the years, mainly through the batting mic, which most players don't like.

I can't say I got much training going in, but that might have been the idea. The advice Richo and Chris gave me was not to try to being too 'presenterish'. Rather, I should just treat my co-commentators and the camera like people in the pub. Pretend I'm in a pub? I can do that! They advised me to wear 'smart casual', so I turned up in jeans, a shirt with rolled-up sleeves and a pair of boots. 'Are you going to be okay standing up in that?' they ask. Apparently, we'll be on our feet for three hours! Anyway, I get given a bat and a ball to do a few demonstrations, which is relaxing and gives me something to do with my hands.

The match we were calling was in Hobart, and it was really interesting to see how they do remote coverage like that. Basically, you stand in front of a bank of ten screens, which surround a big screen with the main feed on it. You know where the field is, you have access to the scoreboard, and a little switch on your microphone gives you access to the producer, so you can request stuff. 'Can you give me Nathan Ellis's last over and his pitch map?' you might ask, so you can talk viewers through how he's varying his pace or his angles.

Cricket commentary is certainly different these days. I remember Richie Benaud's advice that a commentator shouldn't speak unless they were sure they could add something; now, as Richo said, they *do* want you to talk. Chatting afterwards, Chris said: 'Don't imagine you're talking to one of your teammates, who knows everything. Imagine explaining the game to a 14-year-old.' Which is fine by me.

There was one thing that annoyed me. One of the screens was showing the Hawkeye ball-tracking system, which made me wonder, again, why we don't have DRS in the Big Bash League. It doesn't need to be perfect or complete – it just has to eliminate the howler. The technology is actually there. But for whatever reason, we don't have access to it. Except as commentators!

Wednesday, 15 December 2021

Here we are in Melbourne, another state, another set of COVID protocols. Our CEO, Steph Clark, fills us in on the additional detail, although the overriding principles are the same: spend as little time as you can indoors, eat outdoors as often as you can, try to keep things at level four because we don't want them going to level five. Rapid antigen tests basically every day from here on. I find it bemusing. What was the point of being triple-vaccinated? Anyway, off to the MCG ...

We started well, got rid of Stoin and Joe Clarke early, then I bowled Nick Larkin. Maxy played an absolute gem of an innings, 103 from 57 balls, and that really should have put the game beyond us. But Josh Philippe was superb: he won the match sweeping Qais Ahmad for six to end up on 99 not out from 61 balls, which is the franchise's highest score.

I'm so glad for Flip – he's a massively talented ball striker, and a great young fellow to boot. He lost his way a bit on our white-ball tour this year, started doubting himself and struggled a bit with bubble life – he's very close with his girlfriend and family. There was a lot of talk about getting him to play straighter, when there are few players in the world who hit the ball so well over cover. At the Sixers, he's had the support a promising player needs, and it's showed in his results.

Thursday, 16 December 2021

Moey and I pushed our departure time back to 2.30 pm today so we could fit golf in with Maxy and Finch, so we were out there when today's big cricket news came through. Maxy looked at Twitter. 'Pat's out of the Test,' he says. 'He's got COVID.'

Turns out he doesn't – he's just a close contact of someone, a player from Easts whose hand he had shaken in a restaurant in Adelaide, who subsequently learned he had tested positive. Anyway, Pat has to isolate for seven days. Nothing about this makes sense. Had Pat been in any other state, he would have been fine. Had Pat been dining outdoors at the restaurant, as Mitchell Starc and Nathan Lyon were, he would have been fine.

Get back in time to watch the evening session from Adelaide, which ends with Australia on two for 221. It's slow going. England bowl very defensive lengths; they don't seem to be trying to swing it so much as just wobble it round. There aren't many crisp shots; everything just seems to be missing the middle slightly. But Jos Buttler drops Marnus Labuschagne in the penultimate over, leaving him to resume with Steve Smith tomorrow – not a prospect any team would welcome.

Friday, 17 December 2021

Disappointing confirmation that Steve O'Keefe – SOK to everyone – has not recovered from a calf strain sustained against the Stars, so will miss a few games. That's a big out for us. I played against SOK a lot early on in his career. He and John Hastings and Pete Forrest all came from the Hawkesbury around the same time, a couple of years younger than me, and we played lots of grade cricket and Poidevin-Gray Shield, the under-21s competition.

SOK's first-class career of 300 wickets at less than 25 (and 2400 runs with the bat at just over 25) is amazing. He ripped through us when I played for South Australia; he ripped through us when I played for the Vics. His T20 bowling gets better every year, I think. In the practice games we played against the Thunder, Sam Billings was playing some beautiful sweep shots, so SOK started bowling slowly to him wide of off stump. Sam miscued a few, got frustrated, decided to run at one and missed a dart – it was just a great piece of bowling.

SOK's a great teammate too, and very competitive. He's always on during those flat spots in a game, and a fantastic mentor to our younger spinners: Lloyd Pope from South Australia, the young Victorian offie Todd Murphy, and Connor Cook, a teenager from Gordon. We might need a bit from them in his absence.

Saturday, 18 December 2021

Handling Harper's social calendar. My mum has been over a couple of times; my dad's come and gone; Jorgia's mum is with us now. Making plans for Christmas with Mum's sister in Western Sydney. She's 20 years younger than Mum, so to me she's always been more like an older sister – and she has four girls aged between nine and 15 who are really excited to meet their new second cousin.

Sunday, 19 December 2021

Heard today that Tom Curran will be replaced with Shadab Khan, who is a gun: he bats number three in the PSL and bowls good leggies, so he'll be good cover for SOK. Now we're looking around for a pace bowler to succeed Chris Jordan, who is off to Barbados for some family time. There was some talk of Shaheen Shah Afridi, but he may be a little expensive for what you get.

Monday, 20 December 2021

We have incurred a fine for a slow over rate in our match the other night, which is just ridiculous. The BBL is obsessed with schedules, but completely indifferent to how they compromise them. You'll regularly find yourself at the end of your mark waiting for the music to stop or the broadcast to resume after a commercial. Then the umpire will say to you at the end of the over: 'Hey, you're three minutes behind.' And you think: 'Well, what more can we do?'

Every season, too, there's some silly, petty new rule introduced with an eye to time. This season I can't get a drink on the boundary from the 12th or 13th man. Have you ever known a game of cricket to be delayed by someone taking a drink on the boundary in between balls? Imagine trying that in the IPL. Imagine trying to tell Virat he couldn't get a drink. We're professional athletes, for heaven's sake.

Tuesday, 21 December 2021

A great start to our game against the Strikers. When Sean Abbott was bowling the second over, I just had this feeling I was in the play. Matt Short was standing up and driving but the ball was bouncing; I reckon I started moving to my left as I saw him shaping for the shot, and I took it on the run at chest height.

I've taken a different approach to bowling recently. This is the third game in a row where I've bowled almost entirely at full pace – tonight I even clocked mid-130s a few times. Bowling with the pace on and at a hard length, I'm forcing guys to wait for the slower ball rather than have them expect it. I got two wickets in an over bowling to left-handers from round the wicket: Matt Renshaw, beautifully caught at deep mid-wicket by Hayden Kerr, and Harry Neilsen, chopping on. Jonathan Wells smashed the cover off one from Moises but the umpire didn't hear it; fortunately I got him in the next over, off an even louder edge.

I have three or four different actions, all of them based on my load-up. When I'm striving for full pace, I try to reach up high and snap down; when I bowl yorkers, I try to go wide and fall away to push the ball in. The off-cutter I bowl either coming over the top or from wide around the corner. For my slower ball and my leg-cutter, I have what I call my 'Shaun Pollock': arms in front and long. It doesn't look anything like him, but it *feels* like him – the same way I felt like particular bowlers when I imitated them as a kid in the backyard. Feeling is important. I never look at a point on the pitch; I could run in with my eyes shut and bowl the ball.

Of all the deliveries, the yorker is comfortably the hardest to bowl because it's such a massive length difference. Your margin for error with a bouncer is about 1.5 metres; with a yorker it's next to nothing. There are times where I've lost confidence bowling it, and it can be obvious. You'll see a passage of play when you think: 'He should bowl a yorker here.' And I bowl a slower ball or whatever, because the yorker's just not coming out, and the risk of a full-toss or half-volley is too great. But tonight I threw in a good yorker to Matt Kelly because he'd just come to the wicket; they were five for 90, and so the percentages were in my favour. That felt good.

Josh Philippe is feeling good. He played a lap-sweep off Franky Worrall in the first over – that's how confident he is at the moment. We lost our way a bit against Fawad Ahmed and Rashid Khan, who got me first ball with his googly, but we were guided home mainly by Jordan Silk.

I've a funny connection with Silky. I was 12th man for a Test at Bellerive in 2011, was released to go to Perth after day one to play for South Australia, and 19-year-old Silky took my place because of his gun fielding – he has great anticipation, explosive pace and an amazing leap. I played a lot against Silky early in his career with Tasmania, and in a Prime Minister's XI game with him a few years ago. He was always regarded as a steady player, a bit limited, a good technician: his first-class career strike rate is only 43. But over the years, he's shown how good cricketers can adapt to T20. He's a very intelligent guy, reads the game well and has become one of the Sixers's really solid, dependable senior players.

He was joking the other night about the contrast between opening in the Shield and batting at five for the Sixers. He's played his whole career on seaming decks at Bellerive; now he was saying: 'How easy is it in the middle order? You blokes have got it sorted.' This was a classic Silky innings: 36 off 24 balls with five boundaries, just when we needed it most. He got out in the penultimate over, but Sean Abbott hit a couple of fours and Hayden Kerr a six to win it with four balls to spare.

Wednesday, 22 December 2021

The feeling at our reviews is buoyant, not only because we have five wins and just one loss, but also because it feels very much like last year. We could go through all 240 balls of each match and find heaps to improve on, but we're still winning. If we reach our potential, I can't see other teams stopping us from a three-peat.

We have the Scorchers and the Thunder coming up – both good teams. But we've beaten the full-strength Strikers and Stars, and it took an amazing Matthew Wade innings for the Hurricanes to get the better of us.

Thursday, 23 December 2021

Practice day. Our session is moved away from the SCG, where the nets are in poor shape – overused, corrugated, broken fingers waiting to happen. We head out to Homebush, where the facilities are in better shape.

Friday, 24 December 2021

It's confirmed today that James Vince will be leaving us early, having been picked in England's T20I squad for a tour of the Caribbean. That's a loss for us, because he was sensational in the finals last season, but the Thunder (Sam Billings), the Heat (Saqib Mahmood), the Strikers (George Garton), the Renegades (Reece Topley) and the Scorchers (Tymal Mills) are all similarly affected. International cricket always takes precedence, and global fixtures like this one have to be factored in.

Great news out of the Aussie camp, as it looks like my old friend and teammate Scott Boland will make his Test debut – Josh Hazlewood is still unfit, and Jhye Richardson and Michael Neser have pulled up sore from Adelaide. Scott is a fantastic bloke with a really interesting journey. In 2017 he discovered he had an Indigenous grandfather, and has tried to immerse himself in his new heritage. He and his brother Nick came on the 2018 Indigenous tour of England that I led, on the sesquicentenary of the original Aboriginal team, and he embraced the history. He went to Harrow beforehand, learned about Johnny Mullagh and met some of Mullagh's descendants. He was so proud to be a part of it.

He's also a seriously fine bowler, as I learned from playing about 40 Sheffield Shield matches with him, when he and Chris Tremain were our mainstays whenever James Pattinson and Peter Siddle were on Test duty. He's not a huge swinger of the ball but he nips it round. He has a repeatable action, he's always endangering off stump and he's super-fit – as quick in his fourth spell as in his first. I'm just really, really pleased for him; I think he'll be a real surprise packet.

Saturday, 25 December 2021

Last-minute change of Christmas plans. Jorgia, Harper and I had to abandon our idea of catching up with my aunt and her husband: they're both nurses at an intensive-care unit in Liverpool, and the risk of COVID infection is just too high. Moises was in a similar boat, having to pull out of Christmas

A COVID Christmas in Clovelly – Jorgia, Harper and me.

with his family, so we ended up having fish and chips on Clovelly Beach with him, Kristen and Archie. It was really nice, actually, and somehow in keeping with a year in which I've spent more time with Moises than I have my family.

Sunday, 26 December 2021

A gloomy Boxing Day in the east, starting with Australia sending England in under overcast skies at the MCG and bowling them out for 185. Scott picked up his maiden Test wicket, Mark Wood, and he also caught Ollie Robinson and Jos Buttler. Australia's cruising at stumps.

In Sydney, you can also be guaranteed that rain will warp at least one game a season, and tonight's Smash was the night. It looked like we'd never get a game in, and it was a bit hard to get focused: we were interrupted twice, in the third and seventh overs, then the regulations knocked four overs off and suddenly, from one for 49, we needed to make the most of our last nine overs. It was a good challenge, and we rose to it. The pitch had been a typical drop-in – slow, a bit grabby. But with a little bit of rain, the ball really skidded on. Dan Hughes batted superbly, hit four sixes in nine deliveries in a 25-ball half-century. I came in at four for 117 in the 13th over and got 41 not out off 17 deliveries; our final six overs were worth 91. When I hit Nathan McAndrew into the crowd at point and Saqib Mahmood for six over midwicket, they came right out of the middle.

I came into the game having made a slight technical change. This time a year ago, I had two different batting set-ups: a back-and-across trigger when I first came to the wicket, and a standstill open stance for batting at the death. Somewhere along the line, I'd lost the habit of the former – I think because I was doing so much batting at the end. But training in the nets at the SCG, where the odd ball has been flying, somehow triggered a memory. So tonight I reintroduced the back-and-across step, and the effect was immediate: I had lots more time, I was getting my hands high and hitting the ball on top of the bounce.

Four for 168 was a good total in the circumstances, but the Thunder are a really good team. Any XI that includes Sam Billings, who came in at four, as well as Daniel Sams and Ben Cutting at six and seven, is never out of a game.

We also had a bizarre episode that could only have come from this season. We didn't have access to a PCR machine, so we sent our new recruit Shadab Khan for a normal public test, which was meant to come back in four hours. So we had two teams on the whiteboard – one with Shadab as an X-factor, if he got his test result in time, and one with Mickey Edwards, if he didn't. Inevitably, the test didn't come back; then, with the game being shortened, we decided we needed more pace at the back end, as we had already chosen Lloyd Pope and Todd Murphy. In fact, Lloyd got Billings, Mickey got Samsy just as he was looking dangerous, and Hayden Kerr closed out what is probably our most complete performance of the season so far.

Monday, 27 December 2021

The Aussies have been pretty complete at the MCG too. The tail helps them battle their way to 267, then they take four poles in the last hour, with my mate Scott Boland on fire. I remember Scott on his first ODI tour, when he wasn't quite ready for international cricket – he didn't quite know his action. Tonight he just looked top-class. He lost nothing by comparison with Mitchell Starc and Pat Cummins – I can't say fairer than that. The Ashes should wrap up quickly tomorrow.

Tuesday, 28 December 2021

They did, although more quickly than even I expected. What was I saying about Scott being a real surprise packet? His spell today was one of the most enjoyable 40 minutes' cricket watching I've ever had. He finished his spell with six for seven off four overs – scarcely believable figures, least of all on a Test debut! You could tell he was slightly overwhelmed when he was presented with the Mullagh Medal. Four years ago it was a name he barely knew; now he's the first Australian to win it, and a First Australian too. I was proud to message him my congratulations.

At Manuka Oval, meanwhile, the Thunder beat the Scorchers by 34 runs, with Billings and Saqib on top of their games. That puts us back on the top of the BBL ladder, tipping the Scorchers into second on run rate, with the Thunder and Hurricanes third and fourth.

Wednesday, 29 December 2021

One of the strangest BBL games I've played, against the Heat, began in one of the strangest circumstances possible. A few days ago, the Women's Hospital called Jorgia in because there was some concern she might have an infection from the Caesarean; fortunately all the scans were fine, and all she needed was a course of antibiotics. But because she was in hospital for 45 minutes, I had to have a PCR test.

The Sixers have flown in a PCR machine from the Australian Institute of Sport, but it's not always reliable – and inevitably, just when we needed it to work, it malfunctioned. While I waited for the result of a second test, I had to warm up away from the rest of the team, and I was furious – in fact, I let John Orchard know how furious I was. The negative finally arrived ten minutes before the start of the match, so I was wheeling my bag in as my teammates were about to take the field. It was like a grade game.

Anyway, Jimmy Peirson won the toss and batted, but the game was a mess. It was the second time we'd used the pitch, and everything bowled cross-seam seemed to be gripping. Really it should have been a 140 versus 140 game, not the 100 versus 100 game it became. The Heat lost four wickets in the powerplay: Ben Dwarshuis got Pierson in the opening over, Sean Abbott took a brilliant catch to dismiss Lynny and then bowled Tim Cooper, then I bowled Sam Heazlett. Sean picked up Ben Duckett, Max Bryant and Jack Wildermuth too, caught James Bazley and ran Mujeeb

Ur Rahman out in the last over with a flat throw from long-off to me.

We made a mess of the chase. We were too impatient in the powerplay and lost four wickets ourselves, then I leading-edged Xavier Bartlett to deep point and sat there in the dugout fuming about it as we went 12 overs without a boundary. At eight for 47, we were staring at the lowest BBL total in history. But, somehow, we found a way to get back into the match. Sean played sensibly, then nailed Steketee into the Ladies' Stand and Bartlett into the crowd at midwicket. Dwarshius, who as a left-hander can be quite awkward to bowl to, hit three nice boundaries.

The dugout was a funny contrast. I started to talk about what might happen, what we had to look out for, and Dan Hughes, who's very superstitious, told me off: 'Hey, don't say that. You'll make it happen.' I'm not superstitious in that way at all. At UNSW, we used to have an annual award – a striped blazer – which was awarded to the guy who had done the stupidest thing that season. I remember there was a guy who decided one day that he couldn't move while Michael Slater was batting. He stayed in a chair near the sightscreen all day while Slats made a double-hundred and became that year's runaway blazer award winner. So for me, you've got to be joking if you think anything we say off the field affects anything out in the middle.

Anyway, when we started the last over needing two runs to win, Xavier Bartlett bowled three pinpoint yorkers, the second of which broke Sean's bat. Bartlett tried for a fourth, but Sean was able to work the half-volley away through the leg-side for the winning runs. It was a great finish to a chaotic game, which, fair dinkum, only the Heat could have lost. Their mix seems to have been wrong for quite a while. They have Lynny, but he's not someone to build a batting order around. The way he plays, he'll win you a couple of games a season; but when, inevitably, he fails from time to time, they have nobody to fall back on. When I won a BBL in Brisbane ten years ago, they had James Hopes and Chris Hartley and Daniel Vettori in that lower middle order – so much experience and common sense. Now they have good coaches, but the coaches can't do it for them, and they seem to tighten up a bit under pressure.

Thursday, 30 December 2021

Beginning a 15-day spell on the road, taking Jorgia and Harper with me for the first time. Flew early to Coffs Harbour. The Sixers were split across three different Qantas planes, so if there was a case on one, we didn't all become contacts. Jorgia is my 'travel buddy' (Harper too). We took the 8 am plane; others took the 10.30 am and the 3 pm. On landing, the pairs were each allocated a car.

The caution is understandable. When we arrive at the BreakFree Aanuka Hotel, we learn that there's a COVID case in the Stars, so the game they were scheduled to play today against the Scorchers has been postponed. Sam Whiteman missed a Thunder game earlier this season through being a close contact, but this is the first time a match has been moved. Everyone will have to be PCR-tested. Oh well ...

Friday, 31 December 2021

Our first family tour! We have a hire car with a baby seat; we've brought our foldaway stroller with us; Harper is sleeping in a pop-up cot. But the contagion of confusion is spreading. Travis Head in the Australian camp has tested positive, and it looks like Omicron will soon be everywhere. New South Wales alone recorded more than 21,000 cases today, and the ratio of positive test results is now closer to one in five than one in seven. There's a bit of concern around the Sixers's New Year's barbecue at our hotel. 2022 looms. It has to be an improvement on 2021.

Saturday, 1 January 2022

COVID chaos. Raining on and off during our training at Coffs Harbour International Stadium. During the interruptions, blokes go looking for their phones, and every time there seems to be another update. There are now 15 cases in the Stars's camp – eight players and seven support staff – although not Maxy, because he's been at home. It sounds like the cluster is among the interstate players at their hotel. Four Thunder players have now tested positive too.

The Ashes has been disrupted. Most of England's coaching staff are in isolation. Marcus Harris, who had dinner with Travis Head on the night in question, has tested negative, but

Josh Inglis, Mitchell Marsh and Nic Maddinson have been called up as cover for the Sydney Test. As far as the BBL is concerned, there are rumours flying about: every game will be held in Melbourne, the whole competition will be paused for seven days, and so on. There's a pause in our campaign at any rate. The rain keeps up until 25 millimetres has fallen, the ground is judged unfit at 9 pm, and our game against the Renegades is abandoned. A sizeable crowd goes home disappointed. So do we: we'd have strongly backed ourselves against the Renegades, who've had a poor season.

Sunday, 2 January 2022

Driving to the Gold Coast, with Harper in the hire car's baby seat. Stop halfway on our three-hour journey for a feed – all of us, Harper on the breast. Otherwise, she sleeps most of the way. What a girl! Am I worried about bringing Harper with us? Not really. I discussed it with our physiotherapist, Danny Redrup. Apparently, for as long as Harper is breastfeeding, she'll get the benefits of her mum's vaccination. Still, we're going to keep our distance from other players a bit, just to be on the safe side. Jorgia's also going to get her booster while we're here.

The impact of all the outs on the BBL is palpable. Tonight, the poor old Stars, hastily reinforced with emergencies, crumbled by 50 runs to the Scorchers, losing all their wickets for 52 in 10.2 overs after my Notts mate Joe Clarke had given them a reasonable start: he scored 52 from 32 balls, opening with a fill-in player, Tom Rogers. Their net run rate has dragged them down this year, so neither Melbourne team is in contention, and the Strikers and the Heat are barely hanging on.

Monday, 3 January 2022

The situation is changing every minute: Joe Clarke and Tom Rogers have now tested positive, so they'll miss tonight's derby against the Renegades as well! The disturbing thing is that not all teams appear to be equally prepared. We've been having daily RATs for weeks; I've heard that the Heat have only just got some. Tom Cooper was asking us if we had any spare. There's also a rumour that the Strikers haven't had any.

I think we're at the stage now where we should be trying to ride this out. I understand trying to control infection to protect the vulnerable. But we're 160 young male professional athletes already living in a bubble. Who are we a threat to? Nobody's asking me my view, of course. But if they did, I'd restrict tests to those who have symptoms. Because at the rate we're ruling players out, pretty soon we won't have any left at all.

Tuesday, 4 January 2022

What a surprise: the Heat, who we're meant to be playing tonight, have returned four positive cases, with the rumour being that some players broke the bubble in Hobart. There's a panic. Our game against the Heat is put back to give them time to regroup; our game against the Scorchers, previously scheduled for Thursday, is brought forward. They're without Mitch Marsh and Josh Inglis, added to the Test squad. We have Jackson Bird back, and also SOK, although we lose him after he's bowled two overs because of a blow to his finger. We couldn't pick Shadab because he hasn't spent 14 days in Australia, per the Queensland government quarantine requirements. More craziness.

This was a good game for me but a poor game for us. We played on a very average drop-in pitch at Metricon Stadium: two-paced, variable heights. I picked up two wickets in four balls in the 11th over: my old mate Kurtis Patterson caught at point with the pace off, and the Englishman Laurie Evans caught behind with the pace on. We really controlled their innings – we had them five for 83 after 15 overs. I was really pleased to catch my Aussie teammate Ashton Turner, knocking one up in the ring and diving to take the rebound. Hayden Kerr continued his excellent season, getting four wickets, including Colin Munro, the Scorchers's go-to guy this season at number three. But in the power surge Ashton Agar and Aaron Hardie took 20 off an over from Ben Dwarshuis, and we should never have let them get as many as 60 in the last five.

Flip nicked his third ball to the keeper, Jack Edwards punched his third ball to cover, and by the end of the fourth over we'd lost Moises and James Vince as well, with SOK unable to bat. I might have been given out lbw to my first ball from Tymal Mills but got lucky. Then I had to assess the situation.

After the Heat game, there was a team chat led by Moises and Shippy, who wanted to address how we got out through being a bit impatient. Moises was trying to impress on us the need to give ourselves time when we came in, especially when chasing a small total. I disagreed: my argument was that we were only chasing 140, and a quick 20 could have been decisive – break the field up with a couple of big hits early and you can open up new opportunities. Eventually, Moises gave way, but tonight his approach was the right one: Silky and I decided to try to take it deep, so we worked on making sure the required rate didn't blow out to 12. As a result, we were four for 41 from ten overs – not a great scoreline.

Timing was a real struggle. I shanked a lot of balls, and only really nailed a handful: I flicked a six off Mills, smacked one over cow corner off Lance Morris. I was lucky I got a piece of one I hit back to Ashton Agar because it meant he dropped a hot return catch. By this time I'd lost Silky and Sean Abbott, but I still thought we were a chance, particularly when I hit Ashton for consecutive sixes to get the target down to 20 off eight balls. Then I got out to a very good slower bouncer from AJ Tye and our chase petered out. I ended up with 73 off 63, which was okay, but you can also tell what a struggle it was, and how disappointing it was to lose.

Wednesday, 5 January 2022

It's becoming a circus – a very infectious circus. Just heard that the Heat–Sixers game, which had been rescheduled for today, will have to be rescheduled again. The poor old Stars now have eight staff and 13 players positive, including Maxy.

We've now got our first too: Moises, Sean Abbott, and two assistant coaches, Andre Adams and Mitch Claydon. Andre has complained of tiredness and weakness; the other three have had very mild symptoms. But to be available to play again, you have to pass RATs on consecutive days. So that's more time in isolation. Not fun, even when you're as used to hotel rooms as we are.

Thursday, 6 January 2022

Practice and a full round of PCR tests today: no new cases, thankfully. That earlier rumour has been confirmed: it now looks like everyone is headed for Melbourne, to play out all the games at the MCG, Marvel and Kardinia Park. Must be some serious coin involved, which shows how desperate Cricket Australia are to get this done.

Friday, 7 January 2022

Really good Test unfolding in Sydney, Jonny Bairstow making a hundred today to match Usman Khawaja's. Of course, I'm really pleased for Uzzie. I'd have picked him in Brisbane rather than Travis Head, and although Travis made a hundred there, I still think Uzzie is the better player. If it came to it, I'd leave Travis out in the Test at Bellerive Oval. If you get injured, you give up your place with guarantees you'll get it back – and COVID is an injury, really. I know it's bad luck, but show me an injury that isn't.

Also, how good is my mate Scott Boland? Just saying.

Saturday, 8 January 2022

Back to Coffs in the rent-a-car ahead of our return bout with the Scorchers. They're a bloody good team; we'll need to be at our best, which we weren't against them the first time. It's the first day of the week-long First Nations Round, so I sit down to watch Ben McDermott get more runs – 93 off 61 – against a second-string Heat at the Gabba, on top of earlier back-to-back hundreds. Having had a tough time in the Caribbean and Bangladesh, he's been the form batter of this BBL. Lucky he missed the Hurricanes's games against us.

Sunday, 9 January 2022

Had a real good chance against the Scorchers tonight and we blew it a bit. They were, again, missing Marsh and Inglis; also Colin Munro had tested positive, and Jason Behrendorff was a close contact. But you can't afford to slip up against the Scorchers. They're too good.

Dan Hughes, who was leading us in the absence of Moises, probably got it wrong at the toss. In the first innings the pitch was two-paced, and slower balls were holding; when they batted, the dew came in and the ball started skidding on, which made boundaries easier to come by. We also went seven overs in the middle with scoring a boundary, while Ashton Turner came in for them in the fourth over and made 69 from 41.

Silky and I added 50 off the last 28 balls of our innings: I got a bit back against AJ, who got me out with that brilliant ball the other night, by hitting his attempted yorker onto the roof. Still, we probably left our run too late. I caught Kurtis running back in the ring when he top-edged, but we never had enough, and there was a bit of an inquest afterwards about what we're doing wrong. Compared to last season – where we got on a roll, it's true – our batting has lacked fluency. These kind of discussions can get a bit depressing; I tried not to let it.

When Silky started saying how disappointed he was with his boundary count, I cut in, arguing that we've been playing on some pretty ordinary decks. Conditions have been tough here and at Metricon; we've had thatchy ones at the SCG that are gripping; the MCG was shit, slow, as it always is. And if we look around, nobody is making big runs this season, except maybe Ben McDermott. It's been a low-scoring tournament. So I told the group we need to look at our performances in context, and maybe not fight the conditions: they are what they are.

It's good to talk things out when you're not playing well, but you also need to stay positive. It's just a game of cricket. There's always another.

Monday, 10 January 2022

We depart the BreakFree, leaving behind our COVID cases, including Moey and Sean Abbott, who returned negative RATs today but need to return another before they can join us. We head for a special hangar at Coffs Harbour airport and board an Alliance Air charter to Tullamarine, where we land at one of the private jet terminals. The boys are pretty impressed; in the IPL, I tell them, we do this every other day!

Harper was brilliant on the flight, as she always is. Funny, isn't it? Six weeks ago, I hated being anywhere near kids on planes; now it's our little girl, and I feel really protective of her.

On landing, we break up into pairs and drive to Quest Sanctuary Lakes, Point Cook, between Melbourne and Geelong, where our next two venues are. We popped into the Coles for some supplies in the Sanctuary Lakes shopping centre, which was where the roof collapsed a few days ago. The area's blocked off and there are some skips full of bits of ceiling – there are dangers in the world apart from COVID!

Jorgia is the only partner on this tour, and I've got to say she's been awesome, making what could have been pretty difficult very easy for me. She's not allowed to come to our games but she doesn't seem to mind. I was feeling a bit guilty tonight, so I said I'd take Harper with me when I went to see Danny Redrup for some treatment: Harper was almost asleep in the DockATot, and I thought Jorgia might appreciate some alone time.

I was too ambitious. Within three seconds of my arriving in Danny's room, Harper was screaming her lungs out, and I had to ask Jorgia to come down, which she cheerfully did.

'She's pretty adaptable, isn't she?' said Danny after Jorgia took Harper back to our room.

She is.

Tuesday, 11 January 2022

Scrolling through the headlines on our phones in bed this morning, Jorgia and I notice that the ABC is no longer reporting COVID case numbers – only hospitalisations. Interesting. Maybe that's how it's got to be – let's just get on with it. We've basically been told we now need to be ready to play every day. That's fine.

Some good news for us in the morning: Moises and Sean Abbott reported consecutive negative RATs, so they're free to fly down from Coffs, and available for our evening match against the Renegades. Mind you, some of the protocols still seem a bit weird. Because they want us to spend the maximum amount of time outside, we're not allowed in the changing room at Kardinia Park. It's like club cricket.

This was our second game in the First Nations Round, which started on Saturday: the Renegades's shirt looked almost as good as ours. It was good to come up against Josh Lalor, who's a Gamilaraay man from Mount Druitt. He works at Cricket NSW and has been heavily involved in their Reconciliation Action Plan. Josh is 34 now, but picked up Josh Philippe in the first over, and bowled me a couple of terrific yorkers – he's still a very handy cricketer.

Kardinia Park is a great-looking ground with a superb outfield, but the drop-in pitch is slow and hard to score on. I had the third-highest score with 22, which tells you something. We were lucky Moises made it, as his 49 off 35 balls was the best batting of the match. He was well supported by Jack

Edwards, who's come in since James Vince left. Jack is a great kid, always looking for ways to improve. He hasn't made the most of his opportunities but he's only 21. I wonder whether we haven't placed too much pressure on him by batting him up top, although it's a fine line between pressure and faith. Perhaps he's trying a bit hard, assuming he has to score early boundaries when the field is up. I reckon he could afford just to get his first ten runs off ten balls before worrying too much about boundaries.

The Renegades had a good line-up on paper: Finchy, Maddinson, Shaun Marsh. But they struggled with the conditions even more than we did, and Ben Dwarshius went through them in the middle with five for 26 in a competent, no-frills win.

Wednesday, 12 January 2022

The BCCI have announced the details of its 'Mega Auction' – which will feature two new IPL franchises, from Ahmedabad and Lucknow. It will be held in Bengaluru on 12 and 13 February. I've already decided it's not for me. Now that I've got a home, staying there is pretty appealing, and there are some little jobs to do around the place. When the BBL is over, I'll be ready for a break.

Thursday, 13 January 2022

There are so many COVID cases in the BBL at the moment that Cricket Australia have set up a player pool of reserves that any club can draw on – it's something they also did for the Women's BBL. We've picked up Justin Avendano, who's sort of one of ours anyway: a 28-year-old hitter from North Sydney who's been on the fringes of our squad for a while and peeled off some big hundreds in grade cricket this season. He also happens to be one of the best golfer-cricketers I've ever seen – he plays off three. So an excellent addition to the squad in all respects.

Friday, 14 January 2022

The Aussies go into the Fifth Test at Bellerive Oval with Usman as an opener to make room for Travis Head, and Marcus Harris missing out. It's not what I would have done, but Travis justifies his selection with a second counter-punching hundred of the summer, as England's attack loses its early impetus. The pitch is doing a bit ... this match feels like it will be a short one.

Saturday, 15 January 2022

We have a solid win against the Thunder, who, even without Sam Billings, who's joined the England squad for the Fifth Test, are still a bloody good team. We made a tentative start – we were one for eight from four overs – but then Daniel Hughes put on 82 in 58 balls with Josh Philippe, and 77 off 43 with Moises, in what was possibly our most convincing batting display of the season. Silky and I both got out in the penultimate over, but we still added 15, and Moises and Sean then took 20 off the last.

We benefited from the return of SOK. He's insisting that this is his last season but he's as good as ever. My mate Alex Hales got the Thunder off to a flier – one for 42 off five – but SOK bowled him first up with a ball that was perfectly pitched and very slow. He also picked up Sams, Olly Davies and Alex Ross to win us our first Bash Boost point of the summer, and I caught Jason Sangha off Ben Dwarshius diving forward at mid-on in the 13th over to remove the last of their batting. I had Chris Green dropped at point early on, and he stuck around to get 50 off 31, narrowing our winning margin to 60 runs. But we were slick tonight against quality opposition.

Sunday, 16 January 2022

So much for the BBL being concentrated in Melbourne – we're on our way to Adelaide today. It seems like the state associations have been kicking up a stink about losing home games, so our game against the Strikers has been brought forward.

In the evening, we have a chance to watch the last rites of the Ashes, with England left to chase 271. Zak Crawley and Rory Burns work their way to none for 68 at the start of the last over before tea. It's going to be tough in the final session, under lights with the pink ball, but if they can get through it without losing more than a couple of wickets, they're a chance to come back in the daylight against a softer ball tomorrow. But Burns drags a Cameron Green delivery onto his stumps, and in the next 22.4 overs they lose all ten wickets for 56.

My mate Scott bowls Joe Root with one that stays down, then gets Billings and Woakes, but England are a mess, to be honest. Nobody seems to want to fight; they've all got one foot on the flight home. It's a shambles.

Monday, 17 January 2022

I thought the Strikers would be a good unit this summer, and they're starting to prove it. Unfortunately it's at our expense tonight, as they work their way into the Eliminator with an eight-wicket win – their fourth on the bounce. Rashid Khan has gone home, but Fawad Ahmed coming in means that they haven't missed a beat. Talk about old blokes winning shit – he turns 40 next month. He bowled with the breeze, challenging the batters to hit him down the ground, and they couldn't: he bowled Josh Philippe, then got Jack Edwards and Daniel Hughes with consecutive deliveries.

Frankly, we got this pitch wrong. We've played on so many poor strips that we didn't recognise a good one, probably the best we've had all summer. We were slow getting out of the blocks, and left ourselves too much to do in the back half. I was annoyed to get out in the 18th over for 22 off 17 balls. It took Justin Avendano to get us to a respectable total – he slogged 52 off 29.

Given how well Fawad bowled, we may also have missed a trick not picking Lloyd Pope after resting SOK, and the Strikers gave us a bit of a lesson with the bat. Our bowlers have been fantastic this season – at the top of off every game.

But they were challenged by Matt Renshaw, who had just come back from COVID and bowled Moises with his little tweakers. Renshaw then made 50 off 31, unsettling the bowlers and fielders, which made things easier for the batters who came after him.

One of those was Ian Cockbain, a 34-year-old from Gloucestershire who's been playing with Langwarrin Cricket Club on the Mornington Peninsula, and came in as a replacement in the Strikers's last few games. I played with Ian at Gloucestershire ten years ago, and he could always smack it; apparently Franky Worrall, who also plays at Gloucestershire, roped him in when he came to Adelaide with his Aussie wife for the Christmas break. Ian looked like a guy on top of his game as he made an unbeaten 71 off 42.

Still, I really don't know what we were doing in Adelaide. All the fuss about the importance of looking after home fans, and there can't have been 2000 at the game. The hill was empty; I've seen more members at a Sheffield Shield match. The scenes afterwards were chaotic also. We barely had time for a shower before piling aboard a charter flight to Brisbane – me with Jorgia and Harper in tow. When we landed we were still doing our travel buddy thing of two to a car, but Avis Car Rental hadn't installed the baby seat so I had to figure out how to do it, which took a while.

We finally checked in to the Alex Perry Apartments in New Farm at 3 am, after a very long day for all three of us.

Tuesday, 18 January 2022

All that wasn't the ideal preparation for our rescheduled game against the Heat. It was a disadvantage to us, too, that other teams got the chance to play the Heat when they were at half-strength, while we must play them now they're at full-strength. Thanks to our defeat last night, the Scorchers have sewn up top spot. We're neck-and-neck with the third-placed Thunder in pursuit of the right to play the Scorchers in the Qualifier on Saturday night at Marvel Stadium.

The early conclusion to the Ashes has opened up some interesting possibilities. Not only is Nathan Lyon available for us again, but Shippy has been in touch with the English opener Zak Crawley, who looked the best of their players in Sydney and Hobart. We have a gap in our squad as Lawrence Neil-Smith is injured and has returned to Tasmania. Crawley's super-keen, apparently, and it would be a great opportunity for the BBL to up its international quotient. We'll see what happens.

Wednesday, 19 January 2022

The fixture backlog has finally caught up with the BBL. Our game against the Heat at the Gabba is the first of three today – the Thunder play the Renegades later in the afternoon, hoping to leapfrog us into second, while the Stars host the Hurricanes in the evening in what's basically a dead rubber.

When I get on the bus at 9 am for a 12.30 pm start, I again feel like I've gone back to my club cricket days – even more so when, as at Kardinia Park, we're not allowed into the dressing room because of COVID protocols. It seems they're expecting us just to hang around a dugout that's hot enough to fry an egg on. After a while we walk into the dressing room anyway, and nobody stops us.

The regime is catching up with me too. COVID has now prevented us training for a week and a half, and I'm starting to feel really rusty – which I know will sound strange, given the amount of cricket I'm playing, but there are certain things you can only fix when you slow the game down and think about what you're doing. I came in at three for 120 today with Daniel Hughes going well, but I really struggled in the surge – I reckon I failed to connect with eight balls. Not making contact is the worst crime for a T20 batter. If you're not hitting boundaries, you've got to at least be hitting the gaps and getting off strike. I ended up having to play a few lap-sweeps to get going, and thanks to a six and a four off Mark Steketee's last over I finally ended up getting 32 off 24. But I badly need a feel-good session to work on my swing.

It stayed hot all day. There were drinks breaks every five overs, and the bowlers, Ben Dwarshius especially, found it hard to grip the ball, so much were they sweating. Jimmy Peirson caused us to sweat a bit too. We got Marnus Labuschagne and Ben Duckett cheaply, but Jimmy played beautifully, making 42 off 23, until SOK beat him with something a bit slower. Hayden Kerr, who picked up Lynny, continued his excellent season, and Nathan Lyon slotted straight in.

Again, despite all the rigmarole we were put through to get here, there were no more than 2000 spectators in the ground, what with the Brisbane Heat being second-last, and the Brisbane heat being so oppressive. There's a sense in this BBL that we're all staggering towards the finishing line. People are either sick, tired or both.

Nobody can figure out how the reserve player pool is meant to work. The Scorchers, for instance, have been docked a point for using a replacement player, Brayden Stepien, as a keeper. Having lost Josh Inglis to the Test squad, Cameron Bancroft to COVID and then Laurie Evans to injury in the sixth over of a game against the Strikers, they brought Stepien on to keep: although he was on standby for the game as a replacement player, he had not been officially added to the Scorchers's list. It won't affect their finishing top, or prevent us playing them in the Qualifier at Marvel on Saturday night, but it shows how everyone is scrambling to keep up with all the changes.

As we leave Brisbane, I hear that Zak Crawley won't be joining us. Chris Silverwood, England's coach, apparently believes it would be 'a bad look' if Zak stayed to play in the BBL after a 0–4 Ashes defeat. Seriously, how is going back to freezing, cricketless England a better look?

Now that CA has deferred Australia's scheduled white-ball games against New Zealand, however, there are some Aussie players at a loose end: apparently Steve Smith is so keen to join the Sixers that he's flying down to Melbourne tomorrow to train with us. How good would that be? When top-class internationals are in full flight, the BBL gets a huge lift – as Glenn Maxwell proved this evening, making an unbeaten 154 from 64 balls for the Stars in that dead rubber against the Hurricanes; the Stars piled on a competition record score of two for 273. Come in, Smithy, I say.

Thursday, 20 January 2022

A familiar hotel, Sanctuary Lakes, and a new car, a hybrid Toyota Kluger – on my drive to the 13th Beach Golf Links, it took a while for me to get used to it not making any noise! It was a chance to catch up with Moises and Sean Abbott – we all have reciprocal rights from Bonnie Doon. Justin Avendano, who hits a golf ball as cleanly as a cricket ball, joined us.

By now, you've probably worked out that I play a lot of golf. It's relatively recent. I only bought clubs after I left South Australia in 2013. There were a bunch of keen golfers in the Bushrangers's squad, especially Jon Holland, and playing a few rounds together was a good way for me to get to know them.

There's a lot of theories about the interaction of golf and cricket – some people even used to say that playing golf was bad for your cricket. I've found it really good. What I like about golf is the relief it offers from what's most demanding about cricket. In golf, it's only you and a small, stationary ball; there's nothing else to focus on, no match situation to keep in mind, no teammates that you might let down. I find that really relaxing.

This last year, too, golf has helped my sanity – all our sanities, actually. With the travel buddy system we're using this summer, there's hardly been any chance to gather as teammates – even, as I've mentioned, for training. Golf's become a way we keep in touch, chat about stuff, share our news.

Mind you, one bit of news today isn't so great. Apparently, CA has kicked up a fuss about Smithy joining the Sixers because he's not from the reserve player pool. Every year there are complaints, not least from the broadcasters, about the lack of star power in the BBL. Here's an absolute superstar who desperately wants to play and the CEOs of the state associations won't let him. What if Virat Kohli wanted to play? Or AB de Villiers? Would we say, 'Oh, sorry, mate, you have to go into the reserve player pool first'? It's complete madness.

Anyway, Harper has the right attitude. As I walked into our room at Sanctuary Lakes, Jorgia was sitting beside our little girl in the cot and said, 'Daddy's home from golf!' And incredibly, Harper chose that very moment to give us her first smile – Jorgia even got it on her phone. Harper looked so happy you half-expected her to break into laughter. She doesn't care about whether Steve Smith's playing or not. Maybe I shouldn't either.

Friday, 21 January 2022

Finally, a training session, which I've been crying out for. Hop in the super-quiet Kluger for the drive to the MCG at 8 am, doing a radio interview on the way where I argue for Steve to play. No, he was not on our squad list, but that was because it was expected he'd be involved in the New Zealand series. The Sixers is the only BBL team he has ever played for – indeed, Steve led us to the title in the tournament's inaugural season. The only reason he's been deemed ineligible now is this two-week-old pool of reserve players, which has turned out to be a nuisance nobody asked for.

Basically, what the state CEOs – with the exception of Cricket New South Wales – have determined is that we should have included Steve in our squad at the start of the summer, somehow anticipating, four months ahead, that Australia's ODI series with New Zealand would be cancelled. Nobody signed David Warner, Pat Cummins, Josh Hazlewood or Cameron Green either – it was assumed they'd be busy too. And it's not a counterargument that the Strikers kept Travis Head on their books, for instance, or that the Heat had Marnus Labuschagne – they're not first-choice Aussie white-ball players, and there was always a chance they'd be able to take part in the BBL. That's the reason we signed Nathan Lyon.

I'm impressed that Steve wants to play, rather than rest like David, Pat, Josh and Cameron. Moises spoke for us all when he was asked his view: 'You have got a former Australian captain, one of the best players in the world. You have got IPL teams who pay multi-million dollars just to have this guy as part of their franchise. Advertising, bums on seats, eyes on TVs – I mean, you do the math. And we're saying no because of a rule that is two weeks old in some COVID bubble hub. To me, I don't get it. We're in the top two without him ... so I have got absolute belief in our domestic talent and local talent to do the job. I think it's sad for cricket, that's all.'

I had my say on Twitter:

> @bbl can't attract the best OS players in the game for the whole comp due to 'conflicting schedules' (aka we pay less and it goes for too long)
>
> But when 1 of our local Aussie stars unexpectedly becomes available and wants to play, CA says he can't
>
> Ch7 & Fox must be thrilled

It's no good, of course. This is the kind of decision that tests players' faith in Cricket Australia – it seems so pedantic and parochial. I liked this tweet from Joe Burns:

> Am I the only one who thinks it's crazy that we pushed on blindly with replacement players simply for content fulfilment, thus losing competitive integrity, yet we won't allow Steve Smith to be on TVs playing for the team he always represented and led #ReplacementsOverSmudge

Adam Gilchrist, among others, pitched in: 'No @joeburns441 you aren't the only one. #ridiculous.'

CA then had the nerve to tweet: 'Which #Ashes star are you most looking forward to seeing in the BBL finals?'

Pat Cummins, among others, replied: 'Smithy'.

Well, CA, you asked ...

In the evening, the Strikers see off the Hurricanes in the Eliminator to go into Sunday's Knockout with the Thunder. Smithy stays home. What a waste.

Saturday, 22 January 2022

What a waste indeed. The chapter of accidents that is our season continues. On the morning of our Qualifier against the Scorchers, we learn that Jack Edwards has returned an 'inconclusive' COVID test result, so that rules him out, and his brother Mickey as a close contact. Then, during the warm-up, Daniel Hughes turns his ankle. I've seen this happen before. Those little Toblerone-shaped cushions on the boundary rope look protective, but they're just signage, and they're dangerous. Many a player has tripped on them, but player safety will always come second to money.

Instead of Smithy, we rummaged in the player replacement pool and came up with Nick Bertus, who played the last of five first-class games for New South Wales more than two years ago. Nick is a great bloke: he captains Parramatta, where his dad coached Sean Abbott and his brother, Ben, among others. Nick was in our squad last season as a reserve keeper. But he's not Steve, and he would have felt that pressure.

The Scorchers charged out, going at ten an over for their first 12. They had Josh Inglis back and Kurtis Patterson in great form, and both Sean Abbott and Ben Dwarshius were slightly off, as they had been against the Strikers when really challenged by the batters. Hayden Kerr was the best of our bowlers, getting Kurtis and Mitchell Marsh, but even SOK came in for some punishment as the Scorchers raised three for 189. Again our top order proved brittle: we lost Justin Avendano, Flip, Silky and Nick in the first seven overs, and when I holed out the asking rate was more than 13 an over. Moises was caught behind, and from seven for 55 it was only Ben (66 off 28) and Hayden Kerr (22 off 17) who helped us scavenge as many as 140.

Sunday, 23 January 2022

So the Scorchers go straight through to the final. Can we join them? It's weird, but I think we can. We're completely exhausted. We can barely scrape a team together. The whole league's against us. But we're still alive. And it's T20, so anything can happen, right?

In the Knockout at Marvel, the Strikers win their sixth match on the bounce by seeing off the Thunder, Ian Cockbain continuing his remarkable season with 65 off 38, despite a partnership of 90 in ten overs between Jason Sangha and Alex Ross. They'll be our opponent now in the Challenger on Wednesday. How good would it be to knock them off?

Monday, 24 January 2022

Counting the cost now that we've lost Jack and Mickey Edwards to COVID. Where are we up to now? We've lost Tom Curran, Ben Manenti and Lawrence Neil-Smith to injury, and SOK is a 50–50 prospect every game. James Vince and Chris Jordan are playing for England in the Caribbean, Shadab Khan is back in Pakistan, and Nick Winter's contract is up.

We've made another bid to bring in Smithy, but we're resigned to being knocked back. Apparently the main resistance is coming from South Australia and Western Australia. I can't imagine why.

Tuesday, 25 January 2022

This is getting crazy. Just when you think things could get no worse, Josh Philippe has tested positive to COVID. That's our star opener and our keeper. Bizarrely, though, having rejected our second application to bring in Smithy, the league lets us bring in a different player from outside the pool – our assistant coach Jay Lenton – to keep in Josh's absence. In theory, Nick Bertus could have done the job for us, but at training I agreed with Shippy and Moises that Jay was the better bet. Although it was before Christmas that he last played for his club, Manly, he's kept in Shield cricket and has played a lot more BBL. But Jay hadn't even brought his gear to practice! Wonder what awaits him now.

Wednesday, 26 January 2022

Not in Jay's wildest dreams could he have imagined the role he'd play in tonight's Challenger – no one could. It's one of the most amazing games I have ever played. It's true: in T20, anything can happen.

Our one stroke of good fortune is that Ben Dwarshius, Josh's travel buddy, tested negative, so at least he did not need to be replaced. To fill in where Daniel Hughes should be (and Smithy could be), we had another fossick in the player reserve pool and fished out Jake Carder, a leftie from Perth who now plays for South Australia and had been training with the Strikers. I'd never seen him play; nor had most of us. My acquaintance with him did not extend beyond shaking his hand and saying: 'G'day, mate, I'm Dan.'

We made a fantastic start. I caught Alex Carey in the first over off SOK at mid-off, and Matt Short in the second off Sean at slip. That's only the second slips catch I've taken in 379 T20 matches, but Moises took the risk because the pitch seemed like the Test pitch next to it, with good carry and a bit of extra bounce. Travis Head then played an average shot against Sean, as if he couldn't quite get into it – and I'm not surprised, coming off the high of his Compton–Miller Medal in the Ashes series. So the Strikers were three for 21 in the fourth over.

We actually ended up bowling shit. As well as Ian Cockbain batted again, and as good as the partnership was between Jono Wells and Matt Renshaw, we should never have let them get to 167. Our injury calamities continued too. Moises and SOK both strained calves, and Silky did a hamstring while leaping for a pull shot Cockbain hit off me – the first hamstring he's ever done, because he's super-fit. I blame our crazy schedule: inactivity due to travel is highly predictive of soft tissue injuries.

Still, it's amazing the difference two or three early wickets makes to the arc of an innings. You can't go hard as early as you'd like to – you have to keep wickets in hand for the death – and two or three overs with the brake on is hard to make up. So the Strikers would have wanted more at the start, and we knew their total was gettable, depending on how we plugged our numerous gaps.

We'd sat around before the match discussing the importance of keeping depth in our line-up: Moises, Silky, me and Sean in that middle order. But as Shippy kept moving names around the whiteboard, I finally said: 'Shit, Shippy, it doesn't matter who goes where. If we bat well, we'll get 'em. We're not going to come off the field and say we should have batted him here, or him there. Someone just has to have a worlder.'

And someone did. Hayden Kerr's highest score this season had been 22. But a few years ago I played for New South Wales Country against New South Wales City in some pre-season one-dayers and T20s, and Hayden played as an opening bat – he didn't bowl at all. He smacked 60 in one game and looked like a proper player. So I knew he was good. Mind you, I didn't think he was this good.

Carey should have stumped Hayden off the first ball of our reply; Renshaw should have caught Hayden at deep midwicket on 16. But apart from those blemishes, he hardly hit a false shot. He's got superb timing, and a pull shot like Steve Smith's where he doesn't snap his wrists but still hits them a long way. Above all, he's a smart cricketer. He knows where to hit. He knows who to hit. He knows how to time his run. He can find the boundary when he needs it. And he kept us in touch, though a period when Jake got caught in the ring, Moises got a good yorker and I clothed one off Harry Conway. Sean then provided some extra power, smashing 41 off 20.

The target got down to 20 off eight balls. I reckon you should always win from there. I had a 20 off eight equation earlier this season, and was pissed off that I couldn't get us home. Funnily enough, though, sitting in the dugout, I was completely relaxed – almost at peace with losing. We'd done well against all odds. If we lost, the sun would still come up and it would be another day. Then Sean hit a huge six off Henry Thornton and was on strike for the final over from Conway.

Those last six balls were bizarre. Off the first two, Sean was caught in the deep and Ben got run out. With four balls to go, in went Silky on one leg – we were hoping he could swing one to the short side. He shanked it to deep midwicket, limped through for a single and could barely get to the other end. Then Hayden launched Conway for six – a magnificent shot. Four needed off two balls. Surely we were favourites now.

The penultimate ball Hayden hit into space on the leg-side. Two fit runners might have managed a tight three; as it was, Silky could only hobble back for a second, virtually using his bat as a crutch. So we needed two runs from the final ball, and Hayden was on strike.

The coach took no chances: Shippy jumped up and started signalling for Silky to come in – to retire hurt – so we could get a fit runner to the middle for the last ball. You just knew the commentators would be tut-tutting about this – it'd be the spirit of cricket this, the spirit of cricket that. But seriously. With the rules these days, what scope is there for the spirit of cricket? We were told tonight that there's a playing condition this summer that only the batters at numbers nine, ten and 11 can use a runner. That means Silky or Moises would have been allowed to retire hurt and then come back in with a runner. I mean, what the fuck is that rule?

Anyway, T20 allows no time for a discussion of 'the spirit of the game'. You default to what it takes to win. As coach of South Australia, Darren Berry used to talk about this conundrum. You know that convention that if a fielder's throw deflects off a running batter, you don't take an overthrow? Sure, but what if you need that run to win? I reckon 99 per cent of cricketers would say: take the run and win the game.

So in went Jay Lenton, in the kit he had lost the habit of bringing to training. Hayden swung the ball through midwicket. In his hurry to collect the ball and return, Wells let it through his hands for four, and we were into the final.

Just like that. What a night.

Thursday, 27 January 2022

Got to bed about 2 am, airport at 10.30 am. Thanks to the postponement of that Heat game and the relocation of the Strikers game, we've now done Sydney to Adelaide to Brisbane to Melbourne to Sydney to Melbourne in 13 days – so much for that Melbourne hub we were all moving to! Australia's not getting any smaller, and travel during this time of COVID has been abnormally punishing. At least this was a morning flight, which in my experience is better: you have some time on the ground after arrival, and you're in bed relatively early. But it was nice to know I have only one more flight to go, and that will be taking me home.

By 2.30 pm Moises was doing a press conference with Ashton Turner at Docklands, and I was sending out a tweet from my room at the Quest:

> Shout out to anyone* in Melbourne that wants a game of cricket tomorrow night. My team is struggling to get 11 covid free, fit players on the park. Warm up starts at 6.30 pm at Marvel Stadium.
>
> Free beer afterwards, potentially out of a large cup.
>
> DM if keen
>
> *no test cricketers

Despite this last stipulation, I did hear from a few, including AB de Villiers ('I'm keen if u can guarantee me my 4 overs?') and Jofra Archer ('Do I have to pay subs?').

But it's not all joking. 'A lot of you guys won't have been in this situation, scraping through to finals with so many walking wounded,' Shippy said to us last night, and we thought he was about to tell some story from his own playing career, which dates back to the 1970s. Then he said: 'I'm not sure I can remember a team carrying so many injuries.'

At the moment, I'm the only member of our original top six who is fit to play. It also turns out that Jay Lenton did a hip flexor while keeping last night – not surprising, seeing he's been a professional wanger for the last month. Moises will play on one leg if he has to; you could roll SOK out in a wheelchair. But we're struggling.

It's fair to point out that the Scorchers have their own troubles. I was chatting to Mitch Marsh after our last game, and he admitted he'd picked up a hamstring twinge. 'At least I think it's what a twinge feels like,' he said. 'Every other time I've ripped it off the bone.' They've had Cam Bancroft and Lance Morris down with COVID, plus, of course, they've been marooned in the east by Mark McGowan, the WA Premier – they had a grand total of one game in Perth. At least I've had the occasional night in my own bed this season. These guys have been in limbo the whole time.

Really, this can't end soon enough, for any of us.

Friday, 28 January 2022

Final day. Before the match I caught up with another refugee from Western Australia, Justin Langer, who I guess is in town for his meetings with Cricket Australia CEO Nick Hockley about his contract. It was really good to see him. We were on a tough tour last year: everyone's patience was tested, and I didn't agree with everything that happened. But you're not always going to see eye to eye with any coach, and nobody should be scared of that. Strong teams need strong wills.

Strong teams also need willing flesh, and tonight we really didn't have it. CA knocked back another application for us to field Steve Smith: their reason was that we were still capable of 'fielding an XI', which was the kind of thing an association might say to a club team that was in danger of forfeiting.

So we went in with an extra bowler, Jackson Bird, and with me at number five, partly because we were just so unsure of guys getting through the game. Hughesy shouldn't have been playing. Moises and SOK have grade-one calf injuries. Ben Dwarshuis then twinged his hamstring in the warm-ups, and was barely able to get through two overs. We made a great start. When I caught Mitch Marsh at long-on, we had the Scorchers three for 20, and then Nathan Lyon got Colin Munro in the same over. But the longer the game went, the more our fitness told, and the clearer it became that we had four guys on the field who couldn't move five metres on either side.

Take nothing away from the Scorchers, though. They're a great team. They have a lot of depth, they field well, they've got a smart captain in Ashton Turner and a good coach in Adam Voges. There's a fair chance they'd have beaten us at full strength. After their poor beginning, they ended up with six for 171, a par score for Marvel Stadium this season. Laurie Evans smashed 76 not out off 41 balls, and putting on 104 in 59 with Turner. We had our chances – Hughesy dropped Turner's top edge off me at backward square leg, but he would have struggled to get to it fit, let alone playing on one leg.

We lost Hayden Kerr early. Turner made a smart move, coming in with his off-breaks to the left-handers Bertus and Hughes. He picked up Bertus, then Agar got Moises out sweeping, and suddenly I was in with us needing 126 off 78. I've hardly ever nailed a pull shot better than the one I hit off AJ Tye, but my old Blues mate Kurtis Patterson dived forward to take a superb catch at deep midwicket. Had I hit something as hard as that at the start of my career, no one would have caught it; now we take grabs like that for granted. Sean Abbott then called Hughesy through for one to short third man, and our number three simply couldn't do it: run out for 42 off 33.

So there was no three-peat for the Sixers or a tenth title for me, and this was not a game for my personal highlights reel. We did not even get a chance to catch up with the Scorchers after the game, because they're trying to maintain their bubble in order to get home – some of them, apparently, have even tried enrolling in university courses in order to qualify for the student exemption from lock-out restriction. After Marvel security booted us out about 1.30 am we kicked on, pretty weary and very sore, in our conference room at the Quest until about 4.30 am. The poor old Scorchers still can't go home. At least I can.

Saturday, 29 January 2022

A year ago, I was celebrating on the outfield at the SCG with SOK, Moises and Silky. Now I'm in an Uber with them on the way to the airport for our 10.30 am flight – there are probably two good calves and two good hamstrings between us. I'm not sure SOK's been to bed, but it doesn't matter – far as Cricket Australia's concerned, COVID's over.

Nothing in 2021 turned out as I expected. As it began, I seemed fully booked up and locked in: the PSL, the IPL, The Hundred, the Vitality Blast, maybe a sniff of a T20 World Cup, the possibility of a BBL three-peat. But the year turned out to be as crazy for me as it was for everyone else. Sometimes cricket can seem cut off from reality; in fact, we're just as exposed to the world, only in different ways.

What has it meant for my career? A player should always be contemplating their place in the game; a player at my age has to be. I've always played for enjoyment, and I have to say that this year was not, on the whole, all that enjoyable. In the next few months, I guess I'll weigh up what's contributed to that, whether it might change – the schedule, the travel,

COVID. And, of course, my focus has shifted: having a new home I want to spend more time in with our daughter.

My Notts contract arrived a few nights ago, and I'm really looking forward to playing there this year – great club, great people, great ground. I've also had an email from Jo McMullen at Cricket Australia passing on a request from the BCCI to put myself in the IPL auction. But while it's nice to know there's still interest in my signature out there, there are a lot of things I'd like to do in March and April – family things. At some stage they have to take precedence.

As for this year's BBL, it was nowhere near as enjoyable as previous editions. Most of the games were lacking in atmosphere, and in significance. It felt mechanical, like a pre-season, except that we weren't preparing – this was it. You felt like a circus animal: you did your trick, and the carnival rolled on.

The slight relaxation of the bubble, in some ways, only made it worse. When a whole organisation was sealed up tight, we had to look after each other; this season, because we were in these buddy couples, we hardly saw our other teammates outside of playing and training. It was worse than the IPL bubble. The freedom we enjoyed was so minimal that it was meaningless. What we lost were the fun parts: gathering the whole group, being on the road together.

And we knew the restrictions had nothing to do with our safety; it was all about keeping the show on the road. It confirmed that widespread feeling among players that the administrators care about nothing but money. We fill out these apps about our mental wellbeing, but we recognise them as lip service to player welfare. I reckon 80 per cent of guys just say what they think CA wants to hear. Maybe we've relied on money to take some of the bitter taste away. But it seems like COVID has accentuated the worst of cricket – the uneasy sense we're just churning out content for distant paymasters.

Perhaps this is the price you pay for what is, in other respects, an amazing way of life. In 2021, I represented my country, and my Indigenous heritage. It's what I grew up wanting to do; it's a huge thrill, and I'm grateful to JL and George for the chance. I played in an IPL Eliminator and a BBL final. I played a game that I've loved my whole life and still exhilarates me, with teams of fantastic guys in Australia, Pakistan, India, Bangladesh, the West Indies and the UAE. I also visited England, the Maldives, Bahrain, Italy and Portugal, although I didn't see much of some of them, thanks to COVID.

Yet I can't also deny that the best part of my year was, unexpectedly, off the field, with Jorgia, and with Harper – the process of becoming a father and family man, starting to build a home even if I hardly stayed there.

I'm glad I've written this diary, as it will prevent what was a crazy year from becoming a blur. Maybe it will end up mattering most as a record of the year in which my life finally broke through my career.

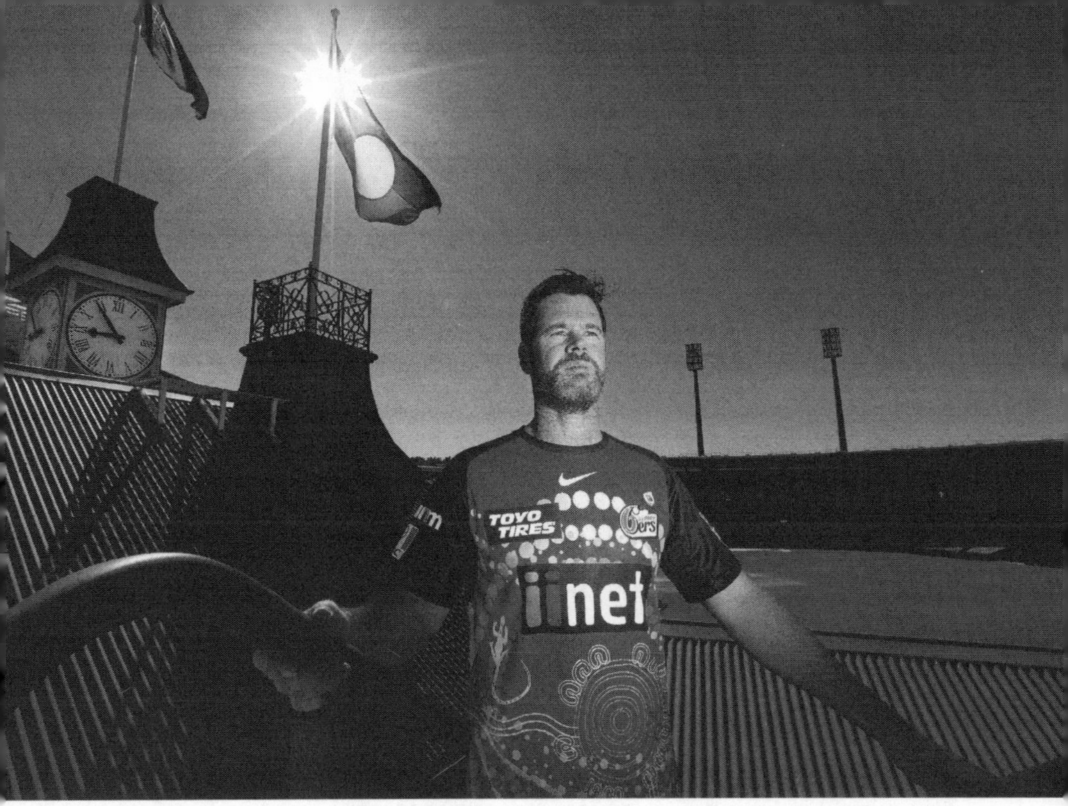

My two cultures meet in the Sydney Sixers Indigenous kit designed by Jordan Ardler, which incorporates Wiradjuri and Muruwari motifs and a circle signifying the Sydney Cricket Ground. *(Phil Hillyard)*

The Sixers form a barefoot circle at the SCG, which is on Gadigal land. The club has strongly supported the cause of reconciliation. *(Phil Hillyard)*

Reunited with Virat Kohli in Chennai, 7 April 2021, eight years after we first shared a dressing room. A fantastic cricketer and an inspirational leader.

No evidence of social distancing in a late-night political rally in Chennai, India, 3 April 2021.

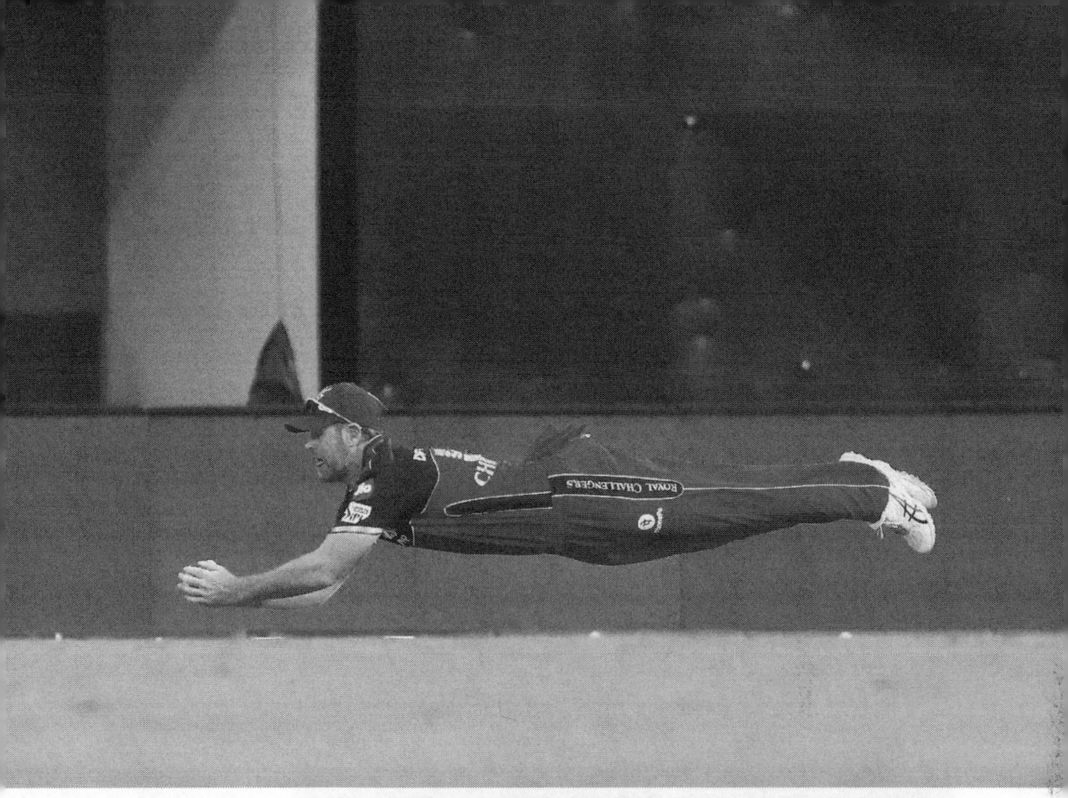

I catch Shubman Gill of the Kolkata Knight Riders off Kyle Jamieson at Chidambaram Stadium, Chennai, 18 April 2021. *(IPL)*

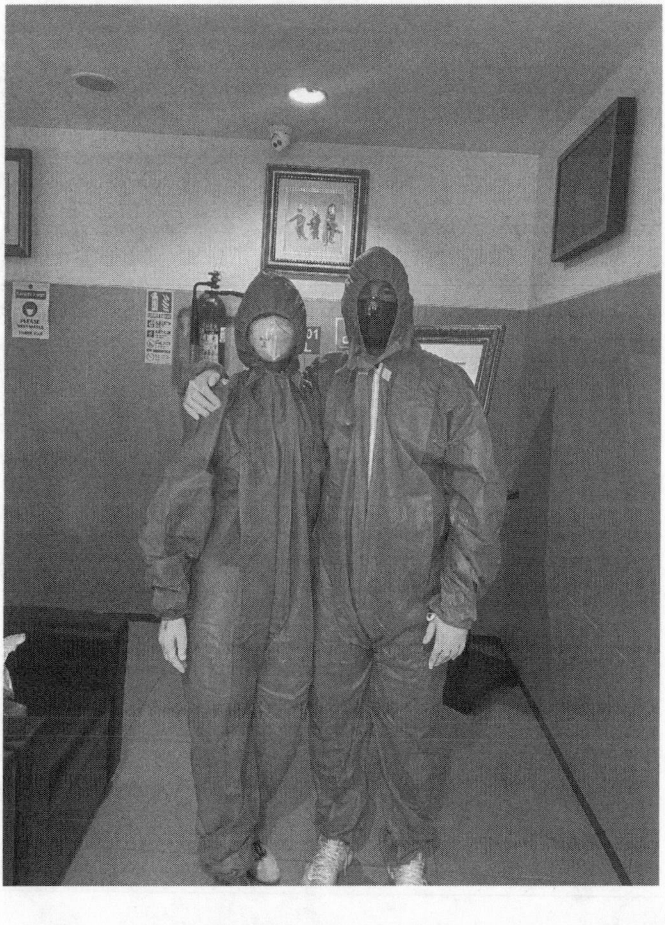

What the best dressed couples are wearing in Chennai in a pandemic. 'Green corridor' for Jorgia's ultrasound, 15 April 2021.

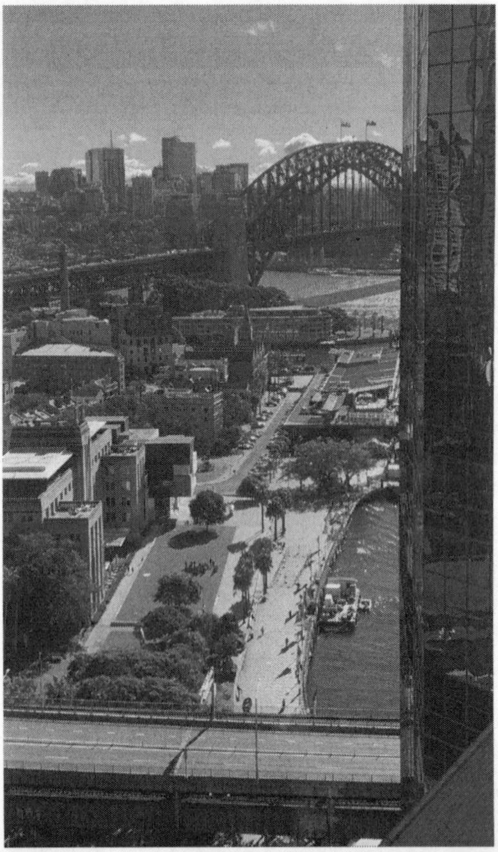

Home, but not as we know it: looking out the window of our quarantine hotel, the Sydney Marriott, 9 June 2021, on the way from England to the West Indies – because flying direct would have been too simple!

Taking a knee in solidarity with the West Indies before the first T20 international, Gros Islet, Saint Lucia, 10 July 2021. *(Randy Brooks / AFP via Getty Images)*

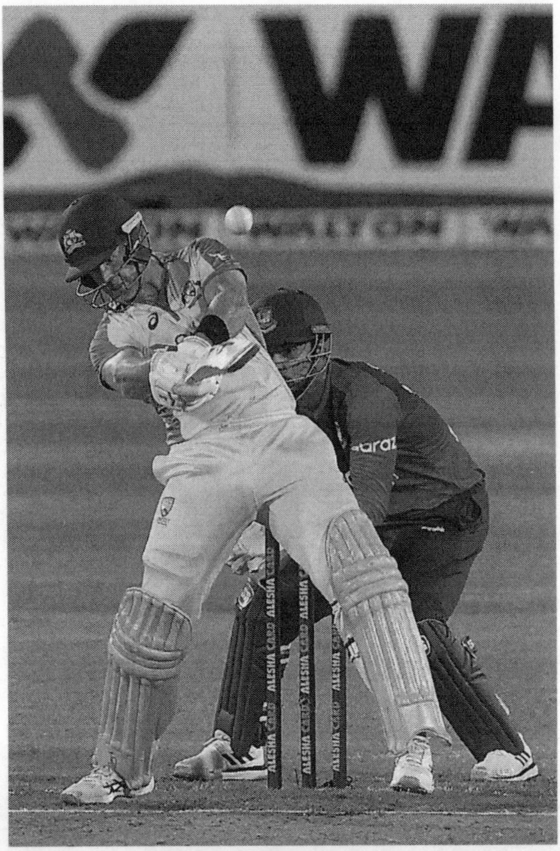

Two of my five sixes in an over from Bangladesh's Shakib al Hasan at Sher-E-Bangla, Dhaka, 7 August 2021. *(Munir Uz Zaman / AFP via Getty Images)*

Almost, but not quite, catching Andre Russell, in the first T20I against the West Indies, 9 July 2021. My relay throw did not quite make it to Ashton Agar. *(Courtesy of Clancy Sinnamon, CA Digital)*

Celebrating the wicket of Rishabh Pant against Delhi Capitals, Dubai, 8 October 2021. *(IPL)*

Trying to up the rate against the Scorchers during the Big Bash League, Coffs Harbour, 9 January 2022. *(Chris Hyde / Getty Images)*

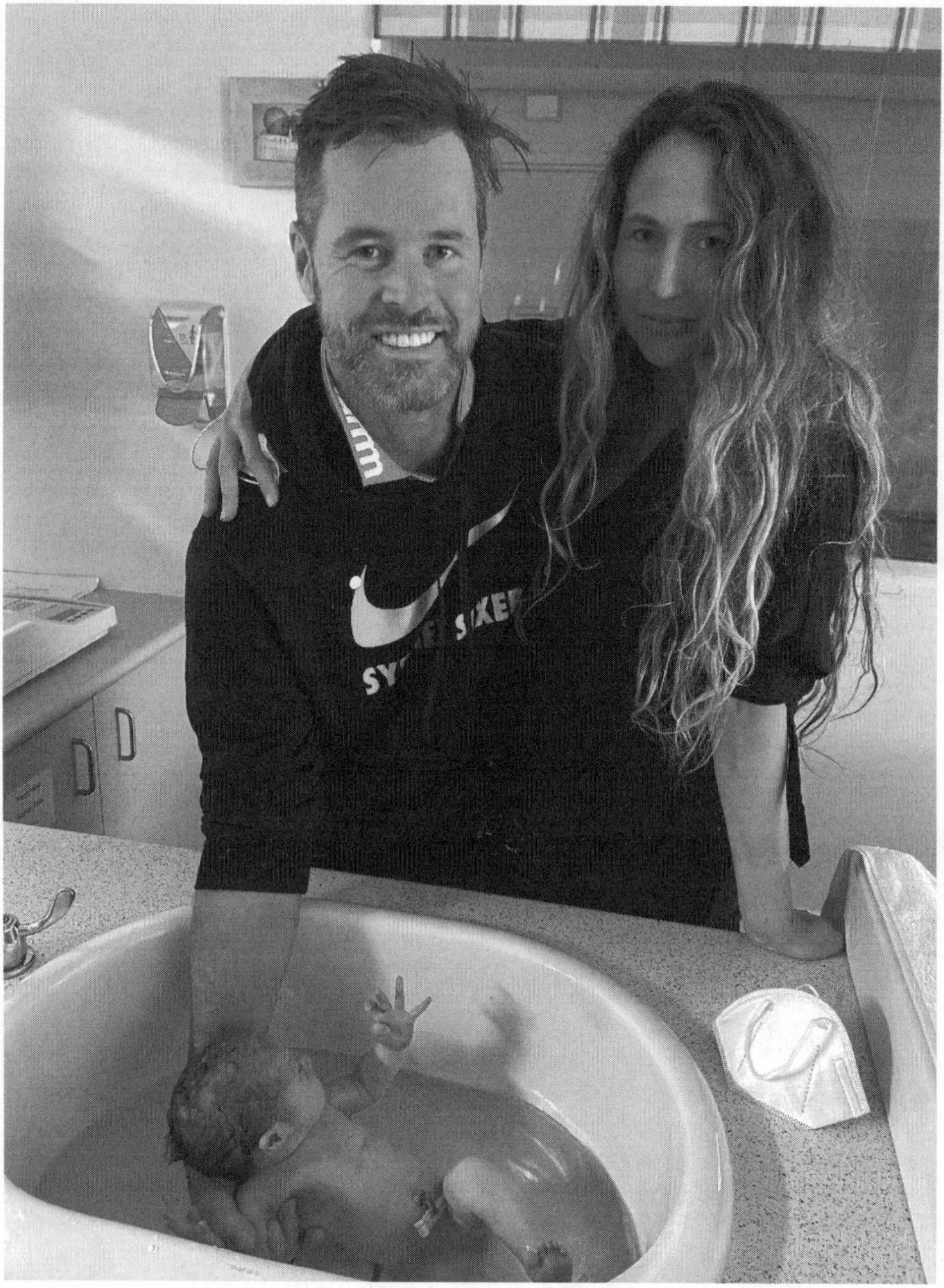

With Harper and Jorgia. A good all-rounder is always learning new skills, 9 December 2021.